All ROUND GUIDE

ISLE of MAN

Editors
Sara Donaldson
and Miles Cowsill

Contributors
Duncan Bridges, Howard Parkin, John Hellowell, David Gooberman, Andrew Scarffe and Chris Sharpe

Photographers
Lily Publications, Dave Kneen, Barry Edwards, Simon Park and Manx National Heritage.

Isle of Man Premier Guide first published 1994, 1st All Round Guide edition 2002, 2nd edition 2004, 3rd edition 2006, 4th edition 2008, 5th edition 2010, 6th edition 2012, 7th edition 2014 and 8th edition 2016, 9th edition 2018, 10th edition 2020. **11th edition: 2023.**

Copyright © 2023 Lily Publications Ltd. All rights reserved.

Any reproduction in whole or in part is strictly prohibited. The content contained herein is based on the best available information at the time of research. The publishers assume no liability whatsoever arising from the publishing of material contained herein. The maps included in this publication have been designed and drawn on an Apple Macintosh computer and neither Lily Publications nor their designers can offer any guarantee as to their accuracy. Readers are strongly advised to use an Ordnance Survey map in conjunction with this guide for further reference. Lily Publications accepts no responsibility for any loss, injury or damage resulting from visits made to places or attractions described or listed in this guide, nor for any loss, injury or damage resulting from participation in activities described or listed in this guide.

All accommodation advertised in this guide participates in the Department of Tourism & Leisure inspection schemes. If you have any concerns about the standards of accommodation, please take the matter up with the provider of the accommodation as soon as possible. Failing satisfaction, please contact Registration and Grading, Dept Tourism & Leisure, St Andrews House, Finch Road, Douglas, IM1 2PX.
Tel: +44 (0)1624 686846.

Published by Lily Publications Ltd.,
Ballachrink Beg, Jurby East, Ramsey,
Isle of Man, IM7 3HD
Tel: +44 (0)1624 898446 www.lilypublications.co.uk

The
ISLE of MAN
a different Kingdom

The Island has its own coins and notes.

Nestled in the Irish Sea, midway between Britain and Ireland, the Isle of Man is a haven for the good life. Popular for its wildlife, water sports, motorsports and breathtaking scenery, it is still something of a hidden gem, with its quiet, unhurried lifestyle and great natural beauty being overlooked by many holidaymakers, making it one of the best kept secrets around.

During the Victorian tourism boom the Island was popular with workers from the British mainland escaping the drudgery of everyday life, then in the post-war years of the 1940s and 50s became a popular destination for many and has remained a favourite for those in the know ever since. Peer beneath Manannan's Cloak (a natural phenomenon and mythological mechanism for hiding the Island from the world in times of trouble) and you will find an island, often unnoticed, that holds a wealth of history, beautiful unspoilt landscapes and a relaxed way of life that is both friendly and inviting.

With their Celtic and Norse roots, and Gaelic language, a relaxed atmosphere pervades the Island encapsulated in the Manx saying traa dy-liooar, meaning time enough.

Size & Population

The Isle of Man is approximately 33 miles long and 13 miles wide at its extremities, giving an area of roughly 200 square miles. The current population is around 84,500.

Government

The Isle of Man is home to the oldest parliament in the world, ruling unbroken for over 1,000 years. Established by Norse settlers, Tynwald is a system of self-government that sets the Island apart from the British Isles, empowering Mona's people to make their own laws and allowing them to remain independent while enjoying close relations with the UK.

Language

English is the spoken language, but Manx Gaelic (derived from Ireland and Scotland) is being revived in the Island's schools. In Manx the Isle of Man is called Ellan Vannin.

Money

Manx currency is the Manx pound, which is the equivalent of UK sterling. All UK currencies and euros are accepted on the Isle of Man, however the Manx pound is not legal tender outside of the Island.

ALL ROUND GUIDE ISLE of MAN

a different Kingdom

Tynwald Day 2022 – the Isle of Man's big annual celebration.

Food

Noted for its fresh home-grown produce, the Isle of Man is a foodie's paradise. Manx kippers, Queenies (Queen scallops), Loaghtan lamb, Island honey, award-winning cheeses and delicious Isle of Man cream all put the Island in the spotlight. Add to that local beer, wine, and gin and you have an Island feast.

The Three Legs

The Isle of Man national flag, the triskelion is based on the C13th Manx coat of arms. It features three armoured legs with spurs upon a red background. It's associated with the motto 'Quocunque Jeceris Stabit' which translates as 'Whithersoever you throw it, it will stand.'

Motorcycle Racing

Famous for the TT race, every year motorcycle enthusiasts descend upon the Island for the thrill and spectacle of two- and four-wheeled racing.

The Island's Capital

Douglas has remained relaxed and welcoming with its transformation from Victorian resort to vibrant international offshore banking and finance centre. With a beautiful sandy bay the Island's capital is steeped in history and modernity.

Manx Cats

The Isle of Man has its very own breed of domestic cat. The Manx cat is missing its tail (in varying degrees) due to an early genetic mutation and comes in all shapes and sizes. Loved by many the breed is one of the world's first show cat breeds.

A manx cat

3

Contents

Ramsey
- The town 6
- Town map 7
- Villages 8
- Places to go, things to do 12

Douglas
- The town 20
- Town map 21
- Villages 26
- Places to go, things to do 29

Castletown
- The town 38
- Town map 39
- Villages 41
- Places to go, things to do 44

Port Erin & Port St Mary
- The towns 50
- Town maps 51/52
- Villages 52
- Places to go, things to do 54

Peel
- The town 56
- Town map 57
- Villages 57
- Places to go, things to do 61

Itineraries
- On foot 64
- By cycle 111
- By trams and trains 115
- By car 123

Wildlife
- Parks to visit 140
- Natural areas 143
- The coast and the sea 151
- Wildlife in the air 156

History
- A proud history 160
- Museums & art galleries 180

Activities
- Trams & trains 184
- Get active 187
- Motorsports 193

Food and drink
- Island hospitality 198

Essentials
- Getting around the Island 212
- Getting to and from the Island 212
- Manx place names 214
- Further Reading and Index 222

4

All ROUND GUIDE ISLE of MAN

Contents

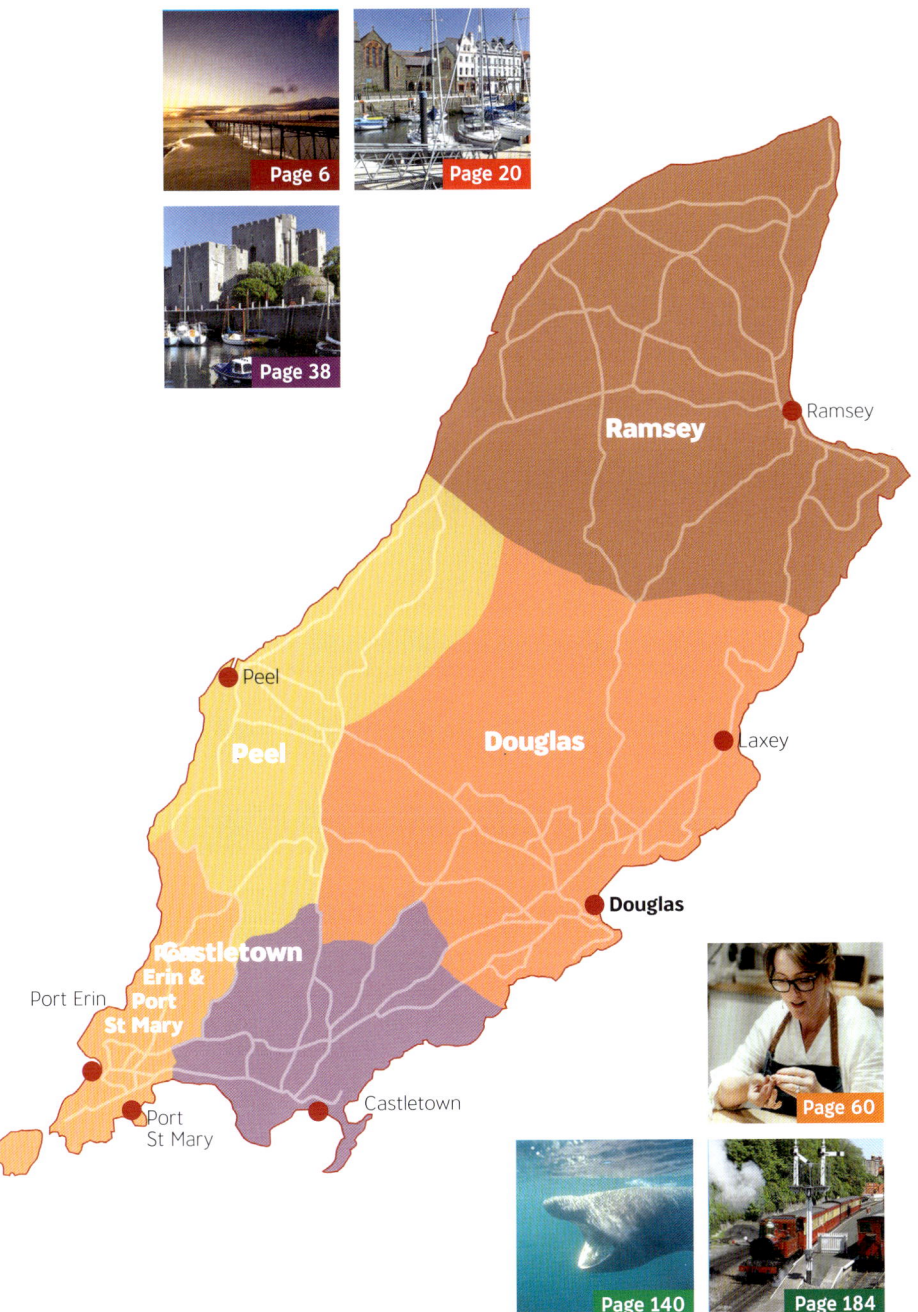

Page 6
Page 20
Page 38
Ramsey
Peel
Douglas
Castletown, Port Erin & Port St Mary
Port Erin
Port St Mary
Castletown
Laxey
Page 60
Page 140
Page 184

5

RAMSEY

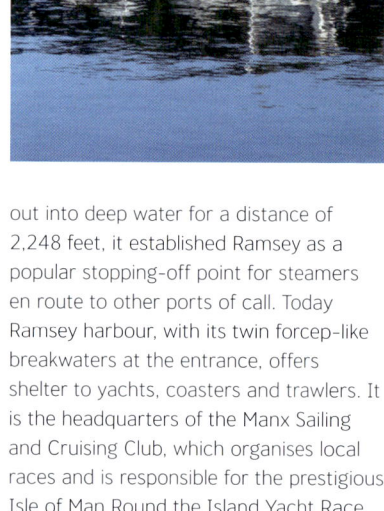

Ramsey, the second largest town on the Isle of Man, is blessed with a wonderful setting: cradled by the 10-mile sweep of the crescent bay, whose sandy shoreline extends to the northernmost Point of Ayre, against the backdrop of the high hills of North Barrule.

Chronicles of Mann of about 1250 records this north-eastern town as Ramsa – seemingly drawn from the old Scandinavian language and meaning Wild Garlic River – yet there are no buildings of great antiquity in Ramsey other than **Ballure Church**. The Burial Register dates from 1611 and in 1637 the building was reported to be in a near ruinous state. At various times over the years it has been restored.

The probable reason for Ramsey's lack of old buildings is that it suffered much turmoil throughout its early history. Olaf, King of Mann, was murdered by his nephew Reginald near the harbour in 1154. Somerled, the 12th-century Thane of Argyll, made a historic landing here, and a century later Robert the Bruce passed through on his way to besiege Castle Rushen.

Centuries on, landing in Ramsey became a lot easier when the magnificent **Queen's Pier** was built in 1886. Thrusting out into deep water for a distance of 2,248 feet, it established Ramsey as a popular stopping-off point for steamers en route to other ports of call. Today Ramsey harbour, with its twin forcep-like breakwaters at the entrance, offers shelter to yachts, coasters and trawlers. It is the headquarters of the Manx Sailing and Cruising Club, which organises local races and is responsible for the prestigious Isle of Man Round the Island Yacht Race every summer.

Another very distinctive feature of Ramsey's harbour is the **iron swing-bridge**, 225 feet long, which came into operation in 1892. On the landward side of the bridge is Ramsey shipyard, which constructed one of the world's first iron ships as well as *Star of India*, now displayed as an attraction in the American port of San Diego. The yard also built the world's first two ships specifically designed as oil tankers.

Flowing into the bay via the harbour is the Island's longest river, the Sulby. In fact, Ramsey was once an island. In 1630

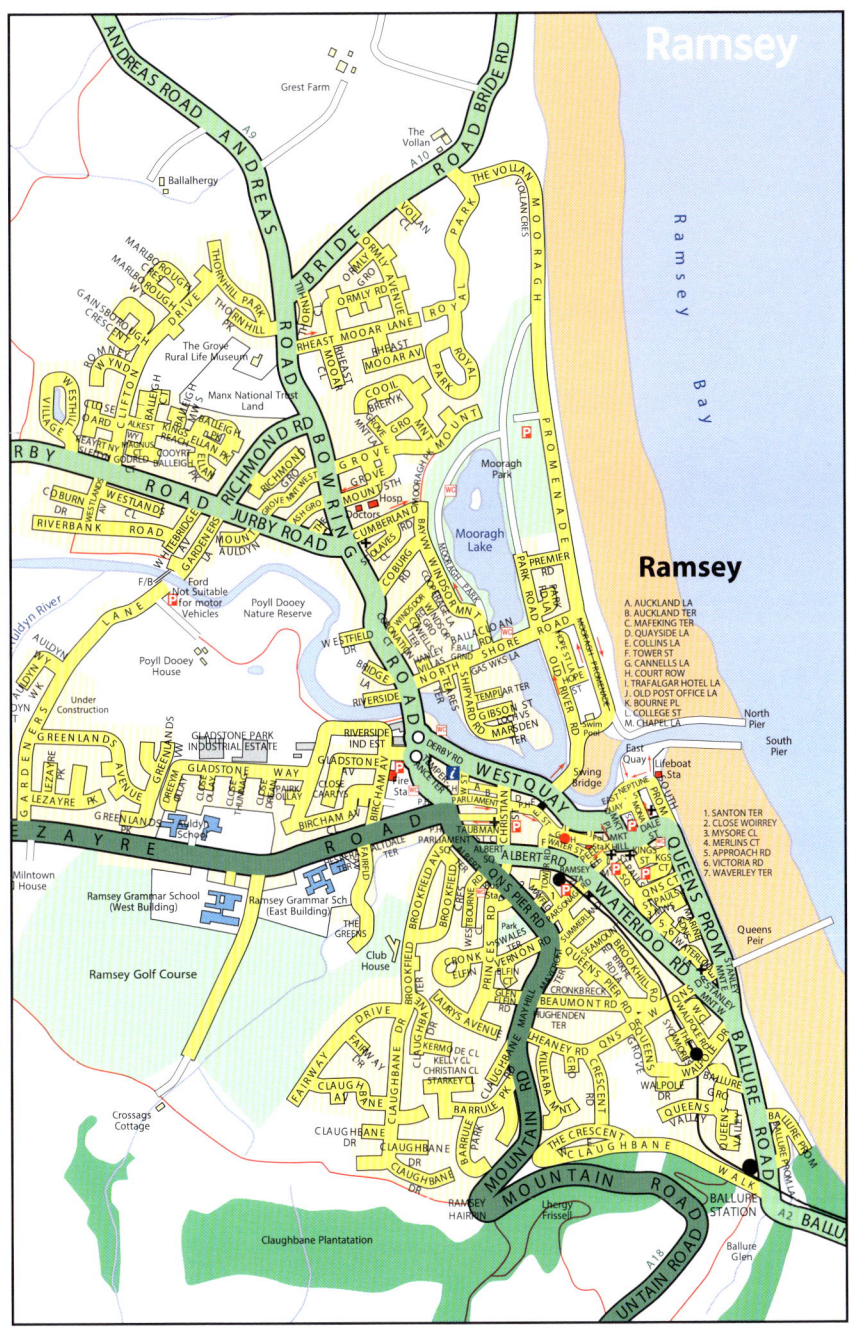

Ramsey from Albert Tower

the town was virtually destroyed by the sea, a continuous threat until the early years of the 19th century.

Villages

Andreas, Bride and Jurby

This is very much farming country. The relatively flat northern plain, easy for walking and cycling, is a maze of roads and lanes zigzagging between the villages. Andreas, Bride and Jurby are the Island's three most northerly parishes (central, east and west respectively) and share virtually the same scenery, the Bride Hills providing the only high ground in the area.

Jurby though is now developing at a pace calculated to transform it from the small community that grew up around the Royal Air Force base in the years of the Second World War into a west coast village in its own right. The famous old airfield, which has served many purposes since those war years, not least as the very popular motorsport and gliding venue which it is today, is the focal point of this activity and is attracting attention for a variety of reasons, one being the Jurby Transport Museum.

Jurby's old garrison church also merits a visit. The porch has a fine collection of stone crosses, and wandering through the churchyard and reading the inscriptions on the old headstones evokes many images of local history. In the new part of the churchyard, the well-kept graves of Polish, Canadian, Anzac and British airmen are laid out in neat rows and Howard Pixton, the pioneer aviator, is buried alongside them. On a clear day, from the back of the church, you can see Scotland's Mull of Galloway and its lighthouse.

Andreas has always been a pleasant village with a peaceful rural existence, largely uninterrupted since the end of the Viking era. In the 1940s, the land to the

All ROUND GUIDE ISLE of MAN

Ramsey

north and east of the village served as a base for the RAF. Roads and lanes accustomed to carrying nothing bigger than a horse and cart were widened, and it was not unusual to see large aircraft being manoeuvred on the roads skirting the edge of this ancient village. In 1995 the old airfields of Andreas and Jurby were used as locations for the film *The Brylcreem Boys*.

The parish church of Kirk Andreas with its Lombardic campanile is unexpected, but the Italian style sits well with the Manx countryside. It was built in 1802 to replace a parish church dating from the 13th century, the time when parishes were first formed on the Island. In 1869 Anglo-Saxon coins were discovered during the building of the bell tower. Dedicated to St Andrew, probably during the period of Scottish rule (circa 1275 to 1334), there are indications that a much earlier church, whose name has been lost, occupied the site. During the Second World War the spire was removed from the church to give a clear flight path for the planes using RAF Jurby and RAF Andreas.

The Andreas carved stones are very fine examples of Dark Age craftsmanship and one, a pillar, is particularly interesting with an inscription in Roman capitals and letters from the Ogham alphabet. Such carvings are seldom found outside Wales.

Not only the hills on whose slopes it sits but also a new rose share their name with the village of **Bride**. But looking at the village's past, the romance ends there. Bride was frequently raided by pirates and marauders, on clear days the smoke from the village's chimneys visible on the Galloway coast and tempting the villainous chieftain Cutlar MacCulloch and his men to set sail for a free Manx feed. On one occasion, arriving at a wedding feast just after soup had been taken, they deprived the guests of the meat by eating it all themselves.

To the west of Bride is Thurot Cottage,

Ramsey

9

Towns & Villages

Milntown

House ◊ Gardens ◊ Café ◊ Apartments

Café and Gardens – Open daily. House Tours available.
Café reservations call 818091 and for all other enquiries please call 812321. Visit our Facebook page and Website for more information
Milntown Estate, Milntown, Lezayre, Isle of Man, IM7 2AB

The Milntown Estate, in Lezayre, boasts 15 acres of beautiful gardens and woodlands encompassing the magnificent House and the Café at the heart.

In a purpose-built conservatory, the Café has wonderful views of the Walled Garden. The menu features a wide range of delicious home cooked seasonal dishes.

Set in the beautiful grounds of the Estate are three fabulous self-catering apartments. Each apartment sleeps up to 4 people: Altadale, Lezayre and Skyhill. Visit our website to check for availability throughout the year and to make a booking.

Come along and explore our RHS Partner Garden as Plant Enthusiasts can watch the gardens transform throughout the seasons. They feature ornamental gardens, water features and enchanted woodland walks. The gardens are always evolving whilst remaining sympathetic to the existing landscape.

Vehicle Enthusiasts will enjoy viewing our rare Vintage Collection of Motorcycles and Motorcars.

ALL ROUND GUIDE **ISLE of MAN**

Ramsey

11

Ramsey

a private house built using timbers from the ship of a defeated French fleet led by the vessel Bellisle, under the command of Captain Thurot. The battle, in February 1760, was witnessed by Bishop Hildesley and probably seen – and certainly heard – from Bride.

Bride church and its Celtic cross are interesting, and this is a very pleasant area for walking.

Ballaugh

The comparatively modern north-west village of Ballaugh is within easy reach of the west coast and straddles the A3 between Kirk Michael and Ramsey. It marks the beginning of the scenery that is so typical of this corner of the Island: remote glens running down to low sandy cliffs and shoreline against the hills of the northern uplands. The new church, built in 1832, is clearly visible from a distance.

Approximately a mile and a half nearer to the sea is old Kirk Ballaugh Church, with its very distinctive 'leaning' gate posts. Ballaugh has the oldest parish register in the Island, dating from 1598.

Maughold

In the north-east of the Island close to Ramsey (Maughold Head overlooks Ramsey Bay) is the village of Maughold. It enjoys stunning views of coast and countryside and was the most important centre of Celtic Christianity on the Isle of Man.

The church, Kirk Maughold, which dates from the 12th century, is dedicated to St Maughold, who is said to have been cast ashore near the headland.

The churchyard contains the remains of four ancient keeills (churches or chapels) and beautiful carved stone crosses found in the area are on display in the cross house. Of both Celtic and Norse origins, they are among the finest examples of the many carved crosses which have been discovered throughout the Island's landscape.

A path from the village takes you to the lighthouse on Maughold Head and those breathtaking views.

Port e Vullen

This small and attractive sheltered bay snuggles between Maughold Head and Ramsey Bay.

Places to go, things to do

Ramsey hosts several major annual events including:

◆ Yn Chruinnaght – the week-long Celtic festival of music, dance, art and literature
◆ Vintage motor rallies
◆ The TT Festival and Manx Grand Prix
◆ Ramsey's Fun Carnival Day in July.

Ballaglass Glen

The **summer angling festival** pulls in many keen fishermen, and golfers now have a choice of two 18-hole courses in the area – Ramsey's long-established club and Glen Truan, a newer course at Bride.

Located on Ramsey's seafront you'll find **Pepsi Max Bowl**. With 10 lanes, pool tables, table tennis, air hockey and a soft play area for the little ones it's a great way to spend some quality indoor time. They are open every day at 11am during Manx school holidays and then Thursday, Friday, Saturday and Sunday at 11am during school term times. There's plenty of parking or they are within easy walking distance of the town centre (accessible via bus or tram). They also have a seafront licensed diner, Sombreros, which has a Tex Mex theme along with some standard old favourites, sandwiches, cakes and of course a children's menu.

Mooragh Park was created in 1881 on reclaimed wasteland, protected by a new promenade and sea wall. It is a very popular spot and a great attraction for all ages, with 40 acres of gardens and a 12-acre boating lake. Canoeing, sailing and other water-based activities are part of the draw, as are the summer concerts and galas held in the park and the Lakeside Centre.

The Grove Museum of Victorian Life on the northern outskirts of Ramsey presents an interesting country house preserved as a period museum. In the 19th century this house was the home of the Gibb family and it retains all of their furniture and belongings. It opened as an attraction in 1979. The Gibb sisters who lived here latterly were keen bee keepers and there are displays reflecting this.

Milntown in Lezayre on Ramsey's

Places to go, things to do

Ballaugh Glen

outskirts (the Milntown estate adjoins the entrance to Glen Auldyn), is the Island's most historic estate and boasts 15 acres of beautiful gardens and woodland which surround the magnificent mansion at its heart. For over 400 years, up to 1886, it was the home of the Christian family, members of which famously included Illiam Dhone (William Christian 1608–1663, the last man to be executed at Hango Hill near Castletown but posthumously found not guilty of treason), Fletcher Christian (leader of the HMS *Bounty* mutiny) and John Christian Curwen (unique in history as both a House of Commons MP and a member of the House of Keys). Milntown has also been a school for young ladies, a hotel and the private home of Lady Kathleen Edwards and subsequently her son, Sir Clive. On his death in 1999 the Milntown Trust was established to maintain the house and estate for the benefit of the Manx people and visitors to the Isle of Man.

There's something for all ages here – children can run free and explore the many wonders hidden in its gardens, feed the ducks on the mill pond and take part in seasonal treasure hunts. Plant enthusiasts can watch the gardens transform throughout the seasons and chat with dedicated and experienced gardeners who are always willing to share their expertise. The onsite cafe offers breakfasts, lunches and tempting afternoon teas and treats all year round. With a selection of light bites, tasty mains and a children's menu, the cafe caters for all. Check the specials boards for alternative options, and seasonal items using the delicious produce from the

Manx Transport History.

Visit Jurby Transport Museum to see our collection of mainly Manx transport history including buses, cars, commercial vehicles, motorcycles, bicycles, trams, memorabilia displays and model railway.

Visit the shop for souvenirs, transport memorabilia and new and second hand books. Hot and cold drinks and confectionary also available.

— **FREE ADMISSION** —

Open on Sundays from Easter until the end of September. Other times by arrangement.

Jurby Transport Museum, Hangar 230,
Jurby Industrial Estate, Jurby, Isle of Man IM7 3BD
Email: jtm.info@manx.net • Web: www.jtmiom.im

Manx Transport Trust Ltd (No. 120821C) registered as a charity in the Isle of Man No. 1034.

kitchen gardens. With a full event calendar for the year there are a wide range of activities catering for all the family, including dining experiences; craft workshops; Hop-tu-naa and Christmas events as well as larger outdoor experiences and festivals. Check their website and Facebook page for seasonal opening hours and for more details on house and garden tours as well as forthcoming events.

All vintage cars and motor cycles of the **Milntown collection** are roadworthy and frequently shown at major events such as the TT Festival. Fine paintings, furniture, ceramics and silver adorn the house.

The restaurant and gardens open March to October, with house tours April to September. As featured on TV's Ghost Hunting, with guests from the cast of Coronation Street, Milntown is reputedly the Isle of Man's most haunted house and ghost tours are very popular.

The **Jurby Transport Museum** displays examples of public and commercial road transport using a combination of vehicles on loan from the Isle of Man Government Department of Community Culture & Leisure, Douglas Corporation, vehicles owned by the Trust and privately owned by individuals or small groups. Jurby is a working museum and some of the restored vehicles can be seen in operation during vintage vehicle events, at Jurby and elsewhere on the Island. This may result in vehicles being absent on occasions.

◆ A number are already restored to operational condition; several are currently under restoration, and some are long term projects stored awaiting attention. The majority of vehicles in the collection are available for viewing, a small number are stored off-site.

◆ The museum seeks to restore, display and inform visitors of the Island's transport history and to promote the necessary interest and skills to enable the maintenance and expansion of the facility for the future.

The museum building itself, a former RAF aircraft hangar, is of interest:

◆ Designed by N S Bellman, the Royal Air Force Directorate of Works structural engineer, it is one of four transportable hangars built at Jurby to the same design and one of around 400 built in total. Head Wrightson & Co. Ltd of Teesdale Iron Works, Thornaby-on-Tees were given the commercial rights to construct the hangars.

◆ The structure is composed of a unit system of rolled steel lattice girders, both the walls and roof using standard units and all joined by standard corner sections. It was 175'0" long, 87'8" wide and has a clear internal height of 25'0".

◆ The four at Jurby were built during the winter of 1939/1940, this one being used as the single engine maintenance flight hangar. It has more recently been used by Ramsey Coal, before being completely refurbished and shortened by about 15'0" by the Isle of Man Government Department of Infrastructure.

Following refurbishment it was leased to MTT for use as a museum.

The museum has a wide range of exhibits including buses, trams, lorries, steam and internal combustion cars and a traction engine. There is also a replica Spitfire, an airborne lifeboat and parts of an Airship (G-MAAC) along with many smaller exhibits. Admission is free from Easter onwards (closed during the winter), though donations are always welcome. Jurby Transport Museum, Hangar 230, Jurby Industrial Estate, Jurby, IM7 3BD. jtminfo@manx.net   www.jtmiom.im

The **Isle of Man Motor Museum** is also

housed in Jurby, and is the home of the Cunningham Classic Car Collection. Comprised of over 100 vehicles, what began as a small collection of classic cars, started 30 years ago by Denis Cunningham, is now the passion of both Denis and his son Darren. Concentrating on rare and unique models from all over the world, and from all eras, the collection boasts cars as well as commercial vehicles, one-offs and prototypes. The museum aims to keep things fresh by rotating exhibits on loan to complement the permanent collection.

Over 250 vehicles are on display, from classic cars and racing motorcycles to larger items such as a Greyhound Bus, fire engines and a steam collection. Set in an exhibition space of over 70,000 sq. ft the ground floor displays a large number of vehicles, with motorcycles being housed on a mezzanine floor. Facilities include a gift shop, refreshment area, toilets, and a car club display area. There is full disabled access throughout.
www.isleofmanmotormuseum.com

One of the biggest attractions for children of all ages is **Curraghs Wildlife Park** in the north. Within its 26 acres are more than 100 species of birds and animals from wetland areas around the world, along with nature and butterfly trails and the Island's smallest passenger-carrying railway – the very popular Orchid Line. The park is open all year round between Easter and October 10am – 6pm, and at weekends from 10am – 4pm during the winter season.
www.curraghswildlifepark.im

Close to the Island's most northerly outpost – **the Point of Ayre** – is the **Ayres Visitor Centre**. Run by Manx Wildlife Trust, it explains the significance of the Ayres National Nature Reserve and its unique variety of habitats and sensitive ecosystem, comprising shingle beach, dunes, lichen heath, dune slacks, conifer plantation and gorse scrub. Whereas to the south-east of Ramsey the **Maughold Brooghs** have the coastal path running through them and are relatively well known.

Killabrega on the slopes of the Sulby Valley, site of a tholtan (abandoned house), is perhaps less familiar to many. For more tholtans, *Lily Publications* have published *Manx Tholtans v1 &v2*.

Eating Out

MILNTOWN: Milntown, Lezayre, IM7 2AB. 01624 818091. www.milntown.org

Having its own kitchen garden ensures that the dishes on offer at Milntown are as fresh as they can be. With the garden team working closely with the chef, the specials board is dictated by the seasonally available produce and always features salads which can be plucked straight from the garden. Set in a light and spacious conservatory, Milntown Café is the ideal place to sit and relax while enjoying a home-cooked meal or tea and cake.

Other Eateries & Cafes

The Dovecote, Main Road, Kirk Michael, IM6 1AB Tel: 01624 878534 www.the-dovecote.business.site/

Victory Cafe is based in a crazy ex Cold War Rotor Radar Station overlooking the 31st Milestone of the TT Racecourse serving homemade British style canteen food. The cafe is also based just by the Bungalow on the Snaefell Mountain Railway. A must visit for food lovers and bike lovers alike! Located on the A18 Mountain Road from Douglas or Ramsey. https://www.facebook.com/VictoryCafeIsleofMan/

Maughold Head

DOUGLAS

In the last few decades the transformation of Douglas from tired Victorian resort to vibrant international offshore banking and finance centre has been dramatic.

Along the sweeping promenade, best viewed from the top of Douglas Head, where the two-mile crescent of **Douglas Bay** spreads out invitingly before you, grand old architecture rubs shoulders with luxury apartments and towering statements of 21st-century corporate clout.

Morning and evening rush hours may be a new and inevitable consequence of this progress, but for all this the Isle of Man capital still retains its relaxed and welcoming 'easy come, easy go' holiday charm and appeal: the great variety of accommodation, pubs, restaurants, entertainment and other attractions new and not so new make sure of it.

It was largely due to its sheltered position on the east coast that Douglas became the Island's major port and the focus of trade in salt, herring, hides, soap and beer. During the 18th century it was also a centre for the 'running trade', by which merchants avoided high British tariffs on imported goods such as tea, tobacco, wine and brandy by importing them legally into the Isle of Man, paying lower taxes to the Lord of Mann, and then 'running' the goods to colleagues waiting along the shore on the British mainland.

'Running' increased the wealth of the town, but in 1765 the British government brought an end to the business by purchasing the rights of the Lord of Mann so that all goods entering the Island paid British taxes. The Royal Navy and British customs officials controlled this, and the effect was a drastic drop in the wealth and living standards in the town. Interestingly, a commander of one of the revenue cutters was Lieutenant William Bligh, later of mutiny on the *Bounty* fame, who married a local girl, Elizabeth Betham. Peter Heywood of Douglas was also on the *Bounty* crew as, of course, was Fletcher Christian, whose family had strong Manx connections.

In 1787, during a terrible storm, a gale off Laxey wrecked the Island's herring fleet. Many boats and lives were lost as they headed for the shelter of Douglas's crumbled pier, and in 1801 a new Douglas pier was constructed.

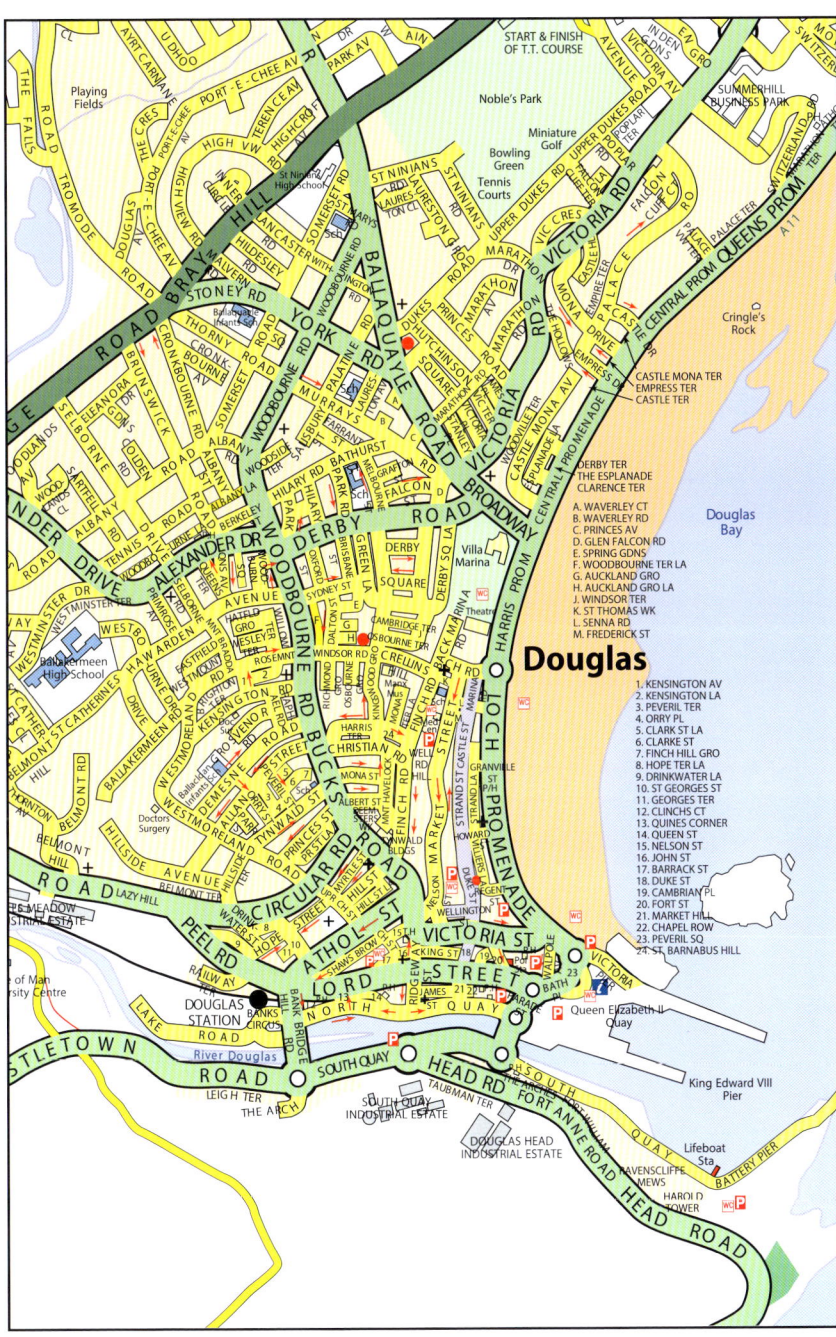

Towns & Villages

View from Douglas Head

Shipwrecks were a fact of life for the Island's sailors. In 1822 a Royal Navy cutter ran aground in the harbour entrance at Douglas and 97 men were saved. The rescue was organised by Sir William Hillary, who had moved to the Isle of Man after triumphs in the Napoleonic wars, and in 1824 he launched the appeal which led to the formation of what was to become the Royal National Lifeboat Institution.

Hillary was involved in many other rescues, including that of the paddle steamer *St. George* in 1832 after it had become stranded on the treacherous Conister Rock reef near the entrance to Douglas harbour. Although a non-swimmer, he took the lifeboat out with his crew and saved all 22 aboard. In 1832 he was also responsible for building the rock's Tower of Refuge for shipwrecked sailors – a sight long familiar to all ferry passengers arriving at the Sea Terminal.

The town spread out from the harbour in the 19th century; first as Georgian residences were built for affluent arrivals from England attracted by the low cost of living, and later for the wealthy holiday visitors from the factory towns of northern England who came on the steamships from Liverpool and Whitehaven. In 1830, to cater for this increased sea traffic, a group of local

The Bee Gees - Douglas Promenade

businessmen decided to build the passenger ship *Mona's Isle* – an enterprise which led eventually to the formation of the Isle of Man Steam Packet Company.

In the decades since, the twin piers of Douglas have welcomed the arrival of millions of holidaymakers, and today cruise ships are regular visitors too. There are two interesting anecdotes relating to the piers: **King Edward Pier** is the only public work named after the uncrowned sovereign, and at **Victoria Pier** the 'Dawsey' memorial commemorates David 'Dawsey' Kewley, a ropeman with the Isle of Man Steam Packet Company, who is reputed to have saved 24 men from drowning.

The holiday trade boomed for Douglas and the Isle of Man in the late 19th century and well on into the 20th. In 1869 Douglas took over from Castletown as the Island's capital, and the latter half of the 19th century saw major developments of hotels and boarding houses, the construction of Victoria Pier in 1872, the erection of splendid theatres and ballrooms, and improvements to municipal facilities and housing for local residents.

The great benefactor Henry Bloom Noble funded the town's public baths, a park, a hospital (recently replaced by a new modern hospital) and, in the middle of the promenade, the original **Villa Marina**, which was a focus of entertainment in Douglas from 1913 up until its decline in the 1990s. The nearby **Gaiety Theatre**, designed by Frank Matcham and another celebration of Douglas's Victorian and Edwardian heritage, was saved from demolition at the eleventh hour in 1971 when Tynwald approved its purchase for the nation. From a sad and sorry state of neglect, the Gaiety was completely and authentically restored under the direction of manager Mervin Russell Stokes, who was rewarded

Douglas inner harbour

with an MBE for his work. The painstaking 10-year restoration culminated in 2000, the theatre's centenary year, and it now stands proud as one of the finest surviving Matcham theatres in the British Isles. The new Villa Marina underwent a similar rebirth in 2004, following significant and sympathetic redevelopment, and is a major modern venue for a wide variety of live shows and other entertainment, including cinema, dance and events.

Other investment in visitor facilities over recent years is apparent in Douglas's fine restaurants, fashionable shops, wine and tapas bars, yacht marina and attractions such as the excellent award-winning **Manx Museum** and restored **Victorian Camera Obscura**.

Traditional attractions are still going strong too. Douglas is the hub of the Island's vintage railways. From here you can enjoy all the delights of both the **Isle of Man Steam Railway**, which takes you to beautiful Port Erin in the south, and the **Manx Electric Railway**. This heads north to Laxey and Ramsey along the spectacular east coast. At Laxey you can temporarily interrupt one great Isle of Man railway journey to experience yet another – by disembarking for the 5-mile ascent to the Island's highest point on the **Snaefell Mountain Railway**.

The emergence of Douglas as an important international offshore banking

Towns & Villages

Founded in 2007 MostlyManx is dedicated to the promotion of Isle of Man Artisans.

At the MostlyManx shop in Douglas customers can enjoy a refreshing return to 'traditional' shopping, with emphasis on quality and a warm, personal service. Gorgeous gift wrapping and a relaxed atmosphere created by the luxurious shop fittings.

Over 30 artisans are represented from foods, jewellery, textiles, glassware and ceramics, MostlyManx is the ideal one-stop gift shop for all things Manx.

**25 NELSON STREET, DOUGLAS, ISLE OF MAN IM1 2AN
01624 674548 (Behind Marks and Spencer)
www.presenceofmann.com/mostlymanx**

FOR GIFTS, HAMPERS, SOUVENIRS, GLASSWARE, MANX TARTANS

THE MANX TARTAN SHOP

Our Sister shop is "The Manx Tartan Shop" At Laxey Woollen Mills where you can find a whole range of products in the two Manx tartans.

Luxurious woollen rugs and scarves made by the last remaining commercial pattern weaver on the Isle of Man. Cushions, ceramics, kitchenware and wedding accessories are all available to purchase

THE MANX TARTAN SHOP
LAXEY WOOLLEN MILLS
GLEN ROAD, LAXEY, ISLE OF MAN. IM4 7AR
01624 860330 www.presenceofmann.com

mostlymanx   themanxtartanshop

and commercial centre is reflected in the town's redevelopment and increased number of designer retail outlets. There are also two shopping centres – the Strand and the more recent Tower House galleria, built round a large central atrium – plus three supermarkets, including the Island's own Shoprite, which also has stores in Onchan, Ramsey, Peel, Port Erin and Castletown.

Villages

Laxey

Laxey ('Salmon River' in old Norse) sprawls along the sides of a deep glen, running down from the mine workings in its upper reaches to the tiny harbour at the north end of a wide bay.

Located on the banks of the Laxey River, St George's Woollen Mills has been a part of village industry since its founding in the late 19th century. Backed by the prominent Victorian social activist and philanthropist, John Ruskin, the mill swiftly replaced the cottage industry of the time. The new industrious and disciplined centre of production drew heavily from Ruskin's social beliefs and even bore the name of his personal society, the Guild of St George.

With the global need to move away from plastics and disposable fashion the mill continues to weave quality pure woollen cloth; Manx Tweed and Manx Tartan both being produced, shipped and sold from the Mill complex. Indeed it is within the Mill shop that you will find rugs, garments, handbags and accessories made from the wool of the famous indigenous Loaghtan sheep. Known for its distinctive brown colour the wool of the Loaghtan sheep lends itself well to rugs and outer garments, its warmth and natural colouring making it highly prized amongst both weavers, tailors and knitters.

Laxey Woollen Mills is the only working mill left on the island, …. the two working pedal looms still used daily to produce rugs, scarves and tweed for coats, jackets, bags, caps, ties and a wide range of accessories. Tweed can also be bought by the metre from the bolts of cloth on display. Within the Laxey Woollen Mills shop you will also find a wide range of exquisite Irish and Scottish knitwear, sheepskin products locally produced garments and accessories plus Manx Loaghtan products and knitting wools.

Located on the first floor, is the Hodgson Loom Art Gallery exhibition space and Gallery Shop. Here you will find a wide variety of work by renowned local artists, sculptors, photographers, ceramicists, jewellers and textile artists.

Gallery Schedule for 2023

11th March – 22nd April. Annual Open Art Competition Exhibition, this year's theme being the word 'Free'

29th April – 10th June. Manx nature artist Chrissie Moss and special guests (TBA)

17th June – 29th July. 'Angel Fields' a collection of new work by the highly acclaimed abstract artist Gary Bennett.

5th August – 16th September. The Manx Art Festival exhibition by members of the Creative Network

23rd September – 4th November. Our Manx Biosphere - Fungi, Moss, Lichen, Liverworts and Slime Moulds. An open exhibition in celebration of these wonderful and bizarre forms of nature.

11th November – January 2024. Manx landscape artist Paul Parker. A new collection of paintings in watercolour, acrylic, pastel and oil.

Further information may be found on the Hodgson Loom Gallery facebook page

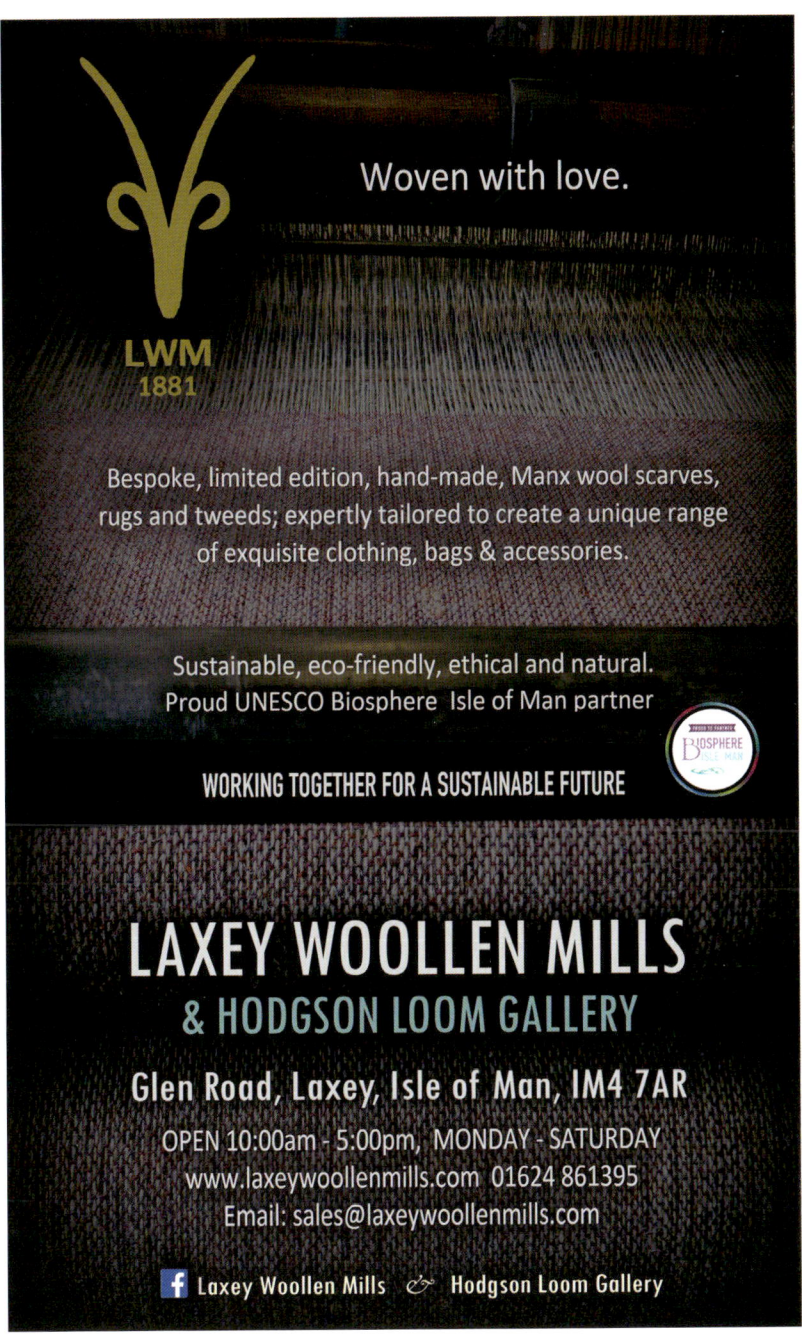

The Mill complex also includes The Manx Tartan Shop replete with all the Manx Tartan products and Manx themed gifts; and Manninkilt for Manx Tartan kilt hire and accessories, by appointment.

It was in about 1780 when the small community of Laxey discovered that a fortune lay at its feet. Substantial deposits of lead, copper, zinc and silver were soon being exploited by a thriving mining industry which reached its peak in the mid-1870s. A thousand men were employed here and the operation was highly profitable, producing as much zinc as all other zinc mines in Britain could muster between them. From 1876 to 1882 the Great Laxey Mines paid out the highest total in dividends of all the lead mines in the British Isles, ensuring a reasonable standard of living for the people of the village.

Transporting the ore from the mines to the washing floors further down the valley, where it was cleaned and made ready for sale, was the work of pit ponies, hauling tramway wagons. But in 1877 they were replaced by Ant and Bee – two 19-inch gauge steam locomotives which remained in service until the mine closed in 1929. Today, thanks to the dedicated work of the Laxey and Lonan Heritage Trust, the quarter-mile surface section of the tramway has been restored and two replica locos take passengers through what is the Island's longest railway tunnel to a picnic site not far from Lady Isabella – better known as the **Great Laxey Wheel**.

One of the world's biggest ever waterwheels, it pumped water from the mines from depths of up to 2,000 feet. At 72 feet in diameter, with 95 steps leading to the viewing platform 75 feet above the ground, the wheel presents a breathtaking sight. Nearby, in Laxey Valley Gardens – once the washing floors – is Lady Evelyn. At a mere 50 feet in diameter, this restored wheel first served the remote Snaefell Mine, which closed in 1908, and then a Cornish china clay works. The Trevithick Society preserved it and returned it to the Isle of Man, where it has been on show at Laxey since 2006.

Another of the village's attractions is the **Laxey Heritage Trail** – a leisurely and fascinating 2-hour circular walk from Lady Isabella. It takes you to a variety of interesting places, such as the woollen and flour mills, Quarry Falls, Old Laxey, Laxey Glen and the former 18th-century water-driven corn mill.

The Laxey and Lonan Heritage Trust, a voluntary organisation, has an information centre and gift shop located in the old fire station on the road just before you arrive at Lady Isabella. Lower down the glen are gardens, the beach and a small folk museum near the station. From the station you can board the scenic electric mountain railway on a 5-mile climb to the summit of Snaefell.

Onchan

This ancient parish immediately north of Douglas has grown rapidly since the Second World War, becoming something of an overspill for the capital although under the separate administration of the Onchan District Commissioners.

The patron saint of the parish was St Christopher, better known by his Gaelic name of Conchenn, meaning dog-head or wolf-head. In the porch of the present parish church, built in 1833, there are Norse carvings which depict dog-like monsters set on Christian crosses.

The church register dates back to 1627 although the first vicar was appointed in 1408. Interestingly, the church features some modern stained glass and in the churchyard there are headstones designed by Archibald Knox and the grave of Lieutenant Edward Reeves RN, the last surviving officer to fight with Nelson at Trafalgar. An earlier church on the site witnessed the marriage of Captain Bligh of *Bounty* fame to Elizabeth Betham, daughter of the Collector of Customs, who lived in Onchan and also lies buried in the churchyard. Beneath the churchyard wall stand two electric lamp standards, originally erected in 1897 to commemorate Queen Victoria's Diamond Jubilee and now the Island's oldest street lamps.

Close by is chapel-like Welch House, a former infant school and Sunday school now used as an office. Above that is Molly Carrooin's Cottage. It is 300 years old and up to 100 years ago had a thatched roof. The recently-created village green connects with the Onchan Wetlands, an urban nature reserve on the site of an old mill dam.

The old part of the village grew up around the church – a process repeated with Onchan's rapid expansion, the old village now fringed by a large number of estates and a modern shopping precinct, as befits the second most populated area of the island.

Onchan, very close to Douglas and easily reached, is of interest to visitors for its country walks, **King Edward Bay Golf Club**, horse riding establishments, and Onchan Park and Stadium.

Port Soderick

Popular with Victorian holidaymakers for its beach, bathing huts, refreshments and walks, Port Soderick lies only three miles south of Douglas on the east coast. This small resort and the capital were connected by road with the construction of Marine Drive, on the headland above

Lady Evelyn, Laxey

Douglas harbour, but separated again when a landslide cut the road in two, as is still the case today. They were also once connected by the Douglas Southern Electric Tramway – the only railway on the Isle of Man ever to use the standard British gauge of track. Despite its demise, Marine Drive still provides an appreciation of the spectacular coastal views the tramway's passengers were treated to.

Port Soderick and Port Soderick Glen are still accessible by road using the A37.

Places to go, things to do

Acquired by the Isle of Man Government in the 1990s and reopened in 2005 after major restoration, the **Great Union Camera Obscura** on Douglas Head, overlooking the harbour and town, was built for the Victorian tourism boom and is one of only four now remaining in the British Isles. Through a series of mirrors and lenses it gives spectacular views over Douglas, open from May to September.

Laxey harbour

Saturdays 1pm – 4pm and 11am – 4pm on Sundays and bank holidays.

Just north of Douglas is **Onchan Park and Stadium**, overlooking Douglas Bay. A big magnet for all ages in summer months with motorboats, karting, squash, tennis, stock car racing, mini golf, flat and crown green bowling and more.

Another park with lots of facilities and attractions is **Noble's Park** in Douglas, and for toddlers the **Villa Marina** has a safe play area.

Laxey has plenty to do with the **Great Laxey Wheel**, **Laxey Woollen Mills**, **Hodgson Loom Gallery**, **Laxey Heritage Trail** and the **electric mountain railway** climb to the summit of Snaefell.

Industry rather than agriculture is the theme of the **Great Laxey Wheel**. The wheel, and the mines for which it was built, show the way of life of a different part of the community – men toiling far underground but joined by women and children in the surface tasks

The northern part of **King Orry's grave** at Laxey has long been readily accessible from the Ballaragh road, and more recently the Manx Heritage purchase of the southern part of the burial site means that this too can be seen.

In recent years Manx Heritage has acquired access to the important **Braaid complex** and you can visit the remains of the Celtic and Viking homes which stood there overlooking Glen Vine.

The Island's history is presented by Manx National Heritage throughout the Island. From the hub – the **Manx Museum** ('Thie Tashtee Vannin', the Treasure House) in Douglas – the story of the Island radiates out to other historic Manx National Heritage sites and museums. Ideally, your starting point is to take a seat in the Manx Museum lecture theatre to view an introductory 20-minute film normally shown every half an hour during the day. It gives you an overview of the Island's history and landscape. The idea then is to proceed through the different areas of the museum, starting with the art gallery, where all the pictures are either of the Isle of Man or are by Manx artists – a policy common to all of the Museum's collections.

Art is followed by maps and geology and a never-ending argument about whether lead or slate is the most important. Prehistory, Celts and Vikings lead through to later history, tourism and wartime internment, with side paths of literature and home design.

Model boats and typical buildings take you to the exhibition gallery, which regularly hosts temporary displays of art or history. A small exhibition links the entrance to the reading room for the library and archives, and nearby are the Bay Room Restaurant and museum shop.

Throughout the museum trail there is generous use of videos and other electronic displays, with links to the other relevant sites, monuments and landscape which are under the protection of Manx National Heritage.

Eating Out

14NORTH: 14 North Quay, Douglas, IM1 4LE. 01624 664414 www.14north.im

Located on Douglas' North Quay, amidst the beautiful laid back setting of a redesigned old building, 14North highlights the finest produce the Isle of Man's farmers and artisanal suppliers have to offer. They believe in keeping things simple and honest, yet delicious. The focus is on modern British cuisine using seasonal flavours, treating produce with respect and using simple cooking methods to allow the produce to be the star.

Laxey wheel

Places to go, things to do & Eating out

Little Fish Cafe, Douglas

LITTLE FISH CAFE: 31 North Quay, Douglas, IM1 4LB. 01624 622518
www.littlefishcafe.com

Little Fish opened in April 2014 with the belief that great food brings people together. With a menu that offers something for everyone, from intimate candlelit dinners with cocktails, lunch with friends, to a quick coffee on the go, the food is humble, yet delicious. Alongside a regular menu they have a rotating specials board which showcases the best of the day's catch. Carefully selected wines and a dedicated cocktail menu complement the food on offer and on weekends there is a well established brunch menu available throughout the day.

COAST: 18–22 Loch Promenade, Douglas, IM1 2LX. 01624 698800
www.claremonthoteldouglas.com

Situated within the 4-Star Gold status Claremont Hotel on Douglas Promenade, officially the highest-rated hotel on the Isle of Man, the philosophy is simply 'Excellence as Standard'. The beautiful Coast Bar & Brasserie is renowned as a first class restaurant featuring all-day dining and friendly attentive service, with stunning panoramic views across the Bay. The perfect location to enjoy breakfast, lunch, afternoon tea or dinner, in a friendly atmosphere.

WINE DOWN: 24 Duke Street, Douglas, IM1 2AY. 01624 624777
www.winedown.im

Over 10 years after the birth of the renowned Macfarlane's Restaurant, they bring you a brand new concept for the Isle of Man.

Combining Roy's 31 years experience in the kitchen with Anne's 36 years working with wine, we bring you excellent quality food to share (or not!) and some of the finest wines to match. The wines are available by the bottle or you can try different wines by the glass to match your menu choices. With well over 100 wines to choose from, Anne will be on hand to help you select one to suit your palate.

PORTOFINO RESTAURANT: Portofino Restaurant, 1 Bridge Road, Quay West, Douglas, IM1 5AG. 01624 617755
www.portofino.im

Located in a fantastic position looking out over the stunning Douglas marina, Portifino is Mario Ciappelli's pride and joy. The modern building houses a stylish interior, which creates a relaxed atmosphere for fine dining. Using the highest quality local produce Mario creates mouth-watering dishes that are sure to impress. Appearing in the Michelin guide for the past three years, Portofino

A CAFE FOR CYCLISTS, A BIKESHOP FOR COFFEE DRINKERS AND A SPACE FOR EVERYONE.

Cycle 360 — Fuel & Freedom

OPEN SEVEN DAYS A WEEK | ISLE OF MAN BUSINESS PARK

Places to go, things to do & Eating out

The Shed, Laxey

specialises in the finest seafood, Mediterranean and international cuisine.

THE TICKETHALL: Douglas Railway Station, Bank Hill, Douglas IM1 4LL. 01624 627888 www.ticket-hall.com

At Douglas Railway Station you will find the tradition of cooking food on the footplate of a steam train has been kept alive. In the Tickethall restaurant, among the usual fare, you can enjoy a full English breakfast served upon a fireman's shovel. Sourcing ingredients from local farms is vitally important to the Tickethall, so while they have their foot firmly in the past, they are also passionate about future sustainability.

SHORE HOTEL AND RESTAURANT, Laxey, IM4 7DA. 01624 861509. www.shorehotellaxey.im

Overlooking the famous Laxey river, The Shore Hotel Restaurant offers patrons a unique and intimate dining experience in a luxurious setting complimented by a menu that makes use of only the best local and seasonal ingredients.

LA MONA LISA. Laxey, IM4 7DA. 01624 862488

La Mona Lisa is a friendly, family run restaurant which has been serving quality Italian cuisine since 1944. The restaurant is located in the picturesque riverside setting near to Laxey harbour. .

Other Eateries & Cafes

The Shed, Laxey Promenade, Laxey IM4 7DD Tel 01624 863751
https://www.facebook.com/theshedlaxey

Cycle 360 Its 80-seater cafe has a daily offering of soups, salads, sandwiches and wholesome lunches, with vegan, gluten free and veggie options. Plus there's plenty of homemade delicious treats to accompany their infamous coffee. For more information see page 33.

All ROUND GUIDE **ISLE of MAN**

Exploring the Isle of Man
with a wide range of maps from Lily Publications

Douglas

Map Offer 1
New editions (2021) of the Isle of Man Outdoor Leisure Maps for both North and South of the Isle of Man available to purchase together at special price. Produced in full colour, scale 2.5 inches to 1 mile. £8.90

Map Offer 2
Weather proof editions (2021) of the Isle of Man Outdoor Leisure Maps for both North and South of the Isle of Man available to purchase together at special price. Produced in full colour, scale 2.5 inches to 1 mile. £15.95

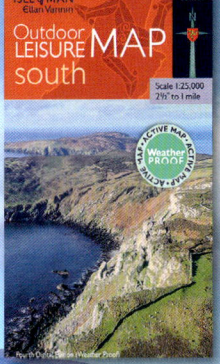

Available at all good book shops on the Isle of Man
Lily Publications Ltd, Ballachrink Beg, Jurby East, Ramsey IM7 3HD
www.lilypublications.co.uk   Tel: 01624 898446

ALL ROUND GUIDE **ISLE of MAN**

CASTLETOWN

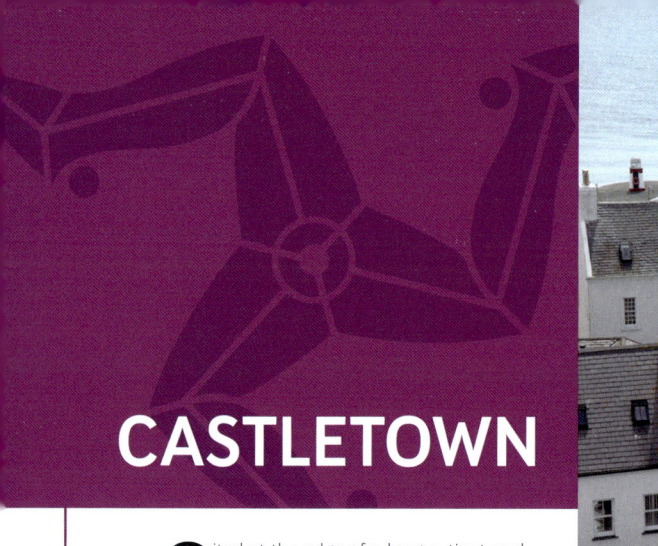

Sited at the edge of a long extinct and almost untraceable volcano, Castletown was for centuries the capital of the Isle of Man, its medieval limestone castle a symbol of strength, power and authority, guardian of the Manx in times of war and peace. It wasn't until the 1860s that the status of capital passed to Douglas, under the governorship of Scotsman Henry Loch.

Castletown today has a quiet but distinctive charm. Not only is the fortress which gave the stronghold its name still standing, it is in remarkably good nick – one of the most complete castles in the British Isles – and well worth seeing for its period recreations, fine views and deep sense of history. Castle Rushen dominates the southern lowlands and is visible for miles around. As well as being an impressive historical attraction it is also a working castle, its courthouse and precincts still in traditional use. A point of early military interest is that the staircases spiral to the right, obliging any uninvited swordsmen with hostile intent to grip their weapons left-handed as they ascended so that right-handed defenders had an obvious advantage.

The castle overlooks the harbour, which is built on a shelf of lava, clearly visible at low water. A walk along the shoreline from the harbour towards Scarlett Point shows you more evidence of this past volcanic activity in the area. Aeons of tide and weather have exposed the volcano's surviving plug, and the **Scarlett Visitor Centre and nature trail** make for an informative excursion.

The virtual end to commercial seaborne traffic into and out of Castletown came in the 1970s. Now banking and finance are the mainstays of the town's fortunes and have helped stimulate a revival in business.

Practically all of the town's ancient buildings are grouped around the harbour and to the seaward side of the castle. Among them is a cluster of small but **fascinating museums. The Nautical Museum, Old House of Keys** and **Old Grammar School** are all significant in the telling of the Island's story and attract many visitors, particularly in summer months.

Castletown's **market square** is little changed since the 1800s. In the centre stands Smelt's Memorial, erected in 1838 to honour Governor Cornelius Smelt (1805 to 1832) – and to this day still incomplete. The people of Castletown refused to contribute for a statue to grace the column, the erection becoming known as the 'Castletown Candlestick'.

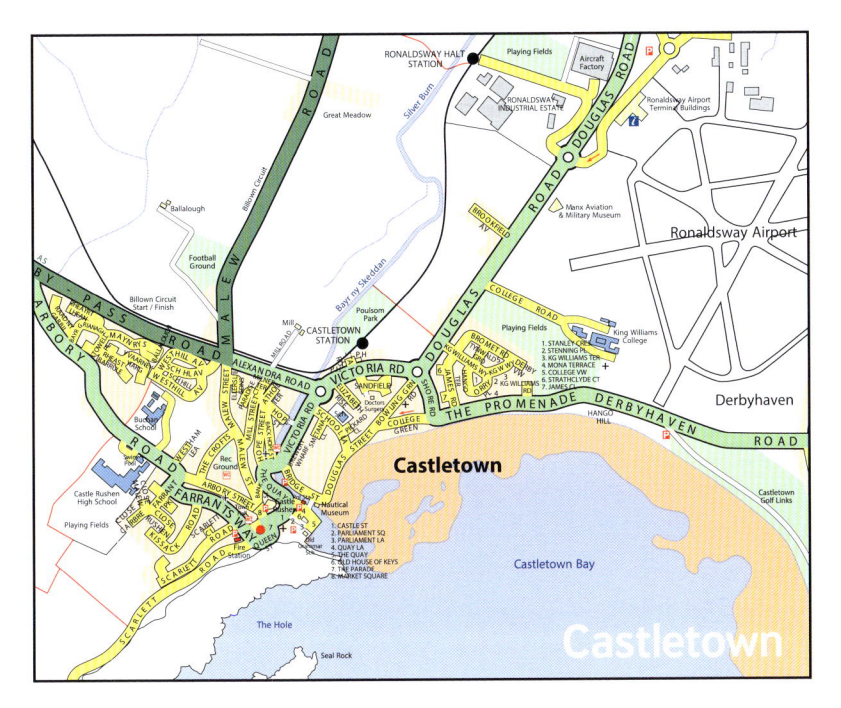

Across from the Smelt Memorial and close to the George Hotel is the former home of Captain John Quilliam RN, who fought at the Battle of Trafalgar and at the height of the fighting saved HMS *Victory* from destruction by rigging a jury (temporary) rudder.

Looking down on the square is a clock presented to the Island by Queen Elizabeth I. Curiously, it has only ever had one finger – but is still going strong after 400 years!

Both anglicised and Norse names are much in evidence in the town and surrounding area – the legacy of Castletown's long association with the seat of government and early colonisation by Viking settlers. Look out for Bowling Green, Great Meadow, Paradise, Red Gap, Witches Mill and the Rope Walk, and homestead names such as Grenaby, Tosaby and Orrisdale.

The outskirts of Castletown have almost as much history as the town itself. Lying to the east is **King William's College**, a long-time site of public school education, its great central tower dominating the landscape. Facing the school is **Hango Hill**, where the Manx patriot William Christian was shot (though posthumously pardoned of treason) for leading a revolt against the Countess of Derby when Charles II was England's king. The Norse name for the hill was Hangaholl, or Hill of Hanging, and Christian was the last person to be executed here. It is also an important archaeological site, with ruins of a blockhouse built by the seventh Earl of

Towns & Villages

Castle Rushen

Derby at the time of the unrest in England.

To the west of the town is the **Balladoole estate**, centred on Balladoole House – for centuries the home of the Stevenson family. Evidence in Douglas's Manx Museum shows that at least six generations of the family lived on the estate prior to 1511.

John Stevenson, Speaker of the House of Keys (1704–1738), is remembered for the manner in which he led the Keys in their patriotic struggle against the tenth Earl of Derby. Bishop Wilson called him 'the father of his country' and at one time he was imprisoned in Castle Rushen for championing the rights of his fellow countrymen.

To the west of Balladoole, where the coastal footpath Raad ny Foillan (Road of the Gull) joins the main A5 road, is the area known as **Poyll Vaaish** – easily reached by car or on foot from Castletown. There are superb views of the surrounding countryside, especially the panorama northwards as the low hills of the coastal areas roll ever upwards to the central mountain range, with Snaefell visible in the far distance.

Poyll Vaaish in English means Death Pool or Bay of Death. There are legends galore about this corner of the Island – stories of shipwrecks, pirates and looters. In fact, the name probably derives from the black marble which comprises the sea bed in the vicinity, the ripples of lava evident at low water. Just after dropping down from the basaltic rock stack of Scarlett, you will come upon a small quarry where the black marble is worked. This was the source from which the steps of London's St Paul's Cathedral were made – a gift from Bishop Wilson – and in recent years replaced due to wear.

Close by the Stevensons' ancestral home is the site of a **Viking ship burial mound** – one of a number of ancient sites which make this area well worth exploring. Also of interest is Strandhall, where a spring flows down to the shore. Legend has it that although the source of the spring lies many feet above sea level, it is a salt water spring with petrifying powers. No doubt the story has taken credence from the fact that at exceptionally low tides – and particularly after a storm has moved the sands – the remains of a large petrified forest can sometimes be seen.

Visiting Castletown and its immediate area is easy, particularly if travelling from Douglas. There is a regular year-round bus service and the steam railway operates in both directions several times a day from early to late summer. Driving is very easy too, although the narrow streets of Castletown itself make 'park and walk' a better option for exploring the town which is also known for hosting major agricultural shows and the slightly more eccentric World Tin Bath Championships.

Villages

Ballasalla

Just north of Castletown and Ronaldsway Airport, on the main A5 road south out of Douglas, is the village of Ballasalla. Within its boundaries are the extensively restored ruins of Rushen Abbey. The interpretive centre explains the site's history and significance, and the Abbey Restaurant helps satisfy more than visitors' curiosity!

It is believed that the abbey was founded in 1098 by Magnus, King of Norway, construction commencing in 1134. As with many ancient sites, over recent centuries it has provided a ready-made source of building materials, but fortunately much of the fabric of the original buildings has survived.

The abbey's Cistercian monks engaged

Castletown

in all sorts of work – draining the land, straightening the course of local rivers and streams, and generally influencing the way of life here. Close to the abbey is an example of their achievements – Monks Bridge, dating from the 14th century. With three arches but a width of just four feet, it crosses the Silverburn River and is one of only a few packhorse bridges still standing anywhere in the British Isles. It is also referred to as the Crossag, a Gaelic word meaning little cross or crossing.

Records prove that a number of kings and abbots lie buried within the abbey's precincts. Excavation in the early 20th century unearthed a skeleton of a man buried with a bronze figure representing the Egyptian god Osiris, pointing to his having been a Crusader. *Chronicon Mannia* (Chronicles of Mann), a valuable reference work of the Island's early history, was written at Rushen Abbey. It contains an account of the murder of Reginald II, King of Mann, by a knight called Ivar.

A little further upstream from the bridge, the Silverburn is joined by the Awin Ruy, or Red River. It flows down from Rozefel – Granite Mountain, or Stoney Mountain as it is called today – and its bed is strewn with boulders. The mountain was

Castletown

the source of much of the building material used in the construction of the new Douglas breakwater in 1979. Norse settlers who recognised the colouring of the granite, exposed as it was to the elements, named the mountain Rjoofjall – Ruddy Mountain.

In summer months, nearby Silverdale is one of the Island's most frequented glens. It was originally the site of the Creg Mill and its dam is now a boating lake, very popular with children. There is also an unusual water-powered carousel here, along with a craft centre, café and wildlife and nature trails.

Ronaldsway Airport is easily reached from the village by bus or taxi. Ronaldsway, meaning Reginald's Ford in Norse, is reputedly the site of King Orry's castle and has been the scene of many battles.

Colby and Ballabeg

To the east of Port Erin (and north-west of Castletown) in the flat lands of the parish of Arbory are the villages of Colby and Ballabeg. Colby (Kolli's Farm) stands at the entrance to the delightful Colby Glen.

A walk up the glen takes you alongside a brook which runs its lower course through wooded glades and higher up where the gorse is a blaze of yellow. Further up the glen again there are the remains of Keeill Catreeney (keeill meaning church or chapel) and a burial ground. The ancient St Catherine's or Colby Fair used to be held here. Nearby is Chibbyrt Catreeney (Catherine's Well), and it was said that anyone who drank from it would be forever afflicted with an unquenchable thirst.

Another fair, which still survives, is Laa Columb Killey (St Columba's Day Fair). Held in a field in either Colby or Ballabeg at the end of June each year, it attracts people from all over the Island and gives a glimpse of Manx country life as it used to be.

Ballabeg is on the ancient quarterland and the village is named in the Manorial Roll of 1511 as Begson's Farm. The area is very rural and foxgloves and wild fuchsia line the quiet sheltered lanes. Weed-killers and pesticides are not used on Manx hedgerows and it is still possible to see wild flowers which have disappeared from other parts of the British Isles; the lanes of Arbory and the neighbouring parishes of Malew and Rushen display excellent examples.

Churches have always played an important part in the life of the south of the Island and none more so than Kirk Arbory. Built in 1757, the present church has an oak beam supporting the roof, the beam having belonged to two previous churches.

An inscription on it mentions Thomas Radcliffe, Abbot of Rushen, and appears to refer to the influential Stanley family crest of an eagle and child. The grave of Captain Quilliam of HMS *Victory* and Trafalgar fame (see under Castletown) is in the churchyard.

Along the road from the church towards Castletown is Friary Farm, and clearly visible from the road are the remains of the Friary of Bemaken, founded by the Grey Friars in 1373. The friars were assisted in its completion by stonemasons who were on the Island working on Castle Rushen. Employed by William de Montacute and later by his son, the masons were on the move around Britain strengthening castles and fortifications between 1368 and 1374. Two Ogham stones were found on the site and are now in the Manx Museum, Douglas. They are inscribed in the ancient Ogham script which was used in much of western Britain from the 4th to early 7th centuries.

Castletown

Derbyhaven and Langness

A close neighbour of both Castletown and the extremities of Ronaldsway Airport is the picturesque hamlet of Derbyhaven, and stretching south behind its sheltered bay into the Irish Sea is the narrow finger of the Langness peninsula.

Ideal for windsurfers and small boats, Derbyhaven was a thriving port in the days of the Vikings and their medieval successors. It was here that blacksmith John Wilks, from whom two former Governors of the Bank of England are directly descended, made the Island's first penny coins, an action which Tynwald authenticated by declaring them legal tender. The remains of the old smelthouse, probably dating from around 1711, are still visible. There is also evidence that Manx coinage was minted here by one John Murrey, a merchant of Douglas in 1668 and the probable owner of the Derbyhaven Mint.

The sandy turf of the Langness peninsula is home to the Castletown Golf Links. Close to the ruins of John Wilks' smelthouse is the 10th hole and it was here, 153 years before it was transferred to Epsom Downs in 1780, that the famous Derby horse race originated. It seems that the seventh Earl of Derby wished to encourage the breeding of Manx horses and as an incentive presented a cup to be won in open competition. One stipulation he put on the race was that only those horses that had been foaled within the Island or on the Calf of Man could be entered. The Manx horses of that period were small and very hardy, renowned for their speed, surefootedness and stamina. It may well be that prior to the Derby the only time horses were in competition was after a wedding when the guests raced back to the bridegroom's home to claim the honour of breaking the bride cake over her head as she entered her new home!

Langness is very well known for its **wildlife**, especially birds – skylarks in particular – and it's often possible to see seals at Dreswick Point, the southernmost tip of the peninsula and indeed of the Isle of Man.

The waters here conceal a reef called the Skerranes which has claimed many lives. In 1853 the crew of the Plymouth schooner *Provider* perished and their bodies were buried in sight of the wreck, the grave marked by a nearby natural tombstone of rock carved with the vessel's name and the date of her loss.

The Langness lighthouse was built in 1880. It became fully automated in 1996, but prior to its construction another landmark was erected on the peninsula and is still here – the cylindrical structure known as the Herring Tower, built in 1811.

Places to go, things to do

Castle Rushen, which gave its name to Castletown, is one of Europe's best-preserved medieval fortresses, its origins dating from the 12th century with the fortification of a strategic site to guard the entrance to the Silverburn River. The oldest part of the castle, believed to have been built during the time of Magnus, the last Viking King of Mann, who died here in 1265, is the keep – a central stone tower standing in an inner courtyard. The castle was developed by successive rulers for a further 300 years, being surrendered to parliamentary forces during the English Civil War. In more recent times the castle has served as a centre of administration, a mint, a law court and a prison, and today it is a major visitor attraction, showing detailed displays which

All ROUND GUIDE ISLE of MAN

Herring Tower

View from Scarlett towards Port St Mary

authentically recreate castle life as it was for the kings and lords of Mann. The spiral staircases may prove difficult for some visitors, but there is a shortened tour using normal staircases if you require it.

More aspects of the Island's history are revealed at **Rushen Abbey**, Ballasalla. Founded in 1134 as a daughter house of Furness in Cumbria, it gives the opportunity to explore the remains of a small but important Cistercian abbey. Introductory displays give the history of the site and explain the background of 'the Church' then and now. At certain times of the year an archaeological dig is likely to be in progress with the possibility of being able to talk to those involved, either direct or via a video link. There are child-friendly areas where to a limited extent you can enjoy experiences such as an archaeological dig, identification of finds, building a Gothic arch and trying to produce your own version of the Chronicles of Mann as written by the monks.

The Old House of Keys building in Castletown was the seat of the Manx government from 1709 until 1869, when population and commercial pressures forced the move to the new capital of Douglas. Visitors are welcome to sit in on live recreations of the debating process. These take place daily from 31st March to 4th November. As times vary, it is advisable to book in advance with tickets for these sessions obtained from the Old Grammar School situated nearby

The Old Grammar School, built in approximately 1200, was originally Castletown's first church. Nearby is the old garrison church of St Mary's, built in 1826 to replace Bishop Wilson's church of 1698 and saved in recent times from dereliction. On his first visit to the Isle of Man in 1777, founder of Methodism John Wesley preached in front of the castle and noted in his journal of the 30th June that year, 'A more loving, simple-hearted people than this I never saw.'

In Castletown the **Nautical Museum's** main exhibit is the remarkable 18th century armed sailing schooner *Peggy*, built in 1789 but rediscovered by chance in 1935, walled up in her original harbour-side boathouse (now the museum) a hundred years after the death of her owner Captain George Quayle. *Peggy* was involved in local smuggling and trade, and is officially recognised by Britain's National Historic Ships Committee as being 'of extraordinary maritime importance'– a distinction shared with more than 50 other historic vessels, including Henry VIII's *Mary Rose*, all deemed worthy of preservation.

An area of coast with access and parking is **Fort Island** on St Michael's Isle, Langness. The 16th-century artillery fort and the 11th-century chapel can be freely seen but not entered.

The **Mann Cat Sanctuary** at Santon, in the south (www.manncat.com), and the **Home of Rest for Old Horses** near Douglas (@iomhorseshome on Facebook) – the retirement destination for the tram-pulling shires – are pleased to welcome visitors.

Scarlett Visitor Centre near Castletown explains how volcanic activity created the spectacular rock formations at Scarlett about 250 million years ago. Along with a nature trail, the centre gives an insight into the area's local flora and dramatic old limestone workings.

Eating Out

THE ABBEY RESTAURANT: Rushen Abbey, Ballasalla, IM9 3DB. 01624 822 www.theabbeyrestaurant.co.im

Situated on land next to Rushen Abbey, and built from the reclaimed stones of the Abbey itself, the Abbey Restaurant is surrounded by history. The main focus of the restaurant each season is to source

Nautical Museum

ingredients from local artisans, farmers and foragers alongside home-grown offerings to bring the diner a true taste of the Isle of Man.

THE FORGE: Santon, IM4 1JE 01624 610031 www.theforge.im

The Forge smokehouse and grill prides itself on marinating, slow cooking, grilling and smoking the best meat, fish and vegetables available. At the heart of the menu are freshly prepared meals, made from scratch on-site, where classic grill dishes are complemented by Mediterranean influences.

LEONARDO'S: Stanley House, Castletown. 01624 827635 @Leonardosrestaurantiom on Facebook

Nestled within the shadow of Castle Rushen, Leonardo's brings a taste of the Mediterranean to the Isle of Man. Here you will find the best Italian food.

Other Eateries & Cafes

Secret Pizza, Barracks Square Castletown, IM9 1NR Tel: 01624 822833 https://www.thesecretpizzaco.im/

Shore Hotel, Shore Rd, Gansey IM9 5LZ Tel: 01624 832269

Niarbyl Bay

ALL ROUND GUIDE **ISLE of MAN**

PORT ERIN & PORT St MARY

Port Erin

Sitting close together but on opposite shoulders of the Mull peninsula – that is to say on its west side and its east side – are the popular summer seaside resorts of Port Erin and Port St Mary.

Whether you approach Port Erin by land or by sea the views are impressive. Port Erin translated means either Lord's Port or Iron Port and in Manx Gaelic is written as Purt Chiarn. Latter-day smugglers came to know Port Erin very well, using the solitude of the bay to mask their activities and hidden from observation by the steep hills and perpendicular cliffs surrounding the village. In the 19th century the village became the playground of the Lancashire mill owners and their employees.

Situated at the head of an almost landlocked bay, which is guarded to the north by lofty Bradda Head and to the south by Castle Rocks and the peninsula, Port Erin offers shelter in most weathers. Pretty white-painted cottages trim the inner edge of the bay, bordered by grassy banks, rising up to a more formal promenade fronting a traditional line of seaside hotels.

The combination of sea, sand, cliffs, hills and heather makes Port Erin very photogenic. Add the appeal of cloud shadows, and brilliant sunsets often framed by Ireland's Mountains of Mourne, and you have some idea of the area's great visual attraction.

Port Erin is also popular for its fine 18-hole **Rowany golf course** and the **Erin Arts Centre**, a venue for regular events, exhibitions and the performing and visual arts, founded by John Bethell in 1971. Run almost entirely by volunteers, and known for its fine acoustics, it now enjoys international recognition and presents an impressive variety of prestigious events, including the Mananan International Festivals, Lionel Tertis International Viola Festival & Competition and Barbirolli International Oboe Festival & Competition. The Sir James Mellon Gallery, opened in 1994, is another of the Centre's valuable assets.

More than a century ago the quality of the waters offshore from Port Erin motivated the establishment of the Marine Biological Station at the seaward end of the bay, which closed in 2006. Directly opposite are the remains of a breakwater started in 1864 and which was meant to turn the bay into the national harbour of refuge. William Milner of Bradda Head was a staunch supporter of the breakwater and he along with everyone else on the Island must have felt a great sense of loss when one night in January 1884 it was destroyed in a storm.

A notable son of Port Erin was William Kermode, born in 1775. Seeking fame and fortune, he crossed the world to take up a grant of land in Van Diemen's Land – now known as Tasmania – and did indeed amass a fortune and contributed valuable service to the Tasmanian Legislative Council. Ambushed in his coach by two bush rangers demanding his money or his life, he smacked their heads together, bound them up and drove to Hobart, where they were arrested.

Port St Mary

Only a few miles from Port Erin across the neck of the Mull peninsula is the attractive fishing village of Port St Mary. The peninsula forms an impressive backdrop, its steep slopes and fields rolling right down into the village. The golf course here is the only 9-hole golf course on the Island, but no less challenging for that, designed by the 1920 British Open Champion George Duncan. And the views from the sixth tee are spectacular.

Once a thriving fishing port and home to both Manx and Scottish vessels, Port St Mary has a factory which processes the delicious local shellfish delicacy known as queenies – a variety of small scallop. The harbour is full of pleasure boats of all types. The breakwater gives good shelter and its deepwater berths are popular with visiting sailors and the few remaining fishing vessels. The inner Alfred Pier, named after a previous Duke of Edinburgh who laid the foundation stone in 1882, shelters the smaller craft and is a very picturesque part of the port.

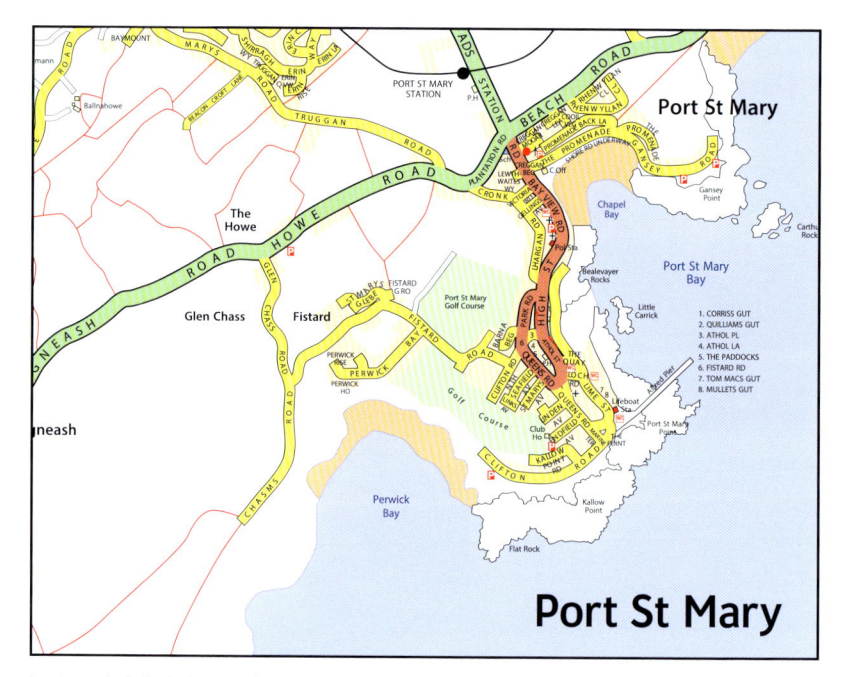

Clustered round the harbour are old Manx cottages, their original thatched roofs having long ago given way to Manx slate. The newer part of Port St Mary lies above the sandy beach of Chapel Bay. Linking the harbour and the bay is a fine walkway winding its way close to the water's edge.

Across the headland from Port St Mary Bay, on the southern side of Kallow Point, is **Perwick Bay**. This owes its name to the old Scandinavian word for Harbour Creek. In recent times the hotel that once stood at the edge of the cliff has been developed for private housing but the beach is still worth a visit, particularly if you have more than a passing interest in geology: there is a noticeable fault on the bay's south-east side. The rocky pools and small caves at the foot of the cliffs make a good play area for children. Sitting high on the hillside above Perwick Bay is the village of Fistard.

Villages

Cregneash

Tucked away on a hillside of the Mull peninsula, in the Isle of Man's south-west corner, is the lovely village of Cregneash – referred to on some maps in its Gaelic spelling of Cregneish, meaning Rock of Ages. You can get to it very easily by road from Port St Mary, the A31 climbing Mull Hill and giving excellent views of the uplands rising to the north. The village is the oldest on the Isle of Man and its 19th-century thatched crofters' cottages are a **folk museum** representing yet another era in the Island's history. The museum has a working farm and in summer there are authentic demonstrations of how life was for the Island's crofters in the 1800s. The cottages nestle in and around a sleepy hollow. Views over the coastline and the nearby Calf of Man and Sound are stunning. Close by this 'modern' village are the remains of an older one. The **Mull Circle** (Meayll in Manx, meaning Bald or Bare Hill) dates back to the late Neolithic or early Bronze Age. Used primarily as a prehistoric burial place, it is unique in archaeological terms, combining the circle form with six pairs of cists (stone coffins), each pair having a passage between which radiates outwards. The prehistoric village was below the circle, and hut foundations and other relics were discovered on the site.

On the hilltop above the village is a radio beacon used by transatlantic

Mull Circle

airliners. The huddle of buildings nearby houses a similar system for Irish Sea shipping. Walking on past the beacons brings you to **Spanish Head**, so called because a galleon of the Spanish Armada was reputedly wrecked here. Also here is an area of land known as the Chasms – huge fissures, some a hundred feet deep, covered by gorse and heather and very dangerous for those foolish enough to ignore the warning signs and stray from the footpath.

View from Bradda Head

From the village of Cregneash the road drops down to the Sound Visitor Centre, with its café and panoramic window overlooking the swirling tidal waters of the Sound and the Calf of Man beyond. This is one of the most scenic spots on the Island and a haven for birds and wildlife. With binoculars you may be lucky enough to spot grey seals sunbathing on the rocks of Kitterland – another small island not far from the shoreline – or even basking sharks, feeding on microscopic plants and animals just below the surface.

Walking from the Sound – the Land's End of the Isle of Man – to Port St Mary or Port Erin is also a pleasure not to be missed.

Places to go, things to do

The Railway Museum Located adjacent to Port Erin station boasts an outstanding collection of locomotives, rolling stock, posters and other memorabilia including the Queen's carriage from the royal visit in 1972 by Her Majesty The Queen. The museum also houses a railway simulator, allowing visitors a 'Drive the Diesel' experience. Open whenever the Steam Railway operates, from March to November between 9.30am and 4.30pm, admittance is £2 for adults and £1 per child.

Cregneash, the first open-air museum in the British Isles is very much a living village with a resident community. Certain of the buildings are kept for display purposes and those not needed for display are maintained in their traditional form externally whilst being brought up to modern standards internally. The farm is part of the complex and is in general worked in the old ways and has period animals and crops, though if modern equipment is needed for a specific task it is used. The aim of this Manx National Heritage site is to show the village and its surrounds as they were about 100 years ago.

The Sound Restaurant and Visitor Centre close to Cregneash has been

Niarbyl

Looking towards the Sound from Bradda Head

created to blend into the landscape and give magnificent views and good facilities. Displays and toilets are available without necessarily patronising the restaurant, although the scenery and the wildlife, especially the seals, are likely to tempt you into staying longer than you originally intended, while the lands at Spanish Head have the coastal path running through them.

While you're in the south you can also visit the Gansey Pottery in Port St Mary

Other Eateries, Bars & Cafes

Foraging Vintners, The Old Coal Shed, The Breakwater, Port Erin, IM9 6JA www.foragingvintners.com

A small craft winery overlooking Port Erin Bay specialising in non-grape based sparkling wines. The wine bar, where visitors are welcome to come and taste the wine and relax in the cosy bar, or take in the stunning view from the outdoor terrace provides wines, beers and spirits from all over the world along with light nibble plates.

The Cafe at the Sound: Sound Road, Port Erin, Isle of Man IM9 5PZ
https://www.facebook.com/TheCafeAtTheSound/

Bradda Glen Restaurant, Bradda, Port Erin, IM9 6PJ. Tel: 01624 837713. www.braddaglen.im/

The restaurant offers panoramic views of Port Erin Bay and the coast, all the way down to the Calf of Man. Wide selection of meals offered.

Whistlestop Coffee Shop, Railway Station, Port Erin IM9 6AH. Tel: 07624 261802. Located at the station, offering fresh coffee, homemade cakes and food served daily.

PEEL

Draw a straight line from west to east approximately half way down a map of the Isle of Man and you will see that Peel and Laxey are exactly opposite each other on their respective coastlines, separated by a distance of about 13 miles. But while Laxey is relatively close to both Douglas and Ramsey, Peel is the west coast's only sizeable town – and the only one on the Isle of Man to have a cathedral.

In fact, Peel has two **cathedrals**. One is the medieval ruin of St German's, located within the walls of Peel Castle on St Patrick's Isle, the isle being accessible via the causeway. The other, the present Pro-Cathedral in the centre of the town, is a fine building which technically speaking gives this ancient fishing port the status of a city.

Peel takes its name from an abbreviated form of St Patrick's Isle and has only been known as this since the name came into regular use in the 19th century. The town has played a significant role in the development of the Island's nationhood, and excavations of the area's Viking settlement have uncovered important burial sites.

One site revealed the remains of a female subsequently known as 'The Pagan Lady'. The grave was unusual in that it was a curious mixture of Christian and Pagan rituals, and a very fine bead necklace was recovered and is one of many artefacts displayed in the Manx Museum in Douglas.

Celebrated prisoners have been incarcerated in **Peel Castle** over the ages. Shakespeare makes mention in Henry VI of one such famous detainee – Eleanor, Duchess of Gloucester, who for 14 years was imprisoned in the cathedral crypt, accused of treason and sorcery against Henry VI as she sought to advance her husband's claim to the English throne. Her fellow plotters were not so fortunate: Roger Bolingbroke was executed and Margery Joudemain, the Witch of Eye, was burnt to death. History records that the duchess was a difficult prisoner, capable of escape or even suicide and in need of careful guarding. Her ghost is said to haunt the cathedral's crypt.

For a long time Peel was the centre of the Isle of Man's once-thriving fishing industry, boasting a great maritime tradition and a considerable fleet. Today the port is still known for its traditional oak-smoked **Manx kippers**, the quayside factory and museum open to summer visitors.

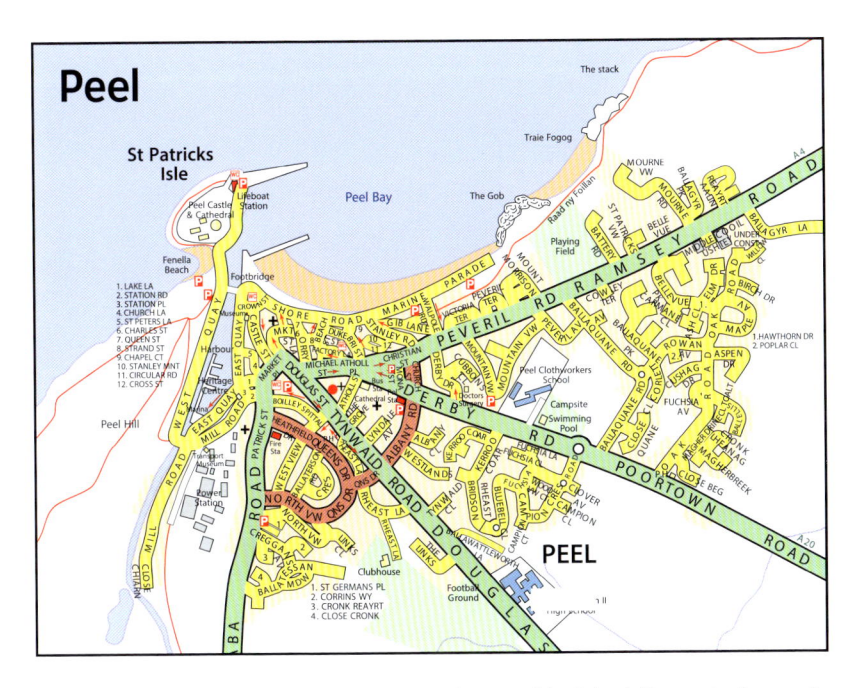

Close to the harbour and kipper factory is the **Manx Transport Museum** – the smallest of the Island's museums, and not to be confused with the much larger Transport Museum in Jurby. Only about 60 square metres in size, the Peel museum's unusual and rare exhibits include a P50 from 1962 – the world's smallest road-legal car ever produced, this example being one of just 100 made by the town's long-defunct Peel Engineering Company.

Peel's place and story in Isle of Man history is brilliantly told in the **House of Manannan** – a waterside attraction that's not to be missed. Named in honour of the ancient sea god, but very much a museum experience for the 21st century, this highly engaging interactive heritage centre presents the town's role within the history of the Island. The centre is one of the Island's major visitor attractions, as well as a successful educational aid for Manx schoolchildren. But if history is not your thing, Peel merits a visit for other reasons too – notably the sands, ice cream, 18-hole golf course, fabulous sunsets and quiet relaxing charm.

Villages

Glen Maye and Niarbyl

Glion Muigh (Glen Maye) means Yellow Glen, and this is a village sitting on steep hillsides at the bottom end of the mining glens of Glen Mooar and Glen Rushen. It is easy to see that the village owes its existence to the farming and mining industries, and much of its original character has been retained.

Beyond the village the river plunges over a series of waterfalls, before finishing its dash to the sea between high cliffs

Peel harbour

which are clad in gorse and heather.

Niarbyl (or to give it its Manx name Yn Arbyl, meaning The Tail, on account of the long reef jutting out from the shoreline) is an ideal place for picnics, with superb views to the north and south and boasting an attractive café and visitor centre on the approach road down to the sea. The grandeur of the west and south-west coast is probably best experienced from this isolated but marvellously relaxing spot – a favourite location for film and TV productions. Massive cliffs stretch away southward in a series of giant headlands and bays before Bradda Head, at Port Erin, briefly interrupts the flow. The Mull Hills continue the vista and from this angle it almost seems as if the Calf of Man is joined to the main island. You'd also be hard pushed to find better walking country than this.

Foxdale

Foxdale is a cunningly misleading name, because it actually translates as Waterfall Dale – very apt in view of the area's abundance of streams. The village was once a centre for lead mining and from the 300 or so tons of ore mined each month, some 15 to 20 ounces of silver per ton were extracted. When the industry ceased in the early part of the 20th century, many of the miners emigrated to the colonies, and it has taken a long time for the village to begin to recover some of its lost prosperity.

St John's

Inland, 5 miles to the east of Peel, you will find the attractive village of St John's. Every year in early July (normally on 5th) this pleasant and quiet community is completely transformed by the colour, splendour and ceremony of **Tynwald Day** – the Island's national celebration of more than 1,000 years of unbroken self-government.

Thousands of people crowd around **Tynwald Hill** to witness an ancient tradition which includes the proclamation,

ELEMENT ISLE
Isle of Man Designer Jewellery

Contemporary and traditional fine jewellery collections that tell the story of our Island, inspired by nature, folklore and evoking memories of the happiest of times.

Based at Tynwald Mills, St Johns with free and easy parking. Tel: 01624 802700

www.elementisle.com

Places to go, things to do & Eating out

in both Manx and English but in summarised form, of laws enacted during the last year. These are read out by the Deemsters – the Manx equivalent of British High Court Judges – and also in attendance are the Lieutenant Governor of the Island and a whole assembly of dignitaries, civil servants and others. On occasions, Her Majesty the Queen or other member of the British royal family is guest of honour.

But it's not all pomp: many of the spectators are here to enjoy all the fun of the fair which is an important element of the day's celebrations.

The village of St John's has several important everyday attractions too, none more popular than **Tynwald Mills Centre** – relaxing country shopping in quality outlets housed under the roof of the spacious former woollen mills.

Element Isle Jewellery is a charming family-run business located at Tynwald Mills in St John's. With a passion for crafting unique and contemporary pieces inspired by the Isle of Man's rich heritage and natural beauty. Claire (Designer and Jeweller) and Scott (Natural Scientist and Gemologist) bring together tradition and innovation to create jewellery that tells a story.

Each of their pieces captures a moment in time, drawing inspiration from the natural world, folklore or evoking a particular memory or emotion. The results are beautiful collections that celebrate the timeless charm and tranquillity of the island. At Element Isle, quality is at the forefront, and the team prides itself on creating jewellery to treasure for years to come.

Element Isle has gained a reputation beyond the shores of the Isle of Man, with an ever-growing following throughout the UK and beyond. Their reputation was cemented further in 2022 when they were commissioned to create the Queen's Platinum Jubilee Brooch, now in the Royal Collection.

The shop itself is a warm and welcoming space, with a homely feel that invites visitors to browse at their leisure. Element Isle Jewellery is a must-visit destination for those seeking an authentic experience of the Isle of Man. Their creations capture the essence of this stunning corner of the world, offering a connection to nature and the island's rich history that is truly unique.

Close by, and within easy walking distance, is St John's stately **Royal Chapel**, the beautiful national arboretum and park, and the showcase **Manx Wild Flower Garden**.

For more information on Tynwald Day see page 168

Kirk Michael

On the west coast and a few miles south of Ballaugh, Kirk Michael (previously called Kirk Michael Towne or Michaeltown) sits at the junction of the spectacular A4 coast road to Peel and the picturesque A3 to St John's and the south.

It is also on the famous TT course, and the spotlight falls on the town in late May and early June every year when the races pass through; the inhabitants of Kirk Michael are said to have the flattest feet in the Isle of Man because their houses edge right up to the race course! A good place from which to watch the racing is the Mitre. Very close to the town is Glen Wyllin (meaning Mill Glen, and sometimes spelt without a break between the words). At one time a bridge carried a railway line high above the glen and helped make it a very popular spot with holidaymakers. Nothing remains of the railway now except for the two redundant sandstone

60

bridge supports, but the beauty of the glen is undiminished and still attracts many visitors, the lower section leading to the shore.

Five bishops are buried within the grounds of the local church. There is a memorial stone to the popular cleric 'The Good' Bishop Wilson, who did much for the people of the Island in his long and beneficial stewardship.

Places to go, things to do

Peel Castle stands on St Patrick's Isle, which in the 6th century was established as a centre of Manx Christianity and survived in this role until the arrival of the pagan Norse Vikings at the end of the 8th century. In the 11th century it became the ruling seat of the Norse Kingdom of Mann and the Isles. A major programme of excavation conducted in the 1980s revealed much about the site's prime importance, and Viking jewellery and other finds are on display in the Manx Museum in Douglas.

Peel's interactive and ingenious **House of Manannan** brings the Island's Celtic and Viking past to life using a combination of video, audio and authentic recreations such as a Celtic roundhouse centred around an imaginary family of the time. The magic and wizardry are led by Manannan himself, shape shifter that he is, as the presenter of the documentary-style tale.

Moving on in time, a replica longship, two-thirds actual size, forms the link between the Vikings and maritime history. The ship, *Odin's Raven*, was built in Norway in 1979 and in that year sailed to the Island to mark the Manx Millennium.

The House of Manannan also uses a dozen or so other characters from differing periods of the past to tell their stories. Other devices and subjects include a busy quayside scene, the natural history of the coasts, kippers and the Steam Packet, all bringing you to a final section which introduces Peel Castle and urges you to make the short journey along the waterfront to visit it. When you do, Manannan's voice takes you wherever you want to go and explains the fortifications and buildings including the old cathedral.

Niarbyl in the west has a **visitor centre and café**. Situated amongst the spectacular coastline, and on one of the most important geological sites on the Isle of Man, looking over to the Irish Mountains of Mourne, this is the perfect spot for watching marine wildlife such as basking sharks and seals.

Eary Cushlin also contains some of the most spectacular coastal scenery and provides access to Lag ny Keeilley, an ancient chapel, burial ground and hermitage.

Eating Out

THE BOATYARD RESTAURANT, Mariners Wharf, East Quay, Peel, IM5 1AR. 01624 845470
theboatyardpeel.com

Situated on the East Quay in Peel, with excellent views looking out over the marina, The menu has been developed around the philosophy of using as many local ingredients as possible, preparing dishes fresh to order. Fresh local fish and seafood features heavily across the menus with specials highlighting the catch of the day.

Dining By Chris Franklin, Peel Harbour, E Quay, Peel, Isle of Man IM5 1AR. Tel: 07624 431146.

Other Eateries & Cafes

The Creek Inn, 14 Lake Ln, Peel, Isle of Man IM5 1AT Tel: 01624 842216

Peel

All ROUND GUIDE **ISLE** of **MAN**

ITINERARIES

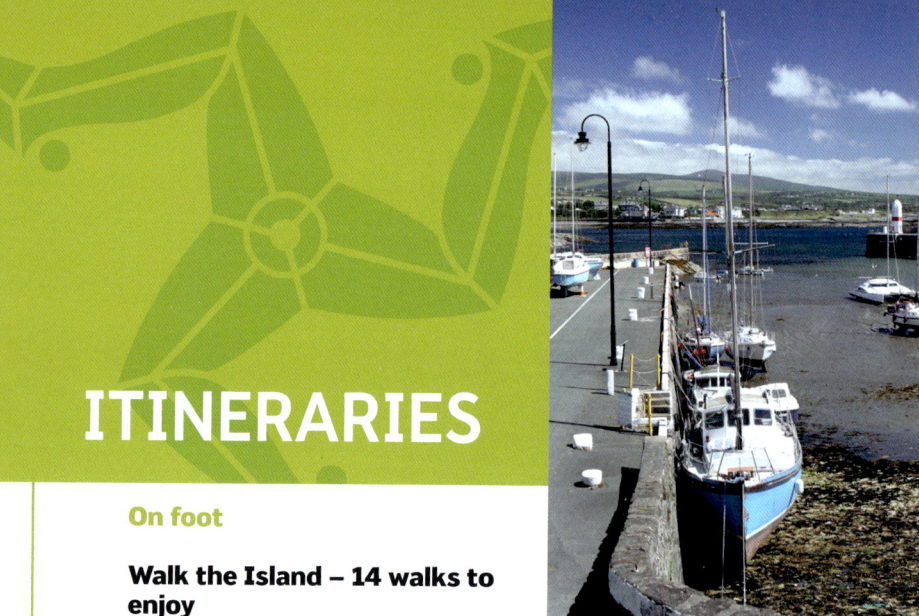

On foot

Walk the Island – 14 walks to enjoy

It doesn't matter whether you're a dedicated or an occasional walker – if you love fresh air and beautiful surroundings, the Isle of Man is a truly invigorating experience. As well as the wonderful variety and richness of the landscape, stepping out to explore offers you a rewarding choice of options. You can simply go where the fancy takes you, along the Island's many public rights of way – countryside, beaches, cliff-tops, glens, high hills – or use this section of the guide to help you conquer and enjoy some of the Island's designated waymarked trails.

FOURTEEN TOP WALKS

The walks described in the following pages touch each end of the spectrum – from the challenging long-distance coast path to much more leisurely circular town walks. The first route covered, broken down into seven manageable sections, is the 95 mile coast path itself, Raad ny Foillan – the Road of the Gull.

Following this are the Heritage Trail (11.5 miles), the Millennium Way (26 miles), the Foxdale Line (just 2.5 miles along disused railway lines) and four town walks – in Douglas, Castletown, Peel and Ramsey.

THE COAST PATH

The Road of the Gull opened in 1986 and embraces most of the Island's dramatic coastal paths, but also takes in unusual rural walks and the vast beach walks of the northern alluvial plain. The total length of 95 miles is approximate and varies according to the options you take along the way.

Serious walkers, using overnight accommodation at the main towns en route, can manage the coast path at a comfortable pace over a week's holiday. Purely for the purposes of this guide it is assumed that you will be (a) walking it in sections, (b) using public transport each day to get you to the start and to return from the finish of the walk, and (c) based at accommodation in Douglas (though bus and train links are good wherever you stay). Options (for half-day or even shorter walks) are noted where appropriate.

Itineraries

KEY TO THE WALKS

WALK 1	PEEL TO PORT ERIN
WALK 2	PORT ERIN TO PORT ST MARY
WALK 3	PORT ST MARY TO DOUGLAS
WALK 4	DOUGLAS TO LAXEY
WALK 5	LAXEY TO RAMSEY
WALK 6	RAMSEY TO BALLAUGH
WALK 7	BALLAUGH TO PEEL
WALK 8	FOXDALE LINE
WALK 9	THE HERITAGE TRAIL
WALK 10	THE MILLENNIUM WAY

Raad ny Foillan

MANX PLACE NAMES

Many of the Island's place names are in Manx Gaelic, or a corrupted form of it, and often describe very aptly either the shape or some other feature of the place. Others describe the origins of the place in relation to the family name of the historical owner. The remaining names have their origins in Norse and date from the Viking period. Where appropriate the English translation is given in the text to add interest and a better understanding of the Manx name.

WHAT TO WEAR

For reasons of safety and comfort you should always wear suitable shoes or, preferably, walking boots. This is particularly important on cliff paths where wet grass can be very slippery and catch out even the most experienced walkers. As for clothing, it is sensible to bear in mind that although you will never be far from civilisation, exposed coastal areas are sometimes subject to rapid changes in the weather and if unprepared you can easily get caught out before reaching shelter.

MAPS AND GUIDES

The Isle of Man Public Rights of Way Map, published by the Island's Department of Local Government and Environment (www.gov.im/maps), contains a wealth of information essential to serious walkers. Ordnance Survey's 1:50,000 Landranger map 95 is also well worth obtaining, whether you're walking, motoring, cycling or exploring the Isle of Man by any other means.

Other maps and guides, available from Lily Publications are:

All Round Map to the Isle of Man
Isle of Man Coastal Path
Isle of Man Outdoor Leisure Map
Isle of Man Street Plans
Favourite Manx Walks

RAAD NY FOILLAN: THE ROAD OF THE GULL

The seven sections into which this guide divides the 95-mile coast path (signposted along its route by a gull symbol) are as follows. The walk time indicated against each section is a guideline only and reflects the terrain, places and points of interest en route.

1: Peel to Port Erin (13 miles, 7 hours)
2: Port Erin to Port St Mary (6 miles, 4 hours): page 70
3: Port St Mary to Douglas (15 miles, 8

hours): page 72

4: Douglas to Laxey (9 miles, 4 hours): page 75

5: Laxey to Ramsey (12 miles, 6 hours): page 77

6: Ramsey to Ballaugh (18 miles, 8 hours): page 79

7: Ballaugh to Peel (13 miles, 5 hours): page 82

Coast Path Section 1
Peel to Port Erin (13 miles, 7 hours)

Take public transport to Peel and alight at the House of Manannan – the site of the former railway station and a Manx National Heritage attraction.

The walk starts from here. There are options to take two half-day walks, one from Peel to Glen Maye and return, and the other from Port Erin around Bradda. Begin by walking alongside the harbour to the bridge at its head. Cross the bridge and head towards the castle. After a short distance, follow the broad track up the hill, being careful to take the grassy track sharp left at the corner as the castle comes into view. You will soon see that there are two distinct parts to the hill which dominates Peel. The first, which you have just passed, is Peel Hill and the next part is Corrin's Hill, surmounted by Corrin's Tower.

From the saddle between the two hills you can either carry straight on to the summit of Corrin's Hill, or take the path to the right that follows the old horse tramroad to the quarry on the back of Corrin's Hill. The latter is by far the more spectacular but the path is close to the cliff edge in places so care is needed, particularly with young children – and this caution applies to many places on the walk.

Either option will bring you to the same spot, overlooking the south-west coast of the Island. Niarbyl (literally meaning the tail– from the tail of rocks stretching out to sea) is clearly visible. Cronk ny Irree Laa (hill of the dawn) dominates the skyline above and the hills stretch south to Fleshwick (green creek) and Bradda, with the Calf of Man just appearing in the far distance.

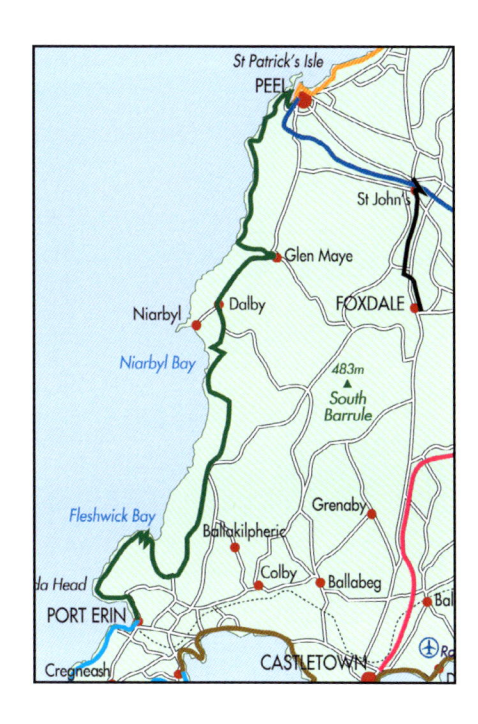

The path now becomes a real cliff path but is easy to follow as it skirts the various bays and inlets. Look for Traie Cabbag (cabbage shore – so named after the wild cabbage that grows here) and the unusual rock known as the Bonnet Rock, which is surrounded by water at most states of the tide. You will see why it has this local name when you find it. Now, as you approach Glen Maye (yellow glen) you have another choice.

The path reverts to the coast road here for a short distance. You can follow the

67

Cronk ny Arrey Laa

path down to the mouth of the glen as you round the headland and take the path up the opposite side of the glen to join the main road. Alternatively, carry on down into the glen and follow the lower path, stopping to admire the waterfall before climbing the steps to the main road.

There is an opportunity here to break for lunch at Glen Maye before returning by public transport or walking back to Peel along the main road. Turn right, follow the road down the hill and climb the other side to continue south parallel to, and in sight of, the coast all the way to Dalby (glen farm).

To continue the main walk, turn right in the village and walk along the road leading to Niarbyl, right down to the sea. Look for the path to the left alongside the small cottage which once belonged to popular music hall artiste Florrie Forde (a regular summer performer in Douglas from 1900–1937) and follow the signs directing you up the path and along the top of the cliff. After a short distance the signposting

directs you down steep steps to the shore Traaie Vane (white beach). Walk along the shore and cross the stream, where in winter the small waterfall can be spectacular. Look for the tall trees behind the beach hut and follow the broad track up again and away from the shore. Signposting takes you to the top of the cliff and a view south, and a steady climb joins a broad path on Manx National Heritage property that takes you south above Feustal (precipice) towards Cronk ny Irrey Laa.

Cross the stone wall over the wooden stile. The path is on the top of a cliff and should be treated with extreme care, swinging inland to cross a stream and wall above Gob ny Ushtey (headland of the waterfall, although the literal translation means beak of the water – the early Manx often described headlands as looking like the bill or beak of a bird and so the description came into common use).

From here strike uphill past the old farmhouse at Eary Cushlin (Cosnahan's shieling), now an outdoor pursuits centre.

Continue uphill, following the signs all the way to the top of Cronk ny Irrey Laa. There are spectacular views all the way up the climb and when you reach the summit you will be at the highest point on the coastal path. Take time out to admire the view back over Niarbyl towards Peel with Corrin's Tower visible in the distance.

Now make your way down towards the Sloc (or Slough, meaning pit or hollow) over open moorland. Flocks of chough frequent this area and they are quite distinctive birds – easily recognisable as members of the crow family but with bright red beaks and legs which contrast sharply with their black plumage. Choughs are increasingly rare in much of Britain, the Isle of Man being one of their last refuges.

At the Sloc you will leave the moorland very briefly to use the road, rejoining the moorland almost immediately by the picnic site on the other side of the boundary wall. Here as so often with the coastal path you are faced with a choice – the easy wide track to the left, or the path to the right which favours more experienced walkers and takes you to the summit of Lhiattee ny Bienee (literally meaning summit on the side), commanding excellent views back towards Cronk ny Irrey Laa and the big bay below.

Next, take the wide track and follow it to Surby (a Norse word – 'Saurbyr' meaning moorland farm), where it joins a surfaced road. At Surby turn right and follow the road to Fleshwick (green creek) down the east side of the valley.

As you approach the end of the valley look for the signs on the left of the road, just after the farm, which will lead you over a stile to start a really steep climb to the top of Bradda. Take your time climbing the path and admire the views behind you of the coast all the way up to Niarbyl and across the valley to Fleshwick. Once you are over the top of this climb, the view down the coast to the Sound opens out in front of you.

The descent into Port Erin is easy and you will pass Milner's Tower on your way. Here again you are faced with a number of alternative paths. Take the one following the coast through Bradda Glen and on to the upper promenade at Port Erin. Walk into the village and follow the signs to the railway station and bus depot, from where you will have a choice of transport back to Douglas.

An optional half-day walk – from Port Erin around Bradda – starts from the railway station as described in the following.

From the station cross the road into Bridson Street past the Cherry Orchard Hotel. Turn right into Bay View Road, left up Harrison Street and on to a public right of way, which takes you across Rowany Golf Course. Be aware of golfers and the possibility of wayward balls, but the path is clearly marked and the views are good.

Keep heading for the valley ahead, avoiding the junctions with other paths, and eventually emerge at Honna Hill, crossing through an old stone-built stile in the boundary wall. Turn left and head up the hill to the top. Look for the sign marking the Ernie Broadbent Walk off to the right. Follow this narrow road down the west side of the Fleshwick valley until joining the surfaced road to Fleshwick beach just past the farm. Turn left and look for the signs showing where Raad ny Foillan leaves the road a little distance further on, and where the longer walk from Peel joins.

There is time to walk down to the beach at Fleshwick and admire the views up the coast towards Niarbyl from sea level. The cliffs below the Carnanes sloping down to the sea are dramatic from here, and you can see where the high-level path from the Sloc descends to Fleshwick and why it is for more experienced walkers.

Coast Path Section 2
Port Erin to Port St Mary (6 miles, 4 hours)

This is perhaps the most beautiful of all the Island walks, whatever the weather and time of year. You should allow about four hours to give yourself enough time to take in the terrific views. The starting point is Port Erin station. An option is to get to Port Erin by first travelling to the Sound (where there is a café and car park) and taking in the village of Cregneash – a folk museum which is well worth seeing. The road from the Sound leads you to the village, from where the Darragh Road (place where oak trees grow) takes you into Port Erin.

From the station, turn left along Station Road and make your way down to the lower promenade and follow the sweep of the bay to the former Marine Biological Station near the lifeboat station. You will have to look very carefully for the start of this next section of the coast path, as it begins from behind an electrical substation! But once you've found it, the path is easy to follow. Climb the rough steps cut in the cliff to the stile in the wall. Follow the path along the wall and up above Kione ny Garee (literally meaning the end of the thicket), where throughout the year fulmars nest on the north-facing shaded cliffs.

The path levels out above Bay Fine and you have a good view back towards Port Erin and Bradda Head before descending towards Aldrick (old people's creek). On the way, look out for an unusual finger of rock known as Jacob's Rock. Ahead is the

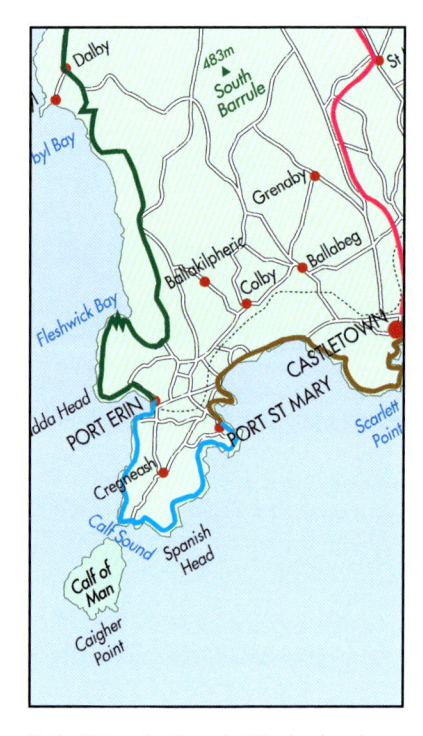

Calf of Man, the Sound, Kitterland and Thousla Rock. You can often see fast-flowing waters as the powerful tides rip and race through here, and if it's at all stormy you'll be treated to spectacular seas and views. An excellent viewpoint is provided by the wide panoramic window of the Manx National Heritage café and visitor centre at the Sound – not only a warm retreat in one of the Isle of Man's wildest places but also welcoming for its choice of hot meals, snacks and refreshments.

Crossing Manx National Heritage land, the path skirts around Burroo Ned (nest hill) and you will see the back of Spanish Head above Baie ny Breechyn (bay of the breeches – so named because it resembles a pair of blue trousers laid out on the sea!).

Pass through a gate and cross a small

stream to commence the very steep assault on the back of Cronk Mooar (big hill, although its local name of Cronk y Feeagh, meaning hill of the raven, is more appropriate as ravens do nest here). This is the southernmost hill in the Island – not very high but you will know it's a hill after you've made the climb!

Pause at the top and take in the views all round over the Sound and the Calf. If you're lucky and the wind's in the right direction, you may hear the baying of common seals as they bask on the Cletts (rocks) on the Calf immediately opposite this point. The path now starts to drop, still skirting the cliff edge and then turning north to start its run up the east coast. The path is very close to the edge above Black Head, so take great care, especially if you have children with you.

The path now starts to fall quickly towards Bay Stakka (a corruption of Baie yn Stackey, referring to the stack of Sugar Loaf Rock) which it skirts and then climbs to the Chasms, which are on the right. Again the path is exposed at this point so tread carefully. Then cross the wall on the substantial stile and head towards the derelict Chasms Café. Go through the wooden gate and follow the waymarked route alongside the wall on your left. This should avoid having to cross any of the Chasms – deep clefts in the rock and quite an unusual phenomenon. Be careful to descend the path beside the wall on your left all the way to a metal kissing gate above Cashtal Kione ny Goagyn (meaning the castle of chasms' head) or Sugar Loaf Rock as it is more popularly known because of its unusual shape. It is inhabited by colonies of guillemots, kittiwakes, fulmars and the occasional razorbill and puffin, and this is perhaps the most spectacular view of the rock, providing you have a good head for heights.

The path crosses the next field diagonally, heading for a gap in the stone

Calf of Man

On foot

wall opposite. Before leaving the cliff edge you can just catch a glimpse of 'the anvil', or as it is sometimes called 'the pulpit rock', which is a rock standing clear of the cliff in the small bay behind the Sugar Loaf.

Follow the well-defined path between walls, leading eventually to a surfaced road to Glenchass (an English corruption of Glion Shast meaning sedge glen) and Port St Mary. At Glenchass take the right fork in the road and follow it downhill for a short distance, looking for a sign on the right to take you to the shoreline at Perwick (harbour creek). The route follows the beach at Perwick and Traie Coon (narrow beach) before swinging up a zigzag path from the stony shoreline to join the path beside the golf course and on to Port St Mary promenade. Walk along the sea wall, passing the disused limekiln and past the breakwater into Lime Street and the inner harbour. Port St Mary remains largely unspoilt but the harbour is now occupied by pleasure craft rather than commercial fishing boats.

Turn left at the end of Lime Street and then right to follow the lower promenade and join the Cain Karran elevated walkway, which gives an impressive entrance into Chapel Bay – without doubt one of the Island's prettiest and most sheltered bays. Walk up into the village, where you'll find a variety of places to eat and a bus to take you back to Douglas.

Coast Path Section 3
Port St Mary to Douglas (15 miles, 8 hours)

If you're arriving at Port St Mary by bus, get off at the harbour. If you're travelling by train, it's only a short walk from the station to the village. Start this section by rejoining the path along Port St Mary's lower promenade and Gansey Point to Bay ny Carrickey (bay of the rock), following the coast road to Fishers Hill for approximately one mile. You will pass the gatehouses and boundary wall to Kentraugh House, and where there's a break in the windswept trees that form the boundary you may just catch a glimpse of this fine mansion. Continue along the sea wall and take the right fork at the bottom of Fishers Hill to follow the single-track surfaced road almost on the shoreline to Poyll Vaaish (literally meaning the pool of death; the name's origin is obscure but one likely explanation is that a slaughter house associated with the farm drained into one of the many sea pools).

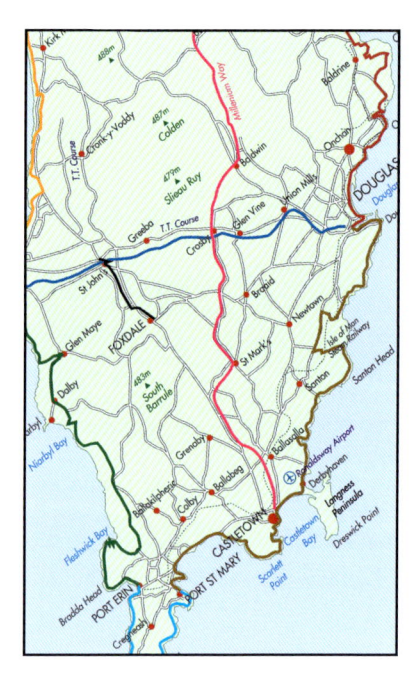

The whole area teems with birdlife, particularly herons fishing patiently in the rock pools and on the edge of the water, competing with curlews and oystercatchers. The path continues through the farm buildings at Poyll Vaaish

Port St Mary

and round the low headland beside the quarry from which the black marble for the steps of St Paul's Cathedral in London was reputedly obtained. Cross the stone stile over the wall on to the grassy headland at Scarlett (cormorant's cleft). The path follows the edge of the fields and skirts the rocks, which change dramatically, showing their volcanic origin and culminating in Scarlett Stack – a volcanic plug to a vent long since extinct. The broken, jagged rocks are the remains of an ancient lava flow. The rock changes from basalt to limestone as you now join a surfaced road once again and approach Castletown, which you will see straight ahead.

Enter the town square and turn right to skirt Castle Rushen, passing the police station. Turn immediate right again, then left over the footbridge to cross the harbour. Turn right into Douglas Street and past the Nautical Museum. Continue along Douglas Street and Bowling Green Road to join the main road to Douglas.

Unfortunately, new runway extensions at Ronaldsway Airport mean that part of the original route of the coastal path from here towards Douglas no longer exists. You now have to walk along the main road past the airport as far as Ballasalla, turning left towards Balthane industrial estate and following the road until it turns left at the airport boundary and on to the entrance of the lime quarry. Look out for the stile to the right and cross it to follow an old road to Santon Gorge.

The path follows the gorge inland, crossing the river over the footbridge and returning to the coast down the other side of the gorge. A raised boardwalk now makes it much easier to cross this very wet and boggy section. The path eventually climbs away from the river and follows the top of the gorge amongst shoulder-high gorse before joining the coast again.

Once at the coast the path is easy to

Marine Drive

follow along the top of the cliffs. You will be rewarded with good views all the way to Douglas.

The next bay you come to is Port Soldrick (sunny creek). Just where the path turns inland to drop down to the shoreline, you will see large caves in the opposite headland, with a view of the coast north towards Santon Head. After travelling along the beach for a short distance, climb back on to the path as it takes you higher still to continue along the cliff top.

The next inlet is Port Grenaugh. Again, after reaching the shoreline, climb up the other side of the bay. Look for the promontory fort and Viking settlement at Cronk ny Merrui (literally the hill of the dead people) on the right as you climb. Continuing along the coast you will pass Purt Veg (little port) and Santon Head before starting the climb up to Ballanhowe, where the path goes inland once again. The single-track road crosses the line of the steam railway before joining the Old Castletown Road. Turning right, follow the road for a little over a mile, but take care as there is no footway.

Descending Crogga Hill (from the Norse Króká meaning winding river), you will pass Crogga House and its decorative lake before seeing a waymarker directing you down towards Port Soderick (which has the same meaning as Soldrick – sunny or south-facing creek) and passing under the line of the steam railway.

Keep to the road and take the left fork along Marine Drive, where the coast path follows the route of the former Marine Drive tramway all the way to Douglas. Proceed along the coast, passing the inlet at Keristal. Note the change again in the rock formations, the contorted strata here in fragmented slate and clearly visible in the cliffs all around you. Problems over the years with rock falling from the cliff faces plus a major landslide in 1977, mean that as a through road Marine Drive has been closed to traffic for quite a time – but take care, as both ends of the drive are still accessible to cars and motorbikes as well as to walkers and sightseers.

The sight of the old toll gatehouse at the end of Marine Drive means that you're almost in Douglas, confirmed by the panorama of the whole bay spread out before you as you round the corner. The coast path now descends the steps between the lighthouse and the Camera Obscura (a restored Victorian attraction) to the breakwater, passing the Lifeboat House. The Douglas Lifeboat is appropriately named *Sir William Hillary* in honour of the Douglas resident who in 1824 was hugely influential in the creation of what was to become the Royal National Lifeboat Institution.

Coast Path Section 4
Douglas to Laxey (9 miles, 4 hours)

This is a good half-day walk and Laxey has a lot to show you, including a fine choice of places to lunch and the fascinating Laxey Wheel and mines area – an important part of the Island's rich industrial past.

Start at the Sea Terminal at the southern end of Douglas's impressively wide and sweeping 2-mile Loch Promenade. The prom was built in the 1870s to enclose part of the foreshore and to extend the lower part of what was then the Island's newly-appointed capital. Some of the original Victorian facade is now giving way to modern development as the changing face of Douglas continues to take shape, but enough survives to give you more than a flavour of Victorian grandeur as you make your way north along the bracing and spacious seafront.

On the opposite side of the promenade note the attractive elevations of the Sefton Hotel and the Gaiety Theatre. The church to the left and set back off the prom was completed in 1849 and dedicated to St Thomas, the patron saint of architecture. It was designed by Ewan Christian R.I.B.A., who was of Manx descent and Architect to the Church Commissioners, noted particularly for his work at Carlisle Cathedral.

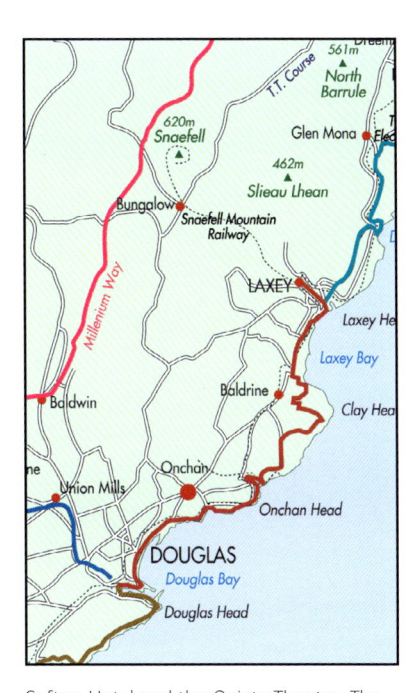

The construction of the church was by local contractor Richard Cowle. It was built to serve the needs of an expanding town, and the arrival of the tourist development along Loch Promenade led to its being referred to as 'the visitors' church'. In 1912, a fire in the tower destroyed the bells, as well as the organ made and installed in 1886 by William Hill of London. The fire damage was repaired and a new peal of bells installed five months later. At the same time the organ was repaired and enlarged, and today recitals and concerts are a regular feature of church life.

As you continue towards the northern end of the crescent-shaped promenade, where stands the terminus of the unique Douglas Bay Horse Tramway, you'll see more evidence of redevelopment. The horse trams are a summer-only attraction and date from 1876. Here also is the southern terminus of the Manx Electric Railway, which has been running north to Ramsey since operation commenced in 1895. Both the horse trams and the railway still use original equipment and, unsurprisingly, they are a Mecca for transport buffs from all over the world.

Continuing past Port Jack and around the loop of Seaview Road, you'll soon see why it is so named, overlooking Douglas Bay. Look for the coast path waymarker directing you along the cliff top and almost through the front gardens of the houses here. The path joins the road again at Lag Birragh (literally the sharp pointed hollow – referring to the rocks below) and continues along King Edward Road to Groudle (narrow glen), where you should follow the narrow road down to the shore by the holiday homes. Cross the river by the footbridge and climb up the path to cross the Groudle Glen Railway. A popular Victorian novelty and attraction, the restored railway is now operated by enthusiasts at various though limited times during summer months and for Santa specials.

Follow the path upwards and on to a narrow surfaced single-track road. Look for the waymarker directing you across the fields to Garwick, and also for the signpost to Lonan Old Church – well worth a detour, not least to see the stone Celtic wheel cross in the grounds.

Walk through the fields to the point where the path joins Clay Head Road, which you must follow towards Baldrine.

Look for the waymarker directing you to Garwick, and follow the fishermen's path to the shore and climbing immediately all the way back up the other side of the glen. Follow the signs to join the main road again.

Turn right at the top and continue towards Laxey on the main road beside the tramway (there's no pavement so be careful). Reaching Fairy Cottage presents you with an option – as long as you know the state of the tide! At low water you can take another fishermen's path down to the beach and walk to Laxey harbour the very pretty way. Alternatively, stay on the coast path and continue down Old Laxey Hill into Old Laxey and the harbour. Follow Glen Road to Laxey village and up the hill under the church to the centre of the village. Christ Church Laxey is situated in what must be a unique setting for any church and its history is entwined with the mining history of Laxey. The village was a very busy place in the mid 1800s as a direct result of mining. The population had increased significantly, and with the temptation of public houses on the doorstep the need for a place of worship within the village was long overdue.

In fact, the Laxey Mining Company and one of its principal shareholders, G.W. Dumbell, were instrumental in promoting a church. Built largely by the miners themselves, right in the middle of the village on land which was formerly part of the garden of the Mines Captain's House, it was designed by architect Ewan Christian. Early English in style, it has an interesting scissorbeam roof and simple internal decor and it merits spending a little time here. Take lunch in the village and complete this leisurely day's coastal walk with a visit to the Great Laxey Wheel & Mines Trail.

In fact, Laxey now boasts not one but

two restored waterwheels. The wheel once used at the Snaefell mine, situated further up the valley, has been painstakingly rebuilt by local enthusiasts and is displayed in the mines' former washing floors – the same location in which (in summer) you can see and travel on a restored section of the Laxey Mines tramway and its authentic replica locomotives of the 1870s.

At the end of the walk, return to the station and take the tram back to Douglas.

Coast Path Section 5
Laxey to Ramsey (12 miles, 6 hours)

From Douglas, travel by bus or electric railway to Laxey station and you're ready to resume your conquest of the coast path. Start by taking the path alongside the station building and down to Captain's Hill. Turn right to join Glen Road opposite St George's Woollen Mills and make your way to the harbour. Note the large factory-type building on the opposite side of the river – built to generate the power for the Laxey section of the Manx Electric Railway.

At the junction by the harbour bridge, look to the opposite side of the road for the coast path waymarker. It directs you up an old packhorse road to Ballaragh (of doubtful origin but best seen as derived from Balley arraght, meaning farm of the spectre or apparition). Continue up through Ballaragh to the top of the hill and the views towards Maughold Head and east across the Irish Sea to Cumbria and the Lake District.

The road curves away from the coast but look for the waymarker on the corner, pointing you over the fence and diagonally down through the fields. Cross the road and the railway track and continue on the footpath until it joins the Dhoon Glen Loop Road. Cross one stile on to the road and then immediately back over the adjacent stile to follow the track down to sea level again. It is worth the effort even though this is another of those down-and-back-up-again detours.

The path skirts Dhoon Glen and you will catch a glimpse of the wheelcase of the Dhoon Rhennie Mine (Dhoon is probably derived from an Irish word meaning fort and rhenny is a ferny place), which extracted lead and zinc but was not productive and eventually abandoned. Then the mouth of the glen opens up and you will have a view of the headland of Kion e Hennin (Kione ny eaynin – headland of the cliff; Kione literally means beak or bill of a bird but by common usage has come to mean headland). Its area, and immediately behind the headland, was a granite boss which for years was quarried for its pink granite.

The path drops to the shore and then

Maughold

returns behind the picnic table. Follow the path within the glen, climbing past the Island's most spectacular waterfall, comprising three falls emptying into a pool beside the path. A further steep climb will take you back to the point where you began this detour. Turn right, back on to the Dhoon Loop Road and follow it over the railway back to the main road, where you turn right. Almost immediately turn right again and at the bottom of the hill take yet another right turn, making sure you follow the right fork by the ford and the single-track road down to Cornaa (an ancient treen name meaning land division).

You are now back at sea level again, but this time with a difference. Behind the shingle bank is a saltmarsh with an attendant variety of birdlife.

The path crosses the river and follows an unsurfaced road known as Benussi's lane all the way up the right-hand side of the valley, heading inland. Cross the railway again, and the main road, to continue up the Raad ny Quakerin (the Quakers' road), noting the Quakers' burial ground at the summit.

Descending through Ballajora (farm of the strangers), you'll enjoy a view of

Ballaglass Glen

Maughold Head and the lighthouse. At the bottom of the hill look for the signs taking you right to Port Mooar (the great harbour). Follow the path round the coast through the tall grass to Gob ny Rona (headland of the seals) where you may very well see some of these marine mammals. At Dhyrnane, before climbing away from the shore, you'll pass derelict workings from an iron ore mine.

Now cross fields past a lime kiln to join the road to the lighthouse, turning right for a short distance before turning left on to Maughold Brooghs. Follow the path over the headland through more old mine workings at Gob Ago (literally edge headland) before joining the road again and turning right towards Ramsey.

Not for the first time, you have a choice of routes: carrying on into Ramsey along the main road or, if the tide is out, going down the slip at Port e Vullen (harbour of the mill) to the shore and following the cliff path around the headland at Tableland to rejoin the road again a little further on.

Either way, it is back up to the main road, passing Belle Vue railway halt and all the way down into Ramsey. At Ballure (Balley euar meaning yew tree estate or farm) you could make a detour into Ballure Glen and on to Ramsey along the beach, but this option is only possible at low water. Once in Ramsey, proceed along the promenade and the harbour. At the end of the promenade is the church of St Maughold and Our Lady Star of the Sea, built in 1900 and designed by Giles Gilbert Scott.

This marks the end of the Laxey–Ramsey section of the coast path, and you can return to Douglas by bus or electric railway from the station in Waterloo Road.

Coast Path Section 6
Ramsey to Ballaugh (18 miles, 8 hours)

Now for something completely different! This section of the Isle of Man coast path embraces the northern alluvial plain – a flatter, gentler landscape

Crosses at Maughold church

On foot

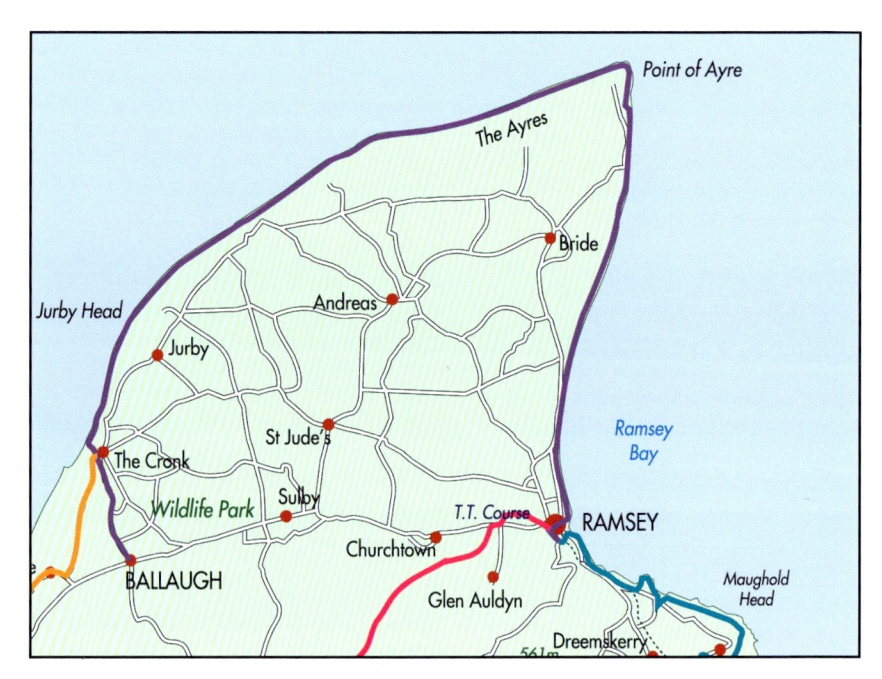

compared with the rest of the Island, the Bride Hills topping a modest 300 feet.

However, the walk is very dependent on tidal conditions and should not be undertaken when the tide is rising. The ideal time to start is shortly after high water, although there are alternatives which avoid the risk areas.

The starting point is Ramsey station – the northern terminus of the Manx Electric Railway, and also close to the bus station. To proceed, make your way from the station to the harbour, follow the quayside and cross the stone arched bridge at the harbour's head. Turn right into North Shore Road to Mooragh Promenade (Mooragh meaning waste land by the sea) and then left, following the promenade as far as the Vollan. The state of the tide will determine which way you go from here. If the tide's out it's possible to walk all the way to the Point of Ayre – the most northerly place on the Isle of Man – along the shingle beach. But if the tide's in, the only option is to walk up the hill, turn right and follow the road to the village of Bride and onward from there to the Point of Ayre.

Of geological interest is the fact that the cliffs of this part of the Island are composed of sand. The high cliffs at Shellag (the original Norse name means seal creek or bay) are quite dramatic – deformed glacial deposits – but because of erosion the bay no longer exists. As you continue along the shore it is clear to see that the whole area is subject to storm erosion.

If you've taken the road to Bride and onwards, you will pick up the coast path again at the Phurt (port) north of Shellag Point. Follow the raised beach and the glacial formation of the northern plain which is clearly evident. The whole of the Ayres was formed by alluvial deposit and here the terrain changes yet again with shingle underfoot all the way around the northernmost tip of the Island.

The lighthouse which marks the Point of Ayre was designed by Robert Stevenson for the Commissioners of Northern Lights and built in 1818. The shingle is constantly on the move, as can be seen by the smaller lighthouse added 72 years after the original and now automated, controlled from a remote central station.

lookout are located, will put sand back underfoot. The whole of the northern plain has been drained by successive generations to reclaim many acres of fertile agricultural land. The last major undertaking was the formation of a lengthy drainage channel which discharges at the Lhen (Lhen Mooar – meaning great ditch). You'll know when you reach it, as the Lhen Trench

Ramsey pier

Continuing along the coast on the shoreline is heavy going underfoot but worth it for the wild natural beauty to seaward, with birdlife in abundance. Look for gannets, whose spectacular dive-bombing action, black-tipped vivid white wings and highly distinctive blue bills set them apart. As you make your way along the beach it's probable that you'll be followed by curious seals and constantly leapfrogged by flocks of oystercatchers – a wonderful sight in flight.

Passing Rue Point and Blue Point, where the rifle range and the old coastguard

discharges across the shore and wading is the only way to get across – so it's boots off and round the neck.

As you approach Jurby Head, the sand cliffs are back with a vengeance and continue almost to Peel. If the tide's well out at Jurby Head look for the remains of the trawler Passages, which was driven ashore in 1929 in a north-west gale, the crew rescued by the rocket brigade of the day.

After passing Jurby Head you approach the Killane (from the Scandinavian kjarrland, meaning brushwood land),

Coast at Jurby

where another drainage ditch discharges to the sea. Shortly after this, look for the signs where the Ballaugh shore road joins the shoreline at the Cronk.

Leave the shore and walk to the village of Ballaugh, passing the old parish church of St Mary de Ballaugh. Dating from the middle of the 18th century, it is noted for its leaning gate pillars. Old photographs and other sources suggest that the pillars must have been in this condition for a hundred years or more.

Walking towards Ballaugh, you can admire the backdrop of the western hills and see the tower of the 'new' parish church. Work on the church commenced in May 1830. The old church was considered too small and, as the village community grew, too far from the centre of the population it was supposed to serve – even though it was no more than a mile away!

Designed by Hanson and Welch, the church is built in local stone in a style unique for the Island. The tall lancet-type windows and intervening buttresses to the nave, and the ornate pinnacles, make it quite distinctive.

You will arrive in the centre of the village opposite the public house and beside Ballaugh Bridge – a famous landmark along the TT course.

Coast Path Section 7
Ballaugh to Peel (13 miles, 5 hours)

To complete your anti-clockwise conquest of the Isle of Man coast path, here's a walk which is easy going all the way. It begins from the centre of the village, beside Ballaugh Bridge. Leave the village by Station Road and proceed to the Cronk, passing the two churches described in Section 6. On the way you will pass the Dollagh (a corruption of Doufloch, meaning black lake), a name rooted in the fact that in much earlier times, a great deal of the northern plain was flooded, the land dominated by several large lakes. No visible signs of these lakes remain, except in periods of heavy rainfall, when remnants appear here and there. Other places such as Ellan Rhenny (ferny island) and Ellan Bane (white island), and even the parish name of Ballaugh (a corruption of Balley ny Loughey – lake farm), give a clue to what this area was like in those days long gone.

At the Cronk turn left and follow the Bollyn Road (Boayl ein – spot of the birds) as far as the Orrisdale Road. There are good views of the western hills which form the backdrop to Bishopscourt, the ancient seat of the Bishop of Sodor and Mann but now a private residence. Turn right at the junction with the Orrisdale Road and follow the road through Orrisdale (from the Scandinavian Orrastör, meaning estate of the moorfowl).

At the corner after the farm look for

the signpost leading to the shore at Glen Trunk. Go through the gate and follow the wide grassy track to the shore, past one of the Island's best-preserved lime kilns.

Once on the shore you will be able to see Peel in the distance. Turn left and walk along the shore, flanked by steep sand cliffs, and note how these are also subject to erosion. For this reason it is advisable to steer a wide berth when walking underneath them.

This is an interesting spot for bird lovers. You're likely to be in the company of oystercatchers, herring gulls and black-backed gulls. Curlews, living on the slopes of the western hills, graze the foreshore in flocks and ringed plover and the occasional chough are often seen in these parts.

As you approach Glen Wyllin (glen of the mill) you will spot sea defence works on the foreshore – an attempt to slow down the rate of erosion. Beyond these, a little further along the shoreline, look for

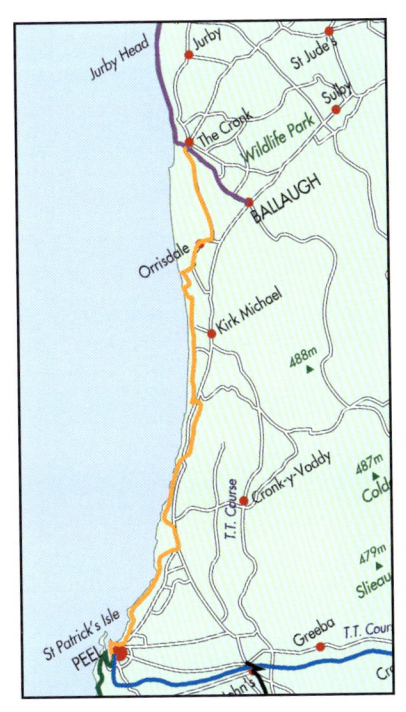

Coastal path north of Peel

Peel

Peel castle

the waymarkers directing you off the shore at Glen Mooar (the great glen).

Leave the shore here and make your way up the narrow surfaced road to the main coast road. Look across the road and you will see a waymarker directing you into the glen. Follow the path as far as the stone pier – one of two piers which once carried the railway across the glen on lattice steel girders. Climb the roughly-cut steps up the side of the embankment to join the disused railway track. This now forms part of the coast path and will take you to the old station at St Germain's Halt, 3 miles away.

Once on the track, look back and this elevated position will show you just how severe the erosion of the sand cliffs is at this point. In places it will not be long before the coast road is threatened.

There are a couple of farm crossings before you approach a rock cutting and the road overbridge at Skerisdale (or more correctly Skeresstaðr from the Norse meaning rocky farm). The railway now runs closer to the sea than the road does and you can imagine just how dramatic a journey it must have been as the train clung to the cliffs and spanned the glens on viaducts and embankments.

Leaving the cutting, the track bed emerges on to an embankment at Glion Cam (the winding glen), opening up views of Peel and the castle on St Patrick's Isle in the distance. The coast road can be seen to the left and above, winding around the head of the glen – hence the local name of the Devil's Elbow.

Half a mile further on, in a shallow cutting which is sometimes quite wet and muddy, the path emerges into the open and really does cling to the cliff. This section, known as the 'donkey bank', suffered continuous settlement problems when the railway was operating, and these are evident as you proceed. Below, as you cross the second of the embankments, you can also see rocks on the shoreline at Gob y Deigan. From here on in the physical features of the coast change yet again – from the sand cliffs to slate and to red sandstone as you get nearer to Peel.

The path continues on the track bed for a further mile, crossing yet another glen on an embankment at Glion Booigh (the dirty glen). It's worth stopping on the embankment to look down at the trees growing in this glen. There's a great variety, with some surprises, and in many ways it is one of the most unspoilt corners of the Island and only really appreciated from this location.

The path now curves left to join the coast road at the site of the former St. Germain's Halt, the old station building and gatehouse just about recognisable as such. Leave the track here and follow the road for a short distance downhill and round the corner at the bottom. Look for the waymarker on the right and go through the kissing gate to join the headland path. The path climbs rough-cut steps and reaches a promontory above Cass Struan (stream end). Stop and look north back along the route you've just walked and you'll see the sand cliffs stretching all the way north to the prominent white outline of Jurby Church and Jurby Head in the distance. Now look down below where you're standing and you'll see the sandstone (referred to earlier) which outcrops here in a glorious burst of russet red.

The path continues to Peel along the headland above Traie Fogog (or more correctly Traie Feoghaig – meaning periwinkle shore), commanding probably the best views over Peel and the castle. Continue on the headland path and descend into the town and the promenade. There are several places to take refreshment and any of the roads off the prom leads to the town centre and the bus station for return to Douglas.

If you've completed all seven sections of Raad ny Foillan, you'll have to admit it's been an adventure. Congratulations – and here's to the next time!

THE HERITAGE TRAIL
Douglas to Peel (10.5 miles, 4 hours)

This easy and leisurely walk along a disused narrow-gauge railway follows the route of the first line which connected Douglas to Peel. When the railway was built in 1873, the Isle of Man Railway Co. had a simple wooden building as its station. But by 1892 it had developed at such a pace that the company had built a new station to rival many of the mainline stations in the British Isles – so where better to start the walk than in the station forecourt, close to Athol Street and the heart of Douglas's business community.

Unfortunately, the first half mile or so of the original line has been extensively built over, so you have to make a detour before joining the line at the Quarterbridge. But as you leave the station, look at the impressive Victorian clock tower, which gives a good idea of the grandeur of the station architecture when it was built.

From the station turn left up Bank Hill and left again into Peel Road. The shops you pass on the left were also built by the enterprising railway company. Continue to the junction with Pulrose Road and turn left over the bridge – built in 1938 to replace an earlier level crossing on the line you'll be joining a little further on. Note the bridge's two arches. The intention was to construct a double track, but it was an ambition never realised. You'll also be able to make out the route of the track bed as it threads its way behind the development in this area, which has taken place over the last 25 years.

Continue on towards the power station and turn right immediately before the bridge over the Douglas River. Follow the pathway behind the Bowl, part of the King George V playing fields. The whole area was reclaimed using waste from the spoil heaps at the Foxdale mines. The Isle of Man Railway locomotive No.15 Caledonia was used almost exclusively to haul thousands of tons of material here between 1935 and 1939.

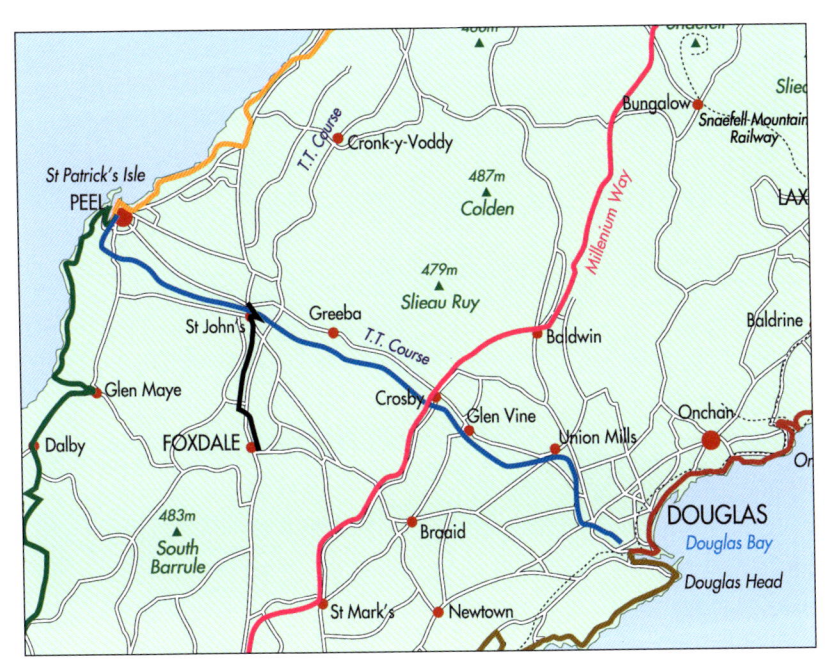

The path takes you to the confluence of the River Dhoo (black river) and the River Glass (green river), and now you can see how the name of the town of Douglas evolved. Follow the right fork alongside the Glass and cross it by the bridge, which leads to the National Sports Centre. Follow the river for a short distance past the rear of the grandstand and join the railway track behind the office building. This is where the railway crossed the river on a skew lattice girder bridge.

Now you can start the walk in earnest. A little way along the old track bed you'll reach the site of the level crossing which took the railway over the Castletown Road. Note the crossing keeper's gatehouse on the left, but take care crossing the very busy road because visibility is restricted.

All of the Island's disused railways are now service corridors for gas, electricity, water and telephones, and nearly all are public rights of way and over time have been improved for walkers. In 1989 this line was the most complete in terms of the overall scheme and was designated the Heritage Trail. It is now also a designated cycle way. The next section of the track bed serves an access road for vehicles to the inside of the TT course when the main road is closed for racing. Continue behind Quarterbridge Lodge and walk between the stone boundary walls. On the left you will see Kirby Estate and possibly catch sight of grey herons, which roost here and range the river. The name Kirby is Scandinavian in origin and means church farm.

As you pass under the road you're

Old Braddan church

approaching the site of what was formerly Braddan Halt. This was used in connection with Open-Air Sunday Services at Braddan parish church, shortly coming into view to the left. It was not uncommon to see 10-coach trains on this short special service from Douglas and hundreds of visitors getting off at the halt, which had no platform, and walking up the steps by the bridge and up Vicarage Road to the fields behind the new parish church.

Carry straight on along the old track bed, which from here on is more recognisable as a disused railway. The River Dhoo, which has never been very far away from you, is now beside the railway. Approaching Union Mills the line curves left after crossing the river on a steel girder bridge. This replaced an earlier stone-built structure which gave rise to flooding in the early years of the railway. A small wayside halt existed here originally to serve a horseracing course at the Strang.

Now, with industry left behind, the scenery becomes more attractive. It's hard to believe that even as late as 1960 there was little or no industrial development between Pulrose Bridge and Union Mills!

Entering Union Mills station through the tall trees which have grown with the railway, you are now 2.5 miles from Douglas. Early photographs show almost no cover at all. Successive station masters took tremendous pride in the station, which became noted for its wonderful rhododendron and floral displays.

The station was on the curve and had a very long passing loop, added some time after 1906. On the left you will see the single platform serving the station. Look for the name of the manufacturer of the non-slip paving slabs which form the edge of the platform. Also on the left, before you reach the platform, there's a roadway accessing the station area. There was a short trailing siding here serving goods traffic and a cattle dock. The wooden station building was situated on the right just before the line passed under the road.

Part of the development of the Heritage Trail has been the inclusion of picnic tables and information boards. Here at Union Mills there is also a static display of a Gibbins breakdown crane – one of two operated by the railway – on a small section of track. Dating from 1893, it was hand operated and had a lifting capacity of 8 tons.

Immediately after crossing the River Dhoo yet again (the original steel structure was removed when the line was being dismantled), continue past a small industrial area where the remaining parts of the old Union Mills are still in use. The name evolved because a corn mill and a woollen mill built on the site by William Kelly both drew water for their machinery from the same dam.

The mills were big employers for this area in the early part of the 19th century. Later they were owned by the Dalrymple family, who continued to operate them until the end of the century. Dalrymple Maitland was a director of the railway and locomotive No. 11 was named after him.

Now cross the Trollaby stream (possibly meaning the stream of the trolls) and enter open country as the line sweeps into the central valley of the Island. The River Dhoo is still on your left and you can see remnants of the curragh (bog) between the river and the railway. Much of the central valley was like this, with wet boggy land, water meadows and willow growing in what was in effect the flood plain of the river. Henry Vignoles, who surveyed the area for the line, chose a route which skirted the valley floor and just managed to keep above the water table.

The line passes Glen Lough (literally Lake Glen) and runs straight for a short distance to cross the road at Closemooar (great enclosure), just after milepost 4. The crossing keeper's gatehouse still

St Trinlan's

Glen Helen

survives and is on the left before the crossing.

There was a short cutting here and the line ran straight towards Marown Church, with Greeba Mountain dominating the view. The track bed here has also been surfaced to allow access to the nearby sewage works, so beware of lorries! The track bed passes behind the parish church and swings left, entering more of the curragh land before approaching another level crossing, where the gatehouse still remains.

Cross the road and enter the playing fields. This was the site of Crosby station, some 4.75 miles from Douglas. Nothing remains to give a clue as to what was here. There was a passing loop and the facing point for this was positioned just before the level crossing, where two tracks crossed the road. This meant that when trains passed here the road was obstructed for longer than usual. If the second train was late the gates would often be opened in between the passing operation. There was a typical IMR wooden station building, painted green and cream, on the right at the point where you entered the playing fields. Just beyond that was a wooden goods shed served by a siding off the passing loop, with a further short siding to a cattle dock, the whole of which was partly screened by a wooden boarded fence.

You are now much closer to Greeba (an obscure Scandinavian word meaning peak) and the hills on both sides are closing in on the railway. You are still climbing and haven't yet reached the summit. On the hill on the left above the Highway Depot you can see the old school which served the parish of Marown.

Leaving the playing fields, you are soon back on the old track bed. Straight ahead is Creg y Whallian (rock of the whelp) with Cooilingill Farm (low nook) on the hillside. You will just be able to see the edge of Archallagan Plantation to the left on the skyline. The River Dhoo has its source in the centre of the plantation before tumbling down the hill below Cooilingel and joining the Greeba River on your left.

The line, now 5 miles out of Douglas, swings right with Greeba and Slieau Ruy (red mountain) straight ahead. As you approach and cross the track leading to Cooilingel Farm, you are into the true remaining curragh of the central valley. This was an accommodation crossing and the gates were always open to the railway. Walk over another short bridge which crosses the Greeba River and continue close under Creg y Whallian. This is the narrowest part of the valley and very near to the summit of the line.

The next level crossing over the Rhenny road (boayl y rhennee – place of the fern) was also an accommodation crossing. The house with the unusual farm buildings on the right is Northop (another Scandinavian word meaning north village). Here is another chance to look at Greeba before the curragh closes in and you pass through a very wet area which was the site of an early settlement. You emerge approaching the Ballacurry Road, another unmanned crossing. The summit of the line, at 185 feet, was marked by the small stream after the Ballacurry Road. The Greeba sportsfield is on your right, just visible through the trees. This is the site of an accident in 1909 when the locomotive Derby (No. 2), acting as pilot engine on a late train running to Peel, had the misfortune to hit a fallen tree. It was completely derailed and toppled on to its side – the second accident in which it was involved (but more of that shortly).

As you pass through Greeba the curragh is still visible in places, but over the years drainage work and farming activity have reclaimed a large portion of it. The wooded hill ahead is Slieau Whallian, although its true summit is further to your left. The hill dominates the village of St John's, and it is up its flank that the Foxdale Railway climbed the gradient of 1 in 49 to the mines. This is the point from where the Isle of Man Railway Co. at one time proposed to build a branch line to Foxdale. It would have gone off to the left, climbing the side of the hill above Kenna (Aodha's hill – Aodha being a name of Irish descent).

Next you cross the Kenna Road, which was yet another unmanned accommodation crossing. After a shallow reverse curve under the trees, the track runs straight all the way to St John's.

Now Slieau Whallian is much closer and you can see the gatehouse for the keeper at the Curragh Road level crossing. The track bed has been surfaced here and an additional road built to serve the adjacent amenity site. Cross the road and the stile on to the right-hand track – the original route of the railway – and pass under the bridge which carried the Foxdale Railway over the Peel line. The bridge is covered with ivy but you can see the brick arch springing from the stone abutments.

You are now approaching the site of St John's station. It grew from very modest beginnings to become the 'Crewe Junction' of the island railways. In its final form the line was single, passing under the bridge and running for a short distance parallel to a three-line steel carriage shed on the right.

There was a fourth carriage siding in the open on the far side of the shed. A small signal box stood in the middle of the grassed area to your right. Here the line split into two, each with a passing loop and served by a single low platform, just one brick high, placed between them. This is where the Ramsey line and the Peel line divided. At each end of the central platform was a water tank supported on a brick structure.

St John's was served by a simple wooden station building situated on the left near the road (the site now part of a housing development). It had a small waiting room, ticket office and station master's office and was never developed or replaced by more impressive facilities despite the relative importance of the station.

Two lines crossed the road on a gated level crossing, the Peel line on the left and the Ramsey line on the right.

To continue the walk you have to make a slight detour from the original route, as the bridges over the river beside the Mart have been removed. Cross the road and go through the gate opposite, leading to the sewage works, and rejoin the track alongside them.

Walking down from the road you can see an interesting red brick building behind the hedge on your right. This was the terminus of the Foxdale Railway and was a grand building compared with the IMR's modest station at St John's.

Passing through the gated stile puts you back on clear track bed again. The two lines were still running parallel here, the line to Peel on the left and to Ramsey on the right. As you approach the two bridges crossing the River Neb at Ballaleece (Leece's farm), you will see the Ramsey line start to rise alongside you in order to pass over the Peel road as it swings away to the right.

The Peel line makes a gradual descent from the river crossing before levelling out on the ancient flood plain of the Neb (the meaning of the river's name is obscure). The river, having looped around to the left towards the Patrick Road and joined with the Foxdale river since the bridge at Ballaleece, is now back alongside the railway on the approach to Shenharra (meaning Old Ballaharra, possibly referring to an ancient earthwork).

View from Peel castle

The river meanders away to the left as you approach the cutting at Ballawyllin (Byllinge's farm), which was a notorious spot in winter for snow. The cutting is through the tail of what appears to be a moraine, deposited at the time of the retreating ice sheet in the last ice age.

Through the crossing at Ballawyllin you can now see the true flood plain extending out towards Patrick, and the full extent of Peel Hill and Corrin's Hill, surmounted by Corrin's Tower. Further to the left are the Creggans (literally rocky place but describing the small rocky outcrop), forming the southern boundary to Knockaloe (Caley or Allowe's hill), the site of a First World War internment camp. A branch of the railway was built to serve the camp and shortly you will see where it joined the Peel line. The line ran straight for a short distance before skirting the sand cliffs of Ballatersen (part of the old Bishop's Barony but literally meaning farm of the crozier), now the location of Peel's golf course.

You'll see that the railway passed through the last remnants of the curragh and if you're particularly observant you might spot the remains of some of the drainage channels dug in the 1940s as a winter employment scheme in a further attempt to drain this area.

The line now ran beneath the cliffs and through boggy ground again – terrain which caused big problems throughout the entire lifetime of the railway. You can get some idea of the nature of the ground as you pass close under the sand cliffs. The willow catkins are a sight to behold in spring and the area abounds with the yellow heads of wild iris.

A little further on and the river is once more back alongside the railway and slowed by a dam built for the Glenfaba Mill (a mixture of English and Manx; it should be Myllin Glenfaba, meaning Mill in the glen of the Neb). The pond is known locally as the 'red dub', and you can see where the mill race was taken off the dam and under the track on its way to the mill. The name for the area, which also gives its name to the weir, is the Congary (rabbit warren).

Before reaching the mill you'll cross a small stream by means of a footbridge. Pay particular attention to the widening of the track bed just after the bridge. This is where the branch railway to Knockaloe Internment Camp left the Peel line by means of a trailing point from this direction. You can just make out the line of the branch as it curved round to cross the river on a wooden trestle bridge to climb for a little over a mile, at a gradient of 1 in 20, to the village of Patrick and Knockaloe.

Next on the right is the Glenfaba Mill. Some indication of what it was like can be gleaned from the size and shape of the building. The waterwheels remain and the overflow from them would have discharged under the track into the river. In fact the railway occupied the original river bed here, the river re-aligned to accommodate it. The railway passed under the Patrick Road and alongside the river, which was also diverted here to allow the line to run through this natural gorge on a gentle curve. It was here, in 1874, that the ill-fated locomotive Derby suffered the first of its two major accidents.

Following heavy rain, the embankment gave way and the loco tumbled into the river. It was the first train of the day and although the driver saw that the track had been washed away he was unable to stop. He and the fireman both fell with the engine but were uninjured, as was the only passenger who fortunately occupied one

Point of Ayre

of the coaches which remained on the track. The railway was temporarily diverted on a reverse curve to the right, almost on the original line of the river, while the present retaining wall was built on the original alignment.

Follow the railway through the remaining fields of Glenfaba farm as you enter Peel, through the back door past the old power station on the left. On your right are the Total Oils storage depot and the new Peel power station. When the railway was running the first buildings encountered would be the brick kilns and tall chimneys of the Glenfaba Brick Company – no doubt aesthetically more pleasing than the concrete chimney now occupying the site.

Straight ahead on the left-hand side of the track is one of Peel's original kipper houses, now operated as a working museum and worth a visit. The modern kipper houses are in the fish yard on the right. The railway finally arrived at Peel station by a level crossing over Mill Road where Peel Heritage Trust have a small transport museum in the old brickworks office.

The station site had been reclaimed from the harbour bed. The water tank, station building and goods shed are all that remain of the station itself, the last two buildings having been incorporated into the House of Manannan heritage centre, which now occupies the site. Behind the water tank there was a small engine shed and on the right a cattle loading dock and the goods shed. This had a loading bay into Mill Road which can still be seen. The station, having undergone several changes throughout its life, ended with four roads and a run-around loop served by a long platform.

The Creek Hotel – originally the Railway Hotel – is a good place to stop for well-earned refreshment. The railway ceased operation between Douglas and Peel in 1972 after five years of uncertainty. The rails had been lifted and sold for scrap before the Isle of Man Government stepped in and purchased everything, which fortunately included the now-thriving Port Erin line of the Isle of Man Steam Railway.

THE MILLENNIUM WAY

RAMSEY TO CASTLETOWN (26 MILES)

This can be undertaken as a full-day walk or as two walks breaking at Crosby. The Millennium Way was the first long-distance path to be introduced on the Isle of Man as part of the celebrations associated with 1,000 years of independent government. Opened in Easter 1979, it is based on the ridgeway used by the Norse kings to travel from their ancient landing place on the Sulby

River near Skyhill to their fortress on the southern plain. The road is recorded in the *Chronicles of Mann* and the Isles – the first written record of Island life, produced by the monks of Rushen Abbey.

NORTHERN SECTION: 14 MILES

Take a bus or tram to Ramsey and make your way from the station to the harbour, which is a short distance along Parliament Street and down Post Office Lane opposite the Courthouse. Turn left at the harbour and follow it to the junction with Bowring Road. Note the shipyard on the opposite side of the harbour which was built on the site of a former salt works.

Cross the road at the top of the harbour and look for the public footpath sign leading to Pooyldhooie (pool of the black ford), where a nature reserve has been constructed on what used to be the town tip. It is now a very pleasant walk and a credit to the local commissioners and the volunteers who have carried out the work.

The path emerges by the Whitebridge, which crosses the Sulby River, and this must have been the most likely place for the Vikings to have made their safe harbour. At the time of their invasions and subsequent settlement the Island was a very different place and the Sulby was by far the biggest river. Here they could sail their longships at least a mile and a half from the open sea and moor them in a sheltered lagoon – something which was not possible anywhere else on the Island.

Walk up Gardeners Lane to the main road and turn right for a short distance, looking for the distinctive waymarkers for the Millennium Way, striking off to the left over the bulk of Skyhill (the Norse named it Skógarfjall – the wooded hill). Follow the path up through the plantation, which was the site of a battle in 1079 when Godred Crovan overcame the native Manx and

Ramsey and the north plains

Druidale

assumed kingship of the Island.

From the plantation the track opens out on the level near some rugged flat-topped pine trees at Park ny Earkan (pasture of the lapwing). Stop and look back over the northern plain, formed by the outwash from the retreating ice sheet at the end of the last ice age. The Point of Ayre is in the far distance.

Carry on to the top mountain gate and enter the open moorland. The track is still discernible and there are waymarkers which you follow to a very wet boggy area. Cross by means of the planked walkway and be careful to follow the waymarkers off to the right, heading for a cairn on the skyline in the saddle between Slieau Managh (mountain of the monks) and Snaefell (snow mountain).

The original kings' road veered off to the left here and followed the line of the mountain road for some distance, travelling around the east flank of Snaefell. The Millennium Way favours the west flank to keep away from the traffic on the mountain road and at the same time introduces you to some of the more inaccessible places in the Island.

Pass the cairn and carry on over the saddle a short distance to join the mountain wall above Block Eary Reservoir (from blakkärg meaning black shieling). Follow the mountain wall where it turns steeply down below the massive bulk of Snaefell. Cross the wall at the bottom by the stile and over the river. The way strikes off steeply from the river and at right-angles to it. It can be wet here at all times of year but only for a short distance. As you climb it is worth looking back across the valley at the route you have just walked. You should just be able to make out the shape of some circular mounds. These are the shielings where the young men used to live with their animals on the mountain pasture during the summer months – another remnant of a past way of life and the best example of such structures on the Island.

Follow the waymarkers across the mountain until you pick up a stone wall and sod dyke which is part of a large earthwork known as Cleigh yn Arragh (stone rampart). Follow this until you reach a Forestry Department track and then the Tholt y Will Road.

Cross the road at the signpost and strike diagonally down the mountainside towards the mountain ahead, which is Beinn y Phott (very loosely interpreted as turf peak). At the bottom of the valley cross the river by means of an old stone bridge, built and used by the miners who operated the mine a short distance upstream. The stone structure you can see is the remains of the wheelcase of the waterwheel. The mine closed in 1867.

Climb up on the left-hand bank of the gulley, being careful at the top to take the left-hand fork, and head for the signpost which you should be able to see on the Brandywell Road. This is where the Millennium Way joins the route of the old ridgeway again. Cross the road and follow the track over the saddle between Beinn y Phott and Carraghyn (meaning scabby, with reference to its stoney top) as far as the mountain gate giving access to a rough track, which you follow for almost two miles. As you skirt the shoulder of Carraghyn, the views open up over the Baldwins and on towards Douglas in the distance.

The track starts to drop down at Cronk Keeill Abban (the hill of St Abban's church)

where an old keeill was located near an ancient Tynwald site on your right. At St Luke's Church, built as a chapel of ease to Kirk Braddan, join a surfaced road taking you downhill into West Baldwin.

At West Baldwin, cross the bridge and the road to follow the signs up a track through Ballagrawe (Balla ny Groa – farm of the cotes or coops) and across the fields of Ballalough (farm of the lakes). After passing the farm, cross the stone stile and follow the lane for a short distance before crossing a ladder stile. Follow the waymarkers across two fields on the eastern flank of Greeba.

There are superb views to the left over Douglas as you head for the saddle between Greeba and Cronk ny Moghlane or Mucaillyn (hill of the sows) and the signpost on the skyline. After the next stile there is a diversion around the edge of the field before reaching the narrow road leading to Cronk Brec (hill of many colours – literally piebald). You must now make a left and right to follow a rough stone track down to Ballaharry. Just before you reach the cottages, look to the right and the sign pointing to an ancient monument. This is the site of the remains of Keeill Vreeshey (the church of St Bridget) and is an example of early Celtic Christianity. There were many such sites on the Island.

At Ballaharry the track joins a surfaced road which takes you into Crosby village at the crossroads with the main Douglas to Peel highway. Here you can finish the walk and return to Douglas by public transport – or if you have the energy, carry on along the southern section to Castletown.

SOUTHERN SECTION: 12 MILES

The southern section of the Millennium Way is totally different in character, and

The Stacks

the old ridgeway passes to your left to cross between the Mount and Slieau Chiarn (the Lord's mountain). It has been incorporated into the present road network, and in order to keep the walk more attractive the Way takes a slightly different but parallel route.

The start of this section is tough. Make your way down Old Church Road, formerly Station Road when the railway was in operation. You will see where the railway crossed the road as you pass the distinctive small crossing keeper's house. Then it is a stiff climb up School Hill, passing the old school built in 1874. Its bleak location may seem a little strange when you look around and see where the centre of population is now. When it was built, however, the school was in the centre of the parish serving numerous remote farmsteads as well as the village. The same factors applied to the old parish church which you will pass at the top of the hill. The church is dedicated to St Runius and dates from the 12th century, although the remains of a keeill dating from the 7th century can be seen on the site.

Continue along the road under the avenue of trees towards the Garth crossroads. Look out for the ancient monument sign on the right as you start to climb the next hill. It directs you to the site of St Patrick's Chair – a small group of stones which according to tradition is the spot where St Patrick first preached and intoduced Christianity to the Isle of Man.

Carry straight on over the crossroads, passing Ballanicholas and drop down the hill to Campbells Bridge, which marks the boundary between the parishes of Marown and Malew. Stop at the bridge, spanning the Santon River, to read the interesting plaque. Look over the bridge and you may just be able to make out the remains of old mine workings.

Continue on past Shenvalley (old farm) and in the distance you will be able to see the tower of the church at St Mark's. The church is a good landmark and you will need to turn left and then right at St Mark's and around the old schoolhouse. The church, school and adjoining houses were built in the 18th century at the instigation of Bishop Hildesley as a chapel of ease to Malew parish church. You need to be careful here and look for the waymarker beside the old parsonage. The path follows the lane beside the parsonage to the Awin Ruy (red river) and crosses it on an old stone slab. The path meanders through the fields of Upper and Lower Ballagarey (farm of the river thicket), crossing hedges through kissing gates and eventually arriving at a surfaced road.

Cross the road and follow the waymarkers through two fields before entering Ballamodha Mooar farmyard and following the farm road through Ballamodha Beg to its junction with the Ballamodha Road (Ballamodha meaning farm of the dog, Mooar meaning big, and Beg little).

Turn left and walk along the road for approximately a mile, taking care as there is no footpath. The Ballamodha Straight was used in the past for hill climb and reliability trials when the motor car was in its infancy.

Continue to the bottom of Silverburn Hill and at the Atholl Bridge turn left to Silverdale and walk on the path alongside the river. Approaching Silverdale you will come to a children's playground, boating lake and café. The boating lake gives the clue as to the function of the old building adjoining the café. Creg Mill was one of two built by the monks of Rushen Abbey, and the lake powered the waterwheel. The little waterwheel which now turns the children's carousel is worth more than a passing glance as it came from the Foxdale Mines when they closed.

Continuing downstream you pass Ballasalla Ochre & Umber Works – an old industrial site now converted into a private residence. The company was a substantial one and had warehousing in Castletown, from where shipments were made. The north quay still carries the name Umber Quay.

Leaving the wooded glen you emerge through a gate at Monks Bridge, dating from the late 14th century and probably the oldest bridge in the Island, built by the monks of Rushen Abbey.

Approaching the site of the abbey, look left to the opposite side of the river to Abbey Mill, now converted to private apartments. It was a substantial mill with an internal waterwheel and gives an indication of the importance of the abbey. The whole area of the abbey has been acquired by Manx National Heritage and archaeological research is further revealing the unfolding story of Mann.

Follow the boundary wall of the abbey to the right and walk around the perimeter – on the way you may be able to catch the odd glimpse of abbey remains through a gate. Cross the road and almost opposite, the waymarkers direct you down a narrow lane and then left to the river again. The Way follows the river into Castletown on a pleasant walk through river meadows. Cross the river on a wooden bridge, continuing on the other side nearer to the steam railway. Look for the weir that took water from the river for the Golden Meadow Mill, visible from the path as you pass Poulsom Park. The railway station is across the park and you can return to Douglas from here or continue into Castletown and finish your walk at the castle.

On foot

SHORT WALKS
THE FOXDALE LINE
(2.5 MILES, 1 HOUR)

This short walk follows the disused railway line which connected the Foxdale lead mines to the rest of the Island's railway network at St John's. The best option is to take a bus to Foxdale and start from the old station, which is adjacent to the primary school.

The Foxdale Line was built in 1886 by the Foxdale Railway Company, an offshoot of the Manx Northern Railway, as an opportunist venture to win lucrative mineral traffic from the Isle of Man Railway.

Prior to the building of the line to Foxdale, all the ore was taken by horse and cart to St John's for onward transmission by the Isle of Man Railway to Douglas station. It then had to be loaded again into horse-drawn carts and hauled to the harbour at Douglas. The contract for the carriage of the ore came up for renewal and the Manx Northern bid was successful. A subsidiary company was formed to build the Foxdale Railway and create a direct rail link between the mines and Ramsey harbour. But it was to prove a financial disaster and resulted in the eventual downfall of the Manx Northern, everything coming into the ownership of the Isle of Man Railway.

When mining came to Foxdale it brought with it a tremendous increase in population. Public houses sprang up in its wake and it soon supported a constable and a jail. Methodism found a strong footing in the area, as in Laxey. The established church appointed a chaplain to Foxdale in 1850 but it was to be 1881 before Foxdale had its own church. Public subscription and a handsome donation from the mining company resulted in the foundation stone being laid in 1874 by Mrs Cecil Hall. The church, designed by James Cowle, was consecrated by Bishop Rowley Hill on Whitsun Tuesday, 7th June 1881 as a chapel of ease to Kirk Patrick Parish Church. The village became a parish district in its own right some years later. The church can be seen on the opposite side of the valley beyond the old school.

It is hard to imagine now what this area was like at the height of the mining boom, lead and silver produced to an annual value of £50,000 at the time the railway was built. There were 350 people employed in the mines. The three main shafts were Potts, Beckwiths and Bawdens. The deepest, Beckwiths, reached a depth of 320 fathoms (1,920 feet) by 1902, yet by 1911 the industry had declined and the Isle of Man Mining Company had ceased working.

The walk starts by the old station building which is opposite the new school in Mines Road, and is all downhill at a steady gradient of 1 in 49. There is quite a wide defined track which runs from the road beside the school. This is the start of the track bed, and the building on the left is the station building. There was a shallow platform with brick edging served by a single line with a runround loop. The area presently occupied by the school was the site of the principal spoil heap from the Beckwiths mine.

A temporary siding was built into this area in the 1930s to assist with the removal of the spoil, which was mostly used in the construction of the playing fields at what is now the National Sports Centre in Douglas. The spoil from the Bawdens shaft formed a massive heap and the station was hemmed in between these two mountains of waste – a scene extremely difficult to imagine today. Beyond the station building was a small brick structure supporting a water tank for the locomotives. A single line climbed behind the back of the station at a gradient of 1 in 12 to cross the road and enter the mines yard. Here the ore was loaded into wagons for Ramsey via St John's. This line was always referred to as 'the back of the moon' – which was exactly how the area looked after the mines had ceased working.

Before starting the walk, go up Mines Road a short distance and you might just be able to see the remnants of the crossing, with the running rails and check rails in the road surface – the only visible remains of the Foxdale Railway.

Return to the station and start to walk down the line. While the first part near the school is somewhat changed, you soon come on to the old track bed, which is quite unmistakably railway as it skirts behind the miners' cottages in Higher Foxdale. On the hillside to the right there is still visible evidence of the oldest mine in the area, particularly near the river.

Now you are very close to the road. The line ran on a high stone-built embankment before swinging left to cross the road on a steel girder skew bridge (Luke's Bridge), the road prescribing a double corner as it dropped under the bridge to continue to Lower Foxdale (the name Foxdale is an anglicised corruption of Forsdalr, a Scandinavian word meaning waterfall dale). The bridge was removed when the track was lifted in the early 1970s. You must climb through the stile in the boundary wall and cross the road to the opposite side where there are steps leading up the old bridge abutment and back to the track bed.

Now the formation can be really appreciated and you continue on an embankment towards Lower Foxdale with a view of Slieau Whallian ahead. Cross

Old mines at Foxdale

over the accommodation road to Ballamore farm (from an Irish family name – More's farm) on a small bridge. The line entered a cutting through rock as it curved left and approached Waterfall Halt, which was the only intermediate stop. Little remains of the halt. Originally planned to have a passing loop, it was completed with only the single line and a small wooden building on the flat area to the right.

Walk straight on across the timber footbridge spanning the Gleneedle stream, a tributary of the Foxdale River. The halt served the community of Lower Foxdale and also attracted visitors to the Hamilton Falls, where the stream cascades down a rock face before joining the main river. Walk under the bridge which carries the Ballanass road over the railway (Balla n eas is Manx Gaelic meaning farm of the waterfall). You are in a short cutting under trees and can probably hear the sound of the waterfall below you on the right. You emerge to curve around the hillside with lovely views towards the central valley dominated by Greeba Mountain. The line was built on an embankment and followed the natural lie of the land. There was an old mine on the left, but nothing remains except a very overgrown spoil heap. The occasional telegraph pole is a reminder of the railway's existence.

You are now approaching Slieauwhallian farm (an obscure word which could refer to a personal name, possibly Mc Aleyn, or it could refer to hill of the whelps) and entering a wooded area. Pass under the bridge which carries an accommodation road associated with the farm and you will see that the construction was of a very simple nature and used concrete for the abutments. After the bridge the line passes through a very attractive section before curving left alongside the plantation – part of the larger Slieauwhallian plantation, neither of which existed in the days of the railway.

Unfortunately, you have to leave the line at the end of the plantation and veer off to the left to join the Slieauwhallian back road.

Follow it to the right, downhill to the Patrick Road and right again to the next junction. Before leaving the track bed, look to the right through the trees and note where the track continued on an embankment almost 40 feet high. Although now much overgrown, it still gives an indication of the amount of material needed for its construction. The line curved to the right to cross the Foxdale River on two steel spans carried on a central stone pier between two abutments.

If you like you can turn right at the junction. Walking a short distance towards the Hope will show you where the line crossed the river, after which it curved in a left-handed sweep to cross over the Peel line and into St John's. If you return to the Patrick Road junction, you can carry on towards the village, passing what is now a car park but was once the site of the St John's station originally built by the Isle of Man Railway.

Walk further up Station Road and cross over the Foxdale Line just before the Post Office. You can look over the right-hand parapet wall and see where the line came into St John's behind Pretoria Terrace, with the embankment climbing away towards Foxdale and over the Peel line. Look over the left-hand parapet and you can clearly see the St John's terminus of the Foxdale Railway. The station was a grand building by comparison with that belonging to the Isle of Man Railway, and similar in style to the station building at Foxdale. There was a passing loop at the station, with goods sidings and the connection to the Manx Northern Railway beyond. Finish the walk here and use public transport to go on to Peel or Douglas.

DOUGLAS TOWN WALK

Starting in front of the Sea Terminal forecourt, it is worth taking time to look at this building, completed in 1962. Now offices, the circular part of the structure immediately below the spire was originally a restaurant commanding unrivalled views of the bay and harbour. The unusual roof earned it the nickname of the lemon squeezer. The building was formally opened by Princess Margaret in 1965.

The short walk around what is now the lower part of Douglas commences along Bath Place towards the bus station. Keep to the left-hand side of the road and head around the corner towards the inner harbour and the new harbour lift-bridge, which replaced an earlier swing-bridge. The accumulator tower and control room for the old bridge can still be seen on the other side of the harbour.

Cross the road at the bridge to the harbourside and read the inscriptions on the plaques, which have been fixed to blocks of Foxdale granite. The inner harbour was until recently a commercial harbour and was tidal. When the new bridge was installed a tidal flap was built and the enclosed basin became a yacht marina – a development which has elevated the harbour as an attractive new focal point for Douglas.

Walk along the side of the harbour behind the parked cars and cross the road opposite the Clarendon Hotel and continue along the North Quay. The old Fish Market (now the Royal British Legion Club) and the market are the next buildings you pass before reaching the British Hotel.

The harbour frontage is gradually changing but some of its past can still be traced on this part of the quay. At the junction of Ridgeway Street is St Matthew's Church, dating from 1895 and built at a time when the old heart of Douglas was being redeveloped and new streets were being driven through the town.

Continue along the quay and look for the plaque on the building on the right just before arriving at Queen Street. You will see that it was the first electricity generating station for the town. At the junction with Queen Street are the last vestiges of the old character of the area. The Liver Hotel formerly stood directly opposite and is now part of the Newson Trading block. To the right is the Saddle Hotel, and the old narrow alignment of Queen Street, winding round the rear of the quay to Quines Corner, completes the picture.

The area had many more public houses then than it has now, earning it the reputation of the 'Barberry Coast'. As you walk along the quay to the top of the harbour you will see that the old and the new have blended together to retain some of the character of the old harbour frontage. Upstream from the Douglas Bridge, a new apartment block nearing completion is further evidence of the changing face of the old riverside property – all part of the grand Development Plan for Douglas.

To continue the town trail, cross Bank Hill and walk into the railway station forecourt and across to the steps on the right leading up to the clock. At the top of the steps pause and look back at the grand building in red facing brick, built at

Tower of Refuge at Douglas

Tynwald buildings, Douglas

the start of the 20th century at the time that the Isle of Man Railway Company acquired the other two railway operators.

Go through the entrance gates and cross into Athol Street and walk along the street on the right-hand side. By the start of the 19th century it represented the upper limits of Douglas, the Georgian-styled houses being the residences of merchants and the wealthy. As the town expanded this area quickly became its business centre, and still is. Much of the street has been redeveloped but here and there you can still see some of the original buildings.

Walk as far as Lower Church Street and turn right past what was once the old Court House but has now been tastefully converted into offices and a restaurant. Note on your right the new multi-storey car park. At the bottom of the hill turn left by the Isola Restaurant. It is probably the oldest surviving building of old Douglas. Opposite is the John Street elevation of the Town Hall and the site of the original fire station for the town.

Turn left and head up Prospect Hill, passing several of the national banks before reaching Athol Street again opposite the Italianate-style Isle of Man Bank headquarters. The opposite side of Prospect Hill has been redeveloped, new office buildings presenting a stark contrast in styles. Continue as far as Hill Street and pause before turning left to look at the 'wedding cake corner' buildings – part of the administrative and parliament buildings of the Isle of Man Government. On the opposite side of the road is St Mary's Roman Catholic Church, designed by Henry Clutton and opened in 1859.

Walking along Hill Street you will note more new office development reflecting the new-found wealth of the town. At the end of Hill Street turn right into Upper Church Street and opposite is St George's Church, from which the street gets its name. Walk up as far as Circular Road and turn right, crossing over to walk on the left-hand side of the road to its junction with Prospect Hill again. Opposite, at the other end of Government Buildings, are the Rolls Office and the new Court House. Now turn left and continue up Bucks Road, once the main route out of Douglas to the north.

Carry on as far as Rosemount, pausing to admire the fine spire of Trinity Methodist Church. Continue straight on past Prospect Terrace and the shops which were originally built as private houses, the extent of the original terrace framed by the pediments at each end. At the junction with Hawarden Avenue is Woodbourne Square, laid out in the late 19th century and one of several which retain the Victorian character of the town. Walk through the square and emerge opposite the Masonic Lodge. Cross the road and walk towards the next town square which you will see behind the Lodge. Hillary Park is totally different from the square you have just seen. Walk through it and emerge opposite the terrace of yellow brick houses and turn right, walking as far as Derby Road, where you turn left.

After a short distance look for the right turn to Derby Square opposite the Bowling Green Hotel and walk to Crellins Hill, at the top of which is the Manx Museum. Walk down the steep hill to St Thomas Church, completed in 1849. Keep to the left-hand pavement, cross the road and walk down Church Road to the promenade. Turn left, and go past the Sefton Hotel to the Gaiety.

If the Gaiety Theatre is open for conducted tours you shouldn't miss the opportunity to see it, it will be time well rewarded. Next to the theatre is the refurbished arcade which is now home to a Wurlitzer theatre organ. The arcade is also an interesting point on the town walk, giving you access to an elevated walkway above the colonnade, with commanding views over the promenade and the Villa Marina gardens. Leave the walkway by the steps at the fountain, opposite the war memorial, or complete the walk by returning to the Sea Terminal

CASTLETOWN WALK

The walk around the former capital of the Island starts at the railway station. This will give you the ideal opportunity to arrive at Castletown by train and sample the delights of Victorian travel. From the station, go over the railway lines into Poulsom Park and cross the park adjacent to the children's play area, through a gate directly opposite on the bank of the Silverburn River. Turn left and walk beside the river.

Pass under the railway bridge, where you will almost certainly be accosted by the resident population of geese and ducks. Walk up to Alexander Road and cross it to join Victoria Road, continuing beside the river. Straight ahead is the imposing grey bulk of Castle Rushen, around which the town grew to become the ancient capital of the Island.

The castle beckons – but first, a detour.

Cross the road at School Lane and walk past Victoria Road Primary School and the unusually named Smetana Close, so called because of the town's close association with many continental musicians and through an annual music festival held in the town. Emerge past the gates of Lorne House, a former residence of the Governors of the Island, on to Douglas Street and turn right. Look out across Castletown Bay at the long peninsula of Langness, its prominent lighthouse at the southernmost tip. Walk along the pavement to the corner with Bridge Street and past the Nautical Museum – which highlights the Island's fishing industry and

Castletown

the amazing *Peggy*, the oldest surviving Manx-built ship. Continue as far as Bridge House.

As you join the harbour turn left, cross the swing-bridge and there's the castle in all its glory. Straight ahead on the corner is the local police station, designed in keeping with the castle by Baillie Scott. Across the road is the castle barbican and entrance. The castle is a must on your list of places to visit. It is one of the best-preserved medieval castles in the British Isles, largely because of its limestone construction, and it has remained in use throughout most of its life.

For now though, leave the castle behind by turning left and walking along the quay. Then turn right up narrow Quay Lane, leading into what is now a public car park. Ahead is the Old Grammar School, one of the Island's oldest buildings, incorporating part of the medieval chapel of St Mary and its structure pre-dating most of the castle.

Turn immediately right and walk into Parliament Square, which forms the forecourt to the Old House of Keys building. This is where the Island's parliament met until Douglas became the capital in 1865. It too merits a visit. Turn left into Castle Street and into the Parade. Cross the road and catch the best view of the castle. Note also the unique one-fingered clock presented to the Island by Queen Elizabeth I in 1597. The castle as it stands now dates from the latter part of the 16th century but parts of it were built as early as 1250. The dominant features are the massive keep and four flanking towers.

If you look to the right, the other end of the Parade is Market Square, which has as its backdrop the former garrison church of St Mary's, dating from 1826 but now deconsecrated and converted into offices.

In the centre of the square you will also see a fine Doric column built to commemorate Cornelius Smelt, the first Governor of the Island. Unfortunately the column never received a statue of the Governor.

Continue along Arbory Street – the road to the left off the Parade. On one side of the street stands the development known as Callow's Yard.

At the end of Arbory Street, turn right into the Crofts and admire the part of the old capital where the wealthy of the day lived. Half way along the Crofts go in through the gate on the right to the municipal bowling green and walk past the café and green to emerge in Malew Street. Turn left and then right to walk down Mill Street.

This area has been redeveloped under the guidance of the local commissioners to bring people back into the centre of the town. At the end of Mill Street turn right into Hope Street and walk back towards the town centre. At the end of the street is a limestone building, formerly the National School and now converted for use as a replacement for St Mary's Church. Turn left and cross the bridge over the harbour to retrace your steps to the starting place at the railway station.

PEEL TOWN WALK

The walk around Peel starts outside the Creek Inn in Station Place – formerly the Railway Hotel and part of the town's railway heritage, though trains no longer run here. Directly opposite is the House of Manannan (a Manx National Heritage attraction), which incorporates part of the old railway station.

To start the walk head away from the harbour and turn right into Mill Road. Passing the back of the House of Manannan, you will see that the goods

Peel castle

shed of the railway has also been incorporated into the museum.

To some extent this is still the 'industrial heart' of Peel, with the gas works on the left together with the kipper yards, the site of the old brickworks and the new electricity generating station. The chimney of the latter lacks much of the elegance of the old brickworks chimney. Peel Heritage Trust has in fact established a small museum in the brickworks weighbridge office, and the former railway station yard opposite is now a boat park, though the railway's water tower has been preserved.

Where Mill Road joins the harbour, Moore's kipper yard is on the left. This is one of very few surviving kipperies which still preserve herring using the traditional oak-smoked method – a process which summer visitors can see for themselves courtesy of a conducted tour of the smokehouse and museum. Turn right here and walk alongside the harbour (back towards the Creek Inn) and over the bridge in the direction of Peel Castle. The hill which dominates Peel (comprising Peel Hill and Corrin's Hill, the latter part distinctive for its tower) is well worth a walk to the top, as described under Coast Path Section 1: Peel to Port Erin on page 67

As you'd expect, the imposing ruins of Peel Castle on St Patrick's Isle are an important landmark along the town walk, accessible over the causeway. Once across, look for the steps leading up to the path around the castle and follow the path to enjoy the views south over the back of the hill and Fenella beach below. The castle is also an unmissable chapter in the story of Mann and well merits half a day's exploration of its ruins and history to reveal such fascinating facts as why Peel can lay claim to city status.

Return from the breakwater to the bridge at the seaward end of the harbour.

The inner harbour is now enclosed by means of a flap gate, a development which has created Peel's new yacht marina. Cross the bridge and turn right on to East Quay. Walk back towards the Creek Inn but look for St Peter's Lane.

You join East Quay after passing the impressive entrance to the House of Manannan. Continue along the quayside for a short distance, passing the remnants of the old warehousing which serviced the fishing industry (for so long the mainstay of Peel's economy) but which are now taking on new life as modern waterside apartments.

At St Peter's Lane turn right and walk up the narrow street past grand stone-built houses, originally the homes of fishermen. At the top of the hill turn left, skirting the whitewashed wall which enclosed the churchyard of St Peter's Church, built as a chapel of ease to the original St German's Cathedral on St Patrick's Isle. It was demolished in 1958 but the clock tower remains and the grounds are retained as a place of quiet reflection.

As you walk along the lane, the architecture of the tower gives an indication of the style of the former church. Turn left into Castle Street and then right into Love Lane and left into Market Street. Continue down the hill to the double corner. On the second corner, continue to the bottom where it joins Crown Street. The Leece Museum, which you pass on your right, is well worth a visit to learn a little more about the town.

Turn right into Crown Street and follow it to the promenade. Turn right, and right again, into Market Street and walk through the opening on the left into Charles Street – a charming part of old Peel. Many of the buildings in Peel are built of sandstone and here the beauty of the stone can be seen to advantage.

Continue through Charles Street and Strand Street into Beach Street and turn left back on to the promenade. Here you will pass some of the oldest fishermen's cottages still remaining in the town. Turn right on the promenade and enjoy the fine view of the castle (which has its origins in a Norse settlement), and continue along the promenade as far as Stanley Road. Turn right and half way up the hill turn right again into Circular Road. Walk up the hill to the corner at the top and cut through the alleyway into Christian Street, turning left and then right into Mona Street. Peel had many Methodist churches, nearly all of which are no longer places of worship, but their spirit remains in their architecture.

Walk up Church Street to emerge opposite the courthouse and police station. Cross the road and enter the grounds of the 'new' St German's Cathedral. Although dating from 1884 and built as the parish church, it was not consecrated as the new cathedral until 1980.

Continue through the grounds and walk down to emerge through the grand entrance gates into Atholl Street, opposite the Methodist church. Turn right to Atholl Place and left down Michael Street, which is the town's main shopping thoroughfare. At the end of the street turn right into Douglas Street and then left at Market Place. Now you can imagine the commanding position which St Peter's Church held overlooking the old part of the town.

Cross the square and follow the church wall to Lake Lane and walk down to Station Place and the completion of the walk.

RAMSEY TOWN WALK

Your tour of the town of Ramsey starts

On foot

in Market Place, opposite St Paul's Church. This dates from 1822, when it was spawned from the parish of Maughold as the town grew and the population centre gradually shifted. In earlier times Market Place was the focal point of the town and the location of an open-air market selling predominantly fish. Some stalls still open here on certain days.

Leave Market Place by way of Dale Street, passing what was once the former municipal swimming pool, now a bowling alley, and the Roman Catholic Church of Our Lady of the Sea, designed by Giles Gilbert Scott and built in 1900.

Arriving at the promenade, walk in the direction of the Queen's Pier. Dating from 1886, it is one of the surviving classic Victorian piers, constructed to allow vessels of the Isle of Man Steam Packet Company to call at all states of the tide. It is now the subject of a preservation campaign.

Opposite the pier, turn right up Queen's Pier Road and then right again into Waterloo Road to return towards the centre of the town. You will pass the old Cross on your right – the site of the Old Town Hall and the point at which one arm of the Sulby River originally discharged into the sea. Just after the Old Cross note the distinctive Mysore Cottages built in memory of Sir Mark Cubbon, Commissioner General and Administrator of Mysore in India. Adjoining is the Old Grammar School dating from 1864 and replaced by the present school in 1922.

At the end of Waterloo Road turn right into Bourne Place and Parliament Street, opposite the terminus of the Manx Electric Railway. The courthouse and police station are on the left as Parliament Street curves around in that direction.

As you continue along Parliament Street, note the facades of the buildings and the dates when they were built. The town still displays a good variety of shops in its main street despite the pressures of supermarkets. Walk along as far as Christian Street before turning left, but pause at the junction and look ahead at the classic buildings of Auckland Terrace – now more than ever the business centre of the town. To the right the old warehouses, still in use, are a reminder of the wealth and importance that this northern town once possessed.

Turn left and on the skyline ahead of you is the Albert Tower, built to commemorate a surprise visit by Queen Victoria's consort when their ship was unable to land at Douglas. Walk as far as the junction with Albert Road and turn left again. Here, on the right, is another reminder of the royal visit, in the shape of Albert Road School. It was built at the turn of the 20th century at the instigation of the then newly-formed School Board.

At the junction with Tower Road, turn right and at the end of the terrace turn left down the narrow lane, emerging in the station of the Manx Electric Railway. After protracted negotiation this was the rather ignominious end of the line when it reached Ramsey, rather than the grand entrance the MER envisaged along the sea front to connect with the Queen's Pier. In the event the railway seems to have faired better than the pier as a visitor attraction and still provides a unique travel experience.

Walk through the station – but be mindful of tramcars moving through the area – and turn right into Parsonage Road, continuing as far as its junction with Queen's Pier Road. Turn right again and proceed past the bus station into Parliament Square. The newly-built Town Hall replaced two earlier buildings on the site and was completed in 2003.

Ramsey

Continue along the road, which now becomes Bowring Road, and at the first roundabout pause to look across to the left at the area occupied by Ramsey Bakery. This was the site of the station for the steam railway which once connected Ramsey and St John's, but the line has long since closed and no trace remains of the station. Carry on past the second roundabout and you cross the Bowring Road Bridge, going straight on as far as Windsor Road.

Turn right and walk along Windsor Road. The style of the properties belies the opulence that the merchants and entrepreneurs who originally developed the town enjoyed when Ramsey was in its infancy. At the end of the road turn right into Windsor Mount. Stop at the house on the corner and read the plaque on the wall proclaiming that this was once the residence of celebrated Manx poet T.E. Brown. Walk down Windsor Mount and Ballacloan Road to North Shore Road. To the left is Mooragh Park, created on land where the second arm of the Sulby River discharged to the sea. On the right you pass the ground of Ayre United Football Club – not be confused with the Scottish club of the same name (but without the 'e'!).

Turn left on North Shore Road to Mooragh Promenade. Turn right along the promenade, which was a late development in the Victorian guesthouse boom and never really realised its potential in the way that Douglas promenade did. All of the houses were built to a very similar design and have come to represent the symbol of the Victorian era on the Island.

Continue back towards the centre of the town, passing the new swimming baths at the end of the promenade before crossing the swing-bridge – a major feature of the harbour. The harbour frontage ahead gives further clues to Ramsey's past wealth. Many of the old warehouse gables remain but only a few retain their original use.

On reaching the other side of the bridge turn left on West Quay to return to Market Place – your starting point.

By cycle

Mountain biking is the perfect way to see the Island, and whether you want to stick to the natural trails or mix it up with a bit of road cycling you are certain to see sights that others rarely do.

Before you head out to ride and explore, here are some key things to remember. While you may be on a small Island the weather changes very fast and it's easy to get caught out, so set out prepared as you would for any mountain bike ride!

On an island in the middle of the Irish Sea weather conditions can vary hour to hour wherever you are on the Island so prepare for the unexpected. Wearing layers of clothing can help maintain your temperature. A quick drying jersey on top of a base layer with a wind and waterproof jacket is ideal. We highly recommend wearing a quality helmet and full finger gloves to protect yourself from injury.

Depending on the expected ride time you're likely to need a few key things.

For a 1-2 hour ride, we'd suggest taking a water bottle, multi-tool tyre levers, a spare inner tube, mini pump, a fully charged mobile phone and some spare cash.

For routes over 2 hours a hydration pack is perfect for carrying extra spares. Taking quick links for your chain, chain ring bolts, zip ties, gaffer tape, shock pump and a spare derailleur hanger for your bike might just save you should you pick up a mechanical issue on the trail.

For rides over 3 hours be prepared to carry enough food and water for your journey, especially if you plan to be out all day. Extras worth packing are sun cream, midge spray for the summer, an extra layer of clothing such as a showerproof coat or an extra pair of gloves in the winter to fight off the cold. Consider taking these items in addition to what you would pack for a short ride. If you forget anything, the local bike shops are very friendly and happy to help!

Mountain biking

Itineraries

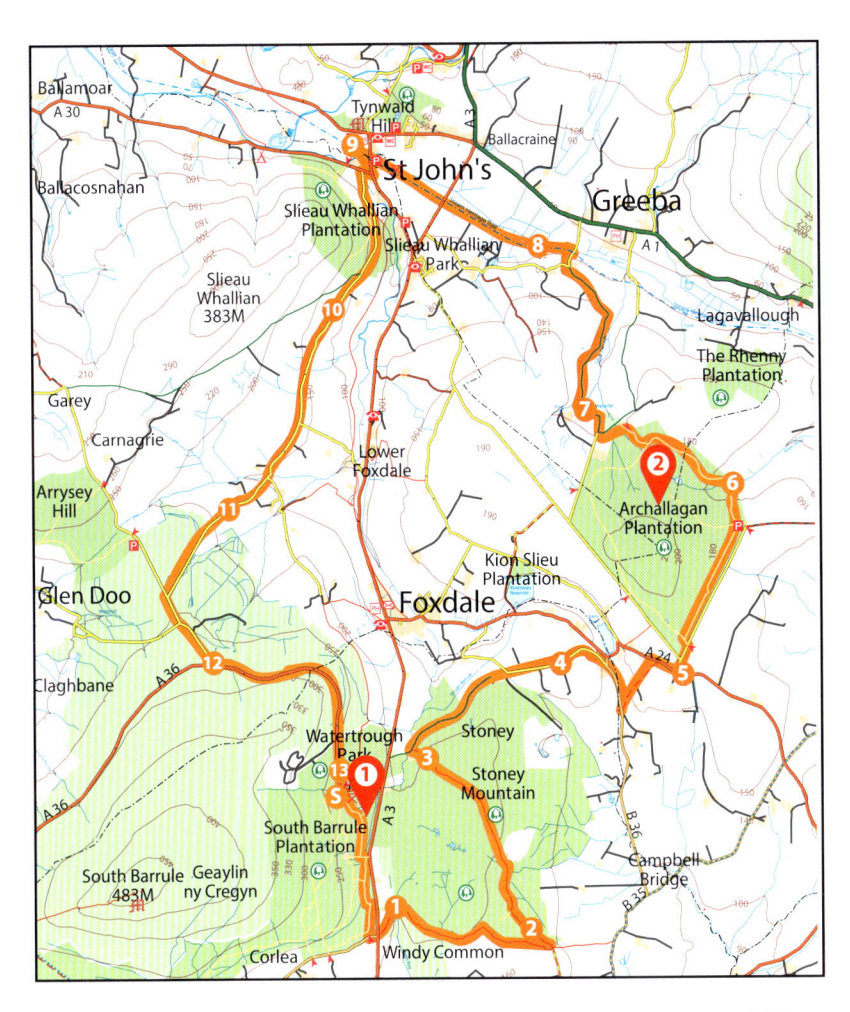

Before you leave your base, be sure to:
Tell someone where you're headed and when they can expect you back. If you don't return they can raise the alarm.

Your bike will need to be in good working order. Hydraulic brakes and a wide gear range are ideal for the hilly routes. Be sure to set your bike up for the style of ride you're doing. The more puncture resistant your bike is, the less likely you are to experience one on our natural trails. Many trails aren't smooth!

Finally, the locals are very grateful that the Isle of Man remains one of very few unspoilt and natural places in the British Isles. Help to keep it that way by riding within your ability, stay on open and legal trails and leave all gates as you find them.

When riding in the forests please follow the Cycle Code, which of course is similar no matter where you ride:

Expect the unexpected – keep your distance.

By cycle

Remember other vehicles use the forest.

Give way to walkers – be friendly towards other forest users.

Be aware of horses and avoid an accident.

Danger! Keep away from forest operations.

Danger! Do not pass a vehicle that is loading timber until you have been told to do so.

Footpaths are for walkers only.

Cycle with care and you can come back again.

The Forestry, Amenity and Lands Directorate is keen to promote responsible access and recreation. For further information on cycling please telephone the Forestry Directorate on +44 1624 695701.

In an emergency dial 999 and ask for the rescue service you need, be it police, ambulance, fire or coastguard.

"Leave nothing but footprints,

Take only pictures, kill only time and share the path with everyone you meet!"

Useful contacts:

If you are looking to link up with local riders to see where to ride there are two clubs that can be contacted:

Manx Mountain Bike Club: https://www.manxmtb.com/

Loaghtan Loaded Mountain Bike Club: http://loaghtanloaded.com/

With the event of social media, most rides are organised through various groups and if they were to be listed here, they would be out of date as soon as this was printed. Therefore you will need to search online or pop into one of the excellent bike shops on the Island and you will be pointed in the right direction by enthusiastic staff.

IOM welcome centre. This is based at the Sea Terminal and will assist you with any query. Tel: +44 1624 686801

If you have any questions on the hills, forests and glens, a good place to start is with the Department of Environment, Food and Agriculture. Tel: +44 1624 801263.

Sample Route from **Mountain Biking on the Isle of Man** - Route 17.

Introduction

This simple loop links South Barrule and Archallagan forests via Stoney Mountain Plantation. The first two of these plantations may indeed be enough with their numerous and often unmarked trails.

An easy ride and a great introduction to mountain bike riding in the plantations. You can either continue in a large loop or come back on yourself, in particular if you get lost in Archallagan.

Points of interest

1. South Barrule MTB skills area: to build up your skills on the pumptrack, graded runs and obstacles.

2. Archallagan plantation with is miles of unmarked single track, Children's MTB race circuit, small adventure playground and the dragonfly pond.

Directions

From the South Barrule car park head South on the fire track past the MTB skills area. At the far corner of the plantation where the track turns 90 degrees to the right carry on through the small gate and turn LEFT down the county lane.

Cross over the road and follow the singletrack round the outside of Stoney Mountain Plantation until you reach the fire track.

Turn LEFT here and follow the fire track up and over through Stoney Mountain

Plantation and when you exit, turn RIGHT along a stony track towards Archallagan Forest.

At the end of the stoney track just follow the road straight and after a mile take the RIGHT at the junction and then look for a small singletrack on your left.

Turn LEFT onto this small climb, onto a minor road before coming out on the A24.

Turn RIGHT and then first LEFT and into Archallagan Forest.

In Archallagan you will find a perimeter fire track with single-track trials crossing left and right. The aim is to get to the far side to exit near Cornelly mines.

At the old mine workings look for the track on the West side and follow this down through the gates until you reach the country lane. Here keep on going down and then take the LEFT onto the old railway lines.

Follow these until you arrive in a large car park at St Johns. Turn LEFT out of the car park, first RIGHT and then first LEFT which take you onto the quiet lane heading up to the mines at Snuff the Wind. At the top of the road by the mines working take the LEFT at the T junction and head towards the A36. After crossing the cattle grid turn LEFT and this road will take you back to South Barrule where you started.

Lily Publications now publishes two books on Mountain Biking on the Isle of Man - visit www.lilypublications.co.uk.

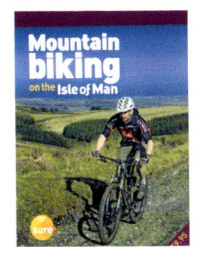

By trams and trains
Heritage railways

The Isle of Man is unique in having retained an extensive network of historic railways with Victorian locomotives, electric trams and rolling stock.

From the moment you step aboard one of the Island's heritage railways you step back in time to a slower paced, gentler world. With a leisurely speed of 25mph on both electric and steam lines, this is a place where you can truly let the train take the strain.

It is possible to travel from the most northerly town Ramsey to Port Erin in the south experiencing four or five different types of rail or tramway.

The ultimate transport challenge, should you choose to attempt it, is to ride on all of them in the same day ... although you will probably find it more enjoyable to take your time and take in some of the attractions, museums and scenery along the way.

Starting in the Island's capital Douglas you will find the terminals for both the Manx Electric Railway and the Steam Railway. Tickets can be purchased at either but it is advisable to stop off at the Welcome Centre in the Sea Terminal to obtain timetables for all trains, trams and buses plus details of any special events or interruptions to service. Here you may also purchase Explorer tickets – which enable unlimited travel on most trams, trains and buses for one adult and an accompanying (free) child. For more details see page 212.

Steam Railway

Officially called the Isle of Man Railway because it was the first established rail service on the Island, the Steam Railway has enormous appeal for today's visitors

By trams and trains

Steam Railway

as much as it did in Victorian times.

First opened in 1874, this remains the longest narrow-gauge (3-feet) steam line in the British Isles. It was the inspiration for the Reverend W. Awdry to pen the Thomas the Tank Engine stories and in 2000 the motion picture Thomas and the Magic Railroad was filmed on location here.

History

The Isle of Man Railway Company was founded in 1870 to build lines from Douglas to Peel. The 11.5 mile Douglas to Peel line opened in 1873 and the 15.75 mile Douglas to Port Erin line that survives today opened in 1874. Celebrations marking its 140th anniversary were held during the Manx Heritage Transport Festival in 2014.

Additionally the Manx Northern Railway was formed in 1877 to create a branch line from St John's to Ramsey. The main competition for the railways came from buses from the 1920s onwards but the rail companies benefited from the thousands of visitors that continued to make the journey by Steam Packet to stay in the Island's many resorts and holiday camps. The post-war years from 1946 were the heyday of Manx tourism as thousands of people were able to enjoy their first holiday for many years but numbers declined when travel to Mediterranean resorts became increasingly popular for British holidaymakers. The last year that more than one million passengers were carried on the Steam Railway was in 1956 and services began to reduce significantly after that. With mounting operational costs, unreliable under-maintained locomotives and falling income, all rail services ceased in November 1965. The Steam Railway was revived in 1967 and its lines reopened but Peel and Ramsey lines closed forever at the end of the 1968 season. Much of these lines are now public footpaths.

Since 1969, the southern line has been the only operational steam line, retained due to it being considered to have the greatest tourist potential and operated by the Isle of Man Government ever since. In 2023 the Steam Railway celebrated its 150th anniversary.

For more historical information visit the Isle of Man Steam Railway Supporters Association http://www.iomsrsa.org/home

A trip on the Steam Railway – points of interest

Generally the first steam train departs Douglas at 9:50am and Port Erin at 10am, with four services daily each way during the early and late season, up to seven a day at busy times. Steam trains operate from early March to early November. In the early and late season there is a five day per week steam train service including weekends, although additional Valentines specials are operated before the scheduled services commence by the restored Dining Car. It is advisable to obtain a free timetable providing information on train times and special events prior to travelling. Timetables are available at Douglas, Castletown and Port Erin stations plus some hotels and commissioners' offices, the Welcome Centre and online at www.iombusandrail.info.

Recent investment and improvements to the track and rolling stock means that steam trains complete the journey between Douglas and Port Erin in exactly one hour.

On departing Douglas the steam train runs through the Nunnery cutting, adjacent to the Nunnery mansion, previously owned by race horse owner Robert Sangster but more recently operated by the Isle of Man Government as a Business School and University Centre.

Around three miles south, Keristal offers stunning sea views before the train stops at Port Soderick. There is a small glen near to the station which leads down to a shingle beach, popular for barbecues and for an excellent cave, which it is possible to explore except at high tide.

The train continues south calling at Santon (5.5 miles) then Ballasalla – a name derived from Manx Gaelic meaning the place of the willows – the half way point. Alight here for Rushen Abbey and the 14th-century Monks Bridge plus Silverdale Glen with its craft centre, boating lake and children's playground.

The Island's ancient capital Castletown is the next stop, well worth visiting for its unspoilt old town and medieval fortress Castle Rushen. There's also the Nautical Museum with its tales of 18th century smuggling plus the Old House of Keys. Coastal walks include taking in Scarlett Visitor Centre and Wildlife Reserve nature trail – within easy walking distance of Castletown, and the place to see the Island's limestone and volcanic rock formations as well as wildflowers and birds.

Past Castletown the train travels through some fine undulating scenery calling at various villages – Ballabeg, Colby and on to Port St Mary and Port Erin. Both ports boast beautiful beaches and scenic walks, while Colby Glen is a good place for a sheltered walk.

Buses connect with Port Erin to take visitors to the Calf Sound and Cregneash folk museum – see timetable for more information or visit www.iombusandrail.info.

The Dining Car

Built in 1905 and meticulously restored during 2013, the Steam Railway's Dining Car was launched in autumn 2013 to great acclaim and excitement. The sumptuous surroundings of its three saloon carriages hark back to the Pullman-style fine dining of yesteryear although there is nothing old fashioned about the fabulous food served on board.

The Dining Car operates a number of Manxman Sunday lunches, afternoon cream teas and Manxman dinner services throughout the year. See the website for more details and booking information www.iombusandrail.info. The Dining Car is also available for wedding parties, corporate and other private hire events, which can be tailored to individual requirements. Bookings and enquiries to steamdining@gov.im or telephone 01624 697457.

Manx Electric Railway

A journey north by Manx Electric Railway starts at the Derby Castle terminus at the northern end of Douglas promenade. The castle that gave it the name has long since disappeared but the MER's rustic booking office, dating from 1897, is still the place to purchase tickets.

History

Construction of the line commenced in 1892 by the Douglas & Laxey Coast Electric Tramway with the first tram running to Groudle Glen in 1893. The company changed its name to the Isle of Man Tramways and Electric Power Co Ltd in 1894, and the line was extended to Laxey in 1894 and to Ramsey in 1898. In 1902 the tramway was taken over by the Manx Electric Railway Company Ltd.

Today it remains the longest inter urban electric tramway operation in the British Isles, following the twists and turns of the Island's rugged east coast on its 75 minute journey through 17.5 miles of spectacular scenery to Ramsey. Two tramcars, numbers 1 and 2 are recognised by the Guinness Book of World Records for being the oldest in continuous operation and the newest of its tramcars was purchased back in 1906. Around half the original rolling stock, 12 motor cars and 13 trailers, are in regular use. Many are stored in the recently rebuilt tram sheds at Derby Castle and can be viewed or ridden on during busy periods, including transport festivals (July/August) or Heritage Open Days (October).

Similar to the Steam Railway, the company struggled to continue operating with dwindling visitors from 1950 onwards. The Island's parliament, Tynwald, approved a Bill in April 1957 for the MER and Snaefell lines to be taken into government ownership and on 1 June 1957 the official handover took place.

The Manx Electric Railway commences operations in mid March and runs most days until early November. Always consult the timetable for latest information, available from main stations, the Welcome Centre and online at www.iombusandrail.info.

A trip on the MER – points of interest

The first tram of the day generally departs Derby Castle at 9.40am from Douglas (8.40am peak season) and at 10.10am from Ramsey (11.10am much of October).

On leaving Douglas, the tram goes up a gradient of 1 in 24 to reach Port Jack, the first of 63 possible boarding or alighting points. The line twists first right then left around Onchan Head and on past Howstrake, the location of a former

Snaefell Mountain Railway

holiday camp, and on to Groudle Glen. This glen boasts a 2-foot gauge miniature railway that opened in 1896 to transport visitors to a small zoo. Recently restored by volunteers, Groudle Glen trains run on Sundays and bank holidays to a newly rebuilt café at Sea Lion Rocks, clearly visible from the electric tramway.

A plaque at Groudle Station marks the fact it was the original terminus of the line in 1893. Opposite is the Groudle Hotel, designed by Mackay Hugh Baillie Scott and around the corner the tram travels across the Groudle Viaduct built in 1894 by Mark Carine.

As you head to Laxey, the Island's only official mountain Snaefell may be seen on clear days, identifiable by the radio masts on the summit.

The trams cross the Groudle road then the main Douglas to Laxey Road to trundle towards Baldrine, a place name derived from Manx Gaelic meaning 'the place of the blackthorns'. A little further on is Garwick, from the Norse Gjar-vik,

meaning cave or creek. Glen Garwick used to be an extensive pleasure garden and a busy stop on the route. However, it closed in 1965 and is now in private ownership. Public access is permitted only to the beach, accessible via a footpath from Clay Head Road, Baldrine. Legend has it the glen was the centre for 18th-century smuggling and Hatterick's Cave (now blocked) is reputed to have been the inspiration for Sir Walter Scott when writing *Guy Mannering*.

The tram goes onwards and upwards providing spectacular bursts of coastal views to Laxey Bay and the cliffs beyond to Maughold Head and lighthouse. Next stop Ballabeg bears the same name as a stop on the Steam Railway. Trams descend towards Laxey, calling at Fairy Cottage and South Cape. It is possible to hike down to the beach from South Cape but the return ascent requires a high level of fitness.

Laxey, which name comes from the Scandinavian Laxa, meaning salmon river, offers a wealth of attractions, starting with the Great Laxey Wheel and Mines Trail. The former Mines Captain's House is now the Mines Tavern offering refreshments from an MER car-shaped bar. The quaint station building has a café and public toilet facilities. A short distance down the hill, past the Valley Gardens which are the old washing floors of the mines, is Laxey Woollen Mills, established in 1881 with the support of John Ruskin and home of the Manx tartan.

In the Valley Gardens, volunteers have restored part of the former mine tramway which once carried ore out of the Great Laxey Mine. Passengers can now travel in a tiny carriage, hauled by replicas of the original steam locomotives Ant and Bee, through the longest railway tunnel on theIsland. The railway operates on Saturdays and bank holidays from Easter Saturday until the end of September plus on Sundays during August.

As you head north out of Laxey, you will first pass Ballaragh village then Bulgham cliffs where the trams run along a narrow ledge 588 feet above the sea, the highest point of the line. Next stop is at Dhoon Glen, which boasts a teashop and is known for a dramatic waterfall in the glen but beware, it is perhaps the most challenging glen to walk and might take longer than you'd expect. The ascent back up the glen from the sea is very steep and can be tiring.

The tram rattles on past Dhoon Quarry, now a storage facility for the railway, past the majestic North Barrule (1,854 feet). After Glen Mona, trams pass under Ballagorry Bridge, the only overbridge to cross the line.

About 55 minutes after leaving Douglas you come to the beautiful Ballaglass Glen. A small single-arched bridge carries the railway over the glen and it heads towards the coast down to Port Cornaa. Ballajora

Enjoying the views on the Snaefell Mountain Railway

is the nearest station to Maughold Village, which has a fine collection of Celtic crosses in its churchyard.

The tram weaves through Dreemskerry, Lewaigue and Bellevue station that serves Port e Vullen, the ideal place to disembark for a walk along the coast to Maughold Head. Rich in wildlife, with an Iron Age fort at its summit, Maughold also boasts a sacred well, said to have been endowed with healing properties by St Maughold.

Soon you will get your first glimpse of Ramsey (name derives from the Norse for wild garlic river) and the Queen's Pier, built in 1886. Ramsey station provides toilet facilities and is a short step from Ramsey's shopping area, with numerous independent traders, cafés and quaint harbour.

The Grove Museum of Victorian Life can be found to the north of the town, while Milntown House is a short distance to the west in Lezayre, on the TT course.

Snaefell Mountain Railway

Completed in 1895, the Snaefell Mountain Railway is the only electric mountain railway in the British Isles and operates on a branch line from Laxey to the summit of the Island's only official mountain, Snaefell (from the Norse for snow mountain) at 2,036 feet above sea level. The gradient averages 1 in 12 for almost its five miles duration.

Routinely there are six or seven tram cars operating each day departing Laxey from 10.15am April to October, linking with trams arriving from Douglas and Ramsey. See timetable for details.

History

The Snaefell Mountain Railway was built in just seven months by the Snaefell Mountain Tramway Association, a separate entity from the Douglas & Laxey Coast Electric Tramway Company. They aimed to provide travellers the view of 'Seven Kingdoms at a Glance', namely England, Ireland, Scotland, Wales, Heaven, Mann and the Sea.

Despite delays caused by heavy snowfall early in 1895, it was opened on 21 August that year, reputedly carrying 900 people per day in its first short season.

The gauge selected for the mountain tramway was 3-foot 6 inches, six inches wider than the Manx Electric Railway to accommodate a central braking rail, known as a Fell rail. John Barraclough Fell invented this braking system for mountain railways and it was first used in 1868 on Mont Cenis between France and Italy and subsequently in Brazil and New Zealand. His son George Noble Fell was the engineer for the Snaefell line and used his father's system to achieve adhesion, which is why the 3-foot 6 gauge mountain railway was adopted. To assist construction the company leased the steam locomotive Caledonia from the Manx Northern Railway to work the line. Use of the three-foot gauge Caledonia required the laying of a temporary rail to three feet gauge during the construction period.

A wooden shelter initially constructed at the summit was replaced with a castellated building in 1905. Gutted by fire in 1982 it has been rebuilt and recently refurbished to a high standard including the provision of under-floor heating and modern toilet facilities.

A trip on the Snaefell Mountain Tramway – points of interest

A trip on the mountain tramway delivers a fresh perspective over the notable landmark that is the Laxey Wheel.

Robert Casement's graceful water wheel, named the Lady Isabella after the wife of the Lieutenant Governor of the day, was constructed in 1854 to pump water from Laxey Mines. It is still the largest working water wheel in the world.

As you progress up the Laxey Valley, you will notice the remains of the Snaefell Mine on the right, along with the ruins of the Mine Captain's house. Lead ore from the mine was crushed and taken in horse-drawn carts along the rough cart track down to Laxey for further processing then export from Laxey harbour.

Snaefell Mine has the tragic claim of being the location of the Island's worst mining disaster. An underground fire in May 1897 had filled the mine with poisonous and deadly carbon monoxide gas and some 20 miners died as they descended into the mine for the morning shift. A memorial marks their loss at the site, unveiled to commemorate the centenary of the disaster in 1997.

Near the top of the valley the tram passes the original power station for the line – its chimney base can be seen on the left of the railway while on the right are the generating boilers. Mountain trams cross the TT course to arrive at Bungalow Station, the only stop on the line. When racing closes the road, tram passengers must disembark and cross to a waiting tram at Bungalow via the road bridge.

Bungalow Station, replaced in 2002, was named after the original Swiss chalet style hotel erected around 1900 on the site by the Isle of Man Tramway and Electrical Power Company.

A short distance above the station Sulby reservoir comes into view. Completed in 1982, it is the Island's largest reservoir holding one billion gallons of water with a surface area of 62 hectares. If it's a clear day, you may be able to see the Mountains of Mourne in Northern Ireland.

Further on the northern plain of the Island can be seen – here most of the Island's arable crops are grown. There are also two disused airfields, Jurby and more central Andreas, which were built in the war time for training RAF pilots. If you look further you may see the Mull of Galloway in the south of Scotland. The Island town that can be seen further on is Ramsey.

As the tram completes its spiral around the mountain, it is sometimes possible to see Douglas Head, Douglas Bay, and beyond that, Langness and Castletown in the south of the Island plus over to the Mountains of Mourne in the west. On very clear days, you can also see Anglesey and beyond.

Journey's end is at the Snaefell Summit Restaurant, which is decorated with historic photographs showing the line's construction. The restaurant offers a selection of home-cooked food plus Sunset Dinners most Wednesdays and Saturdays throughout the season, and special events such as Pie In The Sky stargazing evenings. To book call the Summit Restaurant on (01624) 673631. More information on the website www.iombusandrail.info.

Ultimate Driving Experiences

If riding on the heritage railways isn't enough for you, it is possible to book Ultimate Driving Experiences (UDEs) for the opportunity to drive a Manx Electric Railway tram between Laxey and Ramsey or a steam locomotive between Castletown and Port Erin.

The experiences last a whole day with recipients given safety, history and theory briefings prior to getting to drive on the railway. UDEs were offered for the first

Looking towards Port St Mary

time on the Steam Railway in 2013 but have been available for five years on the MER. They are extremely popular, often purchased for special celebrations and sometimes shared by a small group of family or friends. Due to operational requirements there are limited dates available for UDEs and bookings are made on a first come, first served basis.

For more information and to book Ultimate Driving Experiences contact Marieanne Bridges via email Marieanne.hutton@gov.im or tel: 01624 697419. manxelectricrailway.co.uk/mer-driverexperience/

By car
Drive the Island – Six leisurely tours

As Toad would have it, you can't beat the freedom and pleasure of the open road – or touring the Isle of Man by car or motorcycle!

The six circular routes chosen here cover all regions and can be enjoyed at a leisurely pace, giving ample opportunity to visit points of interest along the way.

The accompanying maps should be sufficient for the purpose, but more detailed information can of course be found in the Ordnance Survey Landranger Map 95.

Tour 1: 35 miles
Douglas – Signpost Corner – The Bungalow – Ramsey – Maughold – Port Mooar – Port Cornaa – Dhoon – Laxey

This tour starts in Douglas at the foot of Broadway, which is adjacent to the new Villa Marina and where the Harris Promenade merges with Central Promenade.

Climbing up Broadway you leave the tourist part of town behind and as Broadway becomes Ballaquayle Road you come to the Bray Hill traffic lights. Turn right and head past the TT Grandstand (on your right).

Some three-quarters of a mile along Glencrutchery Road you arrive at Governor's Bridge. Be careful here that you don't turn too quickly, and take care at the double roundabout before following the road marked Ramsey, turning up – left – by the white-painted stone wall.

For the next few hundred yards on the right you are passing the home of the

By car

Island's Governor. Head on up the A18 to Signpost Corner. Leaving Cronk-ny-Mona behind, there is a distinct change of scenery as the road winds upwards to the famous TT viewing spot of Creg-ny-Baa.

Over to your left, as Kate's Cottage comes into sight, are some very good views of Douglas, and the panorama of the southern half of the Isle of Man lies before you. Take great care in choosing where to stop to take in the views, especially on the TT course as it is a very fast road.

Passing through Keppel Gate you are now in the mountains and some of the finest scenery on the Island. Still on the A18 descend to Ramsey at Brandywell, just past the junction with the B10.

Directly in front of you stands Snaefell and if time permits it is well worth stopping here and catching the electric railway to the summit, from where on a clear day you can see England, Wales, Scotland and Ireland – not to mention the Isle of Man itself, of course! In 1995 the Snaefell Mountain Railway celebrated its centenary and the original rolling stock is still in use.

Past Snaefell the magnificent mountain scenery continues with the views on your right of Laxey and its valley, and the impressive sight of Ramsey and the northern plain spreading out before you. Ramsey is well worth exploring – and if you have still not picked up your free parking disc, call in at Ramsey Town Hall, they will fix you up.

Maughold is the next stop. Drive along Ramsey promenade and past the Queen's Pier, watching for the signs directing traffic to Laxey (A2).

Shortly after, bear left on to the A15. A good tip on these roads is to watch out for the unmanned railway crossings as you will be criss-crossing them for the next few miles.

About half a mile past Maughold there is a small road which takes you down to the peaceful beach at Port Mooar. It's an ideal place to stretch your legs and have a picnic. Back up from the beach turn left on to the A15 and travel to Cornaa. There is a well-preserved burial ground just past the Ballajora crossroads. Look for an old chapel on the corner, keeping it to the left, and travel uphill on the minor road (which in more recent times became the last resting place for

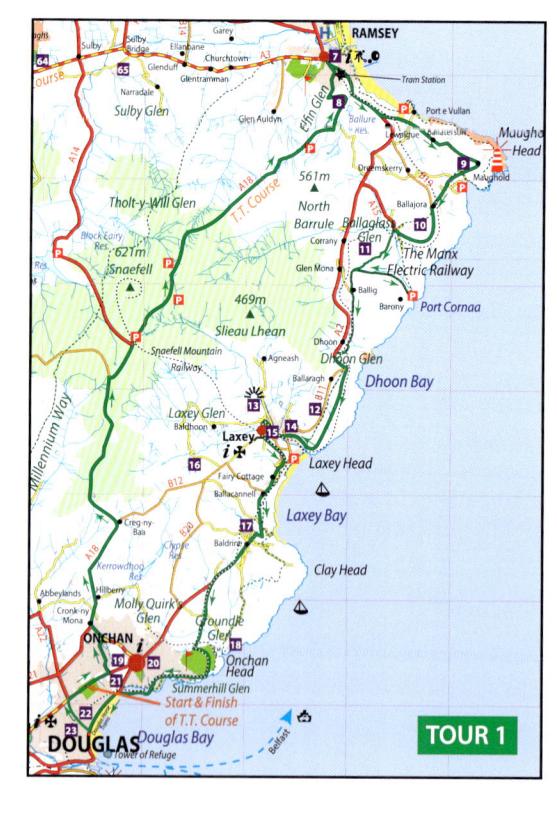

TOUR 1

LOCATIONS THROUGHOUT THE ISLAND

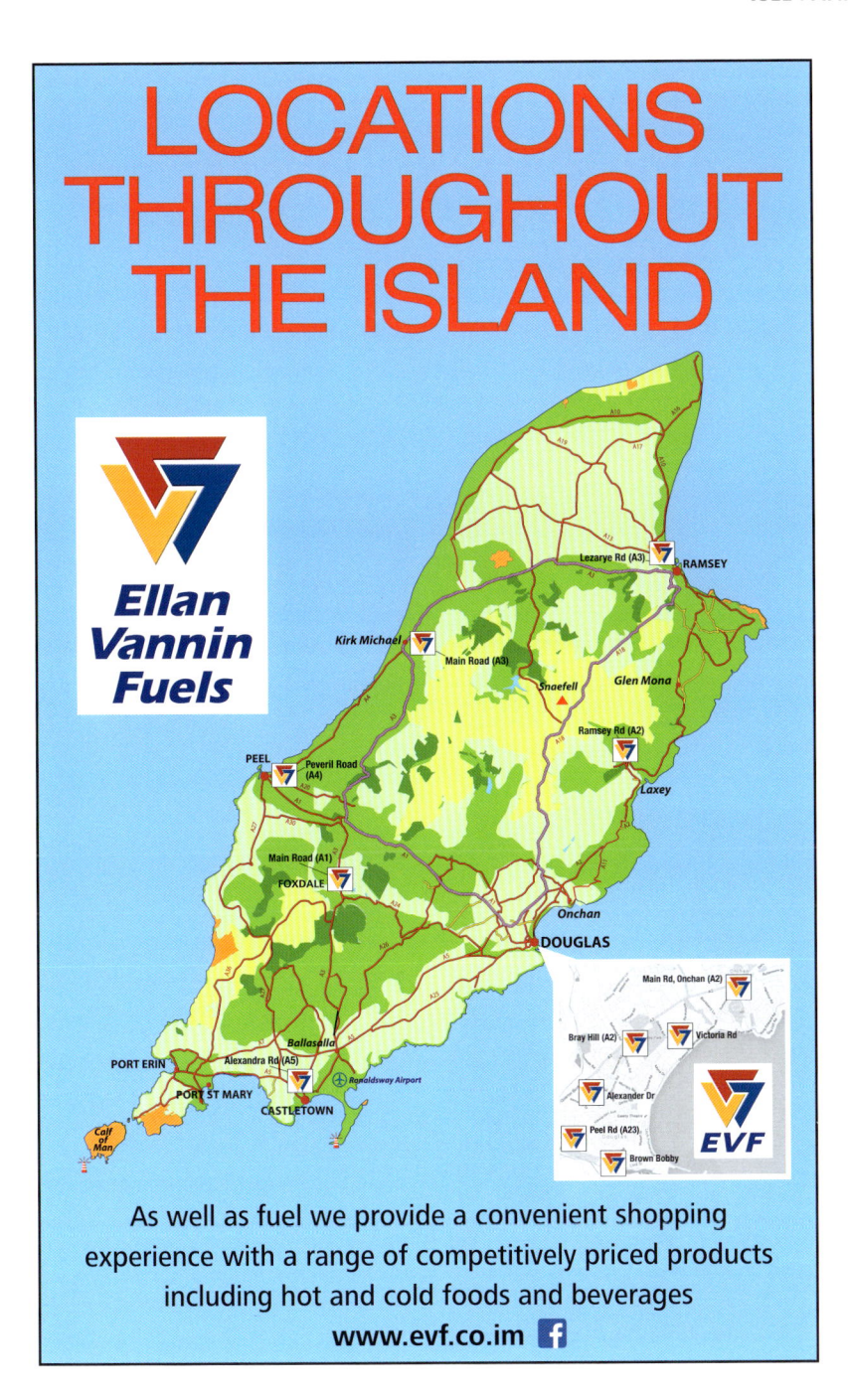

Ellan Vannin Fuels

As well as fuel we provide a convenient shopping experience with a range of competitively priced products including hot and cold foods and beverages

www.evf.co.im

By car

Mylchreests.
Car rental the way YOU want it...

Phone 01624 823533 or email car.rental@mylchreests.com for a quotation

- Low cost Weekend rentals available
- All rates include insurance and VAT
- Child Seats free of charge
- Vauxhall and Mitsubishi cars
- Vans and Minibuses available
- Automatic Cars available
- Island-wide Delivery
- Sat Nav available
- Our Customers come first!

Find us on MylchreestsGroup

We can book your car in the UK or World-wide through our partners

Europcar · Thrifty · AVIS Budget

Mylchreests CAR RENTAL

RONALDSWAY AIRPORT ISLE OF MAN IM9 2AS WEBSITE MYLCHREESTS.COM

---

those Quakers who remained on the Island, the majority of their fellow believers escaping persecution by seeking a new life in America).

Take care approaching Cornaa as the roads are very narrow. Turn off the A15 at Cornaa railway halt and turn down the minor road to the left.

Pass the Ballaglass Glen car park on your right and drive on until you reach a small ford where you turn sharp right for Port Cornaa. The drive down to the beach is well worth the effort, but be careful where you park, it is a popular spot with locals and sometimes the stony upper beach can cause problems if you pick the wrong place.

When coming back up this lovely wooded valley continue past the ford – on your right– and climb back up to the A2, watching out for the signs to the Dhoon and Laxey. If you are feeling energetic park opposite Dhoon station and enjoy a walk down to the shore, but remember to leave extra time for the return journey ... it can fool you! The A2 soon takes you to Laxey and there are great views all along the coast.

Laxey wheel

There is a choice of how you leave Laxey. If you are in Old Laxey then the steep road up from the harbour soon comes out on the A2 at Fairy Cottage. Or if you have been exploring around the mines then rejoin by the Electric Railway station.

On through the picturesque villages of Lonan, Garwick and Baldrine and over the railway crossing just out of Baldrine, take a left turn and over a second crossing in the vicinity of the Halfway House to Laxey (Liverpool Arms) – the road A11 is signposted to Groudle and Douglas. Groudle has a beautiful natural glen and the revitalised miniature Groudle Glen Railway.

Tour 2: 38 miles
Douglas – East Baldwin – Injebreck – Druidale – Ballaugh – Kirk Michael – Peel – St John's

This journey takes its starting point at the bottom of Broadway and proceeds in just the same manner as that described in Tour 1 until the traffic lights at Parkfield Corner (St Ninian's Church) are reached. Get into the left filter lane and enjoy the run down Bray Hill to the bottom of the dip where you take a right turn. (TT racers speed down this hill at over 150 mph – but only on race days!).

The road now winds along through an area known as Port-e-Chee, which translated from the Gaelic means Haven of Peace. Cronkbourne Village is the next destination and this is soon reached. Turn right and go up the steep Johnny Watterson's Lane (A21), turning left at the halt sign, then drive along Ballanard Road (A22) towards Abbeylands for just over a mile. At the crossroads turn left and, heading over Sir George's Bridge, make a right turn on to the B21 – the East Baldwin Road.

Between 1900 and 1905 a three-foot narrow-gauge railway wound its way around these small valleys, carrying workers and building materials for the Injebreck Reservoir.

Keep on the B21 and move in a northerly direction until you reach the old and disused East Baldwin Chapel. Park here awhile and see if you can spot 'The White Man of East Baldwin' – a figure built into a mountain wall on the hillside as a memorial to a deemster, who perished with his horse in a snowstorm whilst on an errand of mercy. The walk up to the cairn from the bottom of the valley is strenuous, and mind you don't get your feet wet when crossing the Baldwin River, but the views are worth the effort.

Retrace your track back to Algare Hill – the small connecting road between the two valleys – and a right turn at the top brings you along to St Luke's Church, on the site of an ancient Tynwald. Drop down to the valley floor and join the B22 by heading once more in a northerly direction. There are lots of good picnic spots around here but be careful where you park as the roads are narrow. If you like fishing, Injebreck is a good spot. From the reservoir the road climbs up between the peaks of Colden and Carraghan, eventually bringing you out on to the Brandywell Road (B10).

Just before the junction there is a small slip road which you should turn into and, by turning right and then almost immediately left, you are now on the Druidale Road. This is a single-track road for its entire length. A short drive down Ballaugh Glen brings you to the village.

Turning left at the famous Ballaugh Bridge – where TT racers become airborne for some distance! – you head south-west towards Kirk Michael, home of runic

127

By car

crosses and the last resting place of five bishops. Take the right fork here as the A3 becomes the A4 and head down towards Peel. This is a good road, but if you are not in a hurry stop off at Glen Wyllin, Glen Mooar or the Devil's Elbow.

It's worth spending some time in Peel. This is the only 'city' on the Island, with two cathedrals, and there are some interesting shops, narrow streets, a harbour and a very fine castle. If you are out on an evening run, stay for the sunset, you won't be disappointed!

Leaving Peel behind, take the A1 to St John's, a village of great political importance to the Island. An alternative route to the village is via the A20 and the connecting road through Tynwald Mills, which is well signposted from Peel. Alongside Tynwald Hill lies the Royal Chapel of St John. The village is little changed in the best part of a century.

The last part of the drive takes you along the central valley. Ten thousand years ago this was the sea bed, dividing the Isle of Man into two main parts. Moving along the A1 towards Ballacraine you come up against an Island rarity – a set of traffic lights. Carry straight on towards Douglas, but just after Greeba Castle look to your left and there is the ancient roofless church of St Trinian standing in splendid isolation in its own meadow.

From here there is a choice of routes back to the capital. The main road follows the A1 to the Sea Terminal via Glen Vine, Union Mills, Braddan Bridge and the Quarterbridge. Alternatively, if time permits, why not take the A23 (the Nab Road) by turning left at Crosby and heading towards Douglas via Eyreton, the Nab, the Strang and Braddan. The A23 rejoins the A1 at the Jubilee Oak Braddan Bridge.

Tour 3: 38 miles
Ramsey – Point of Ayre – Jurby – The Cronk – The Curraghs – Sulby – Tholt-e-Will – The Bungalow

As you wander around the northern plain the scenery changes frequently, from the fine sands of the Lhen, gravel beaches of the Point of Ayre and up to the wooded slopes of Sky Hill, Glen Auldyn, Carrick, Rock and Mount Karrin, and St Ciaran's Mount. Coupled with the winding lanes of the Curraghs it is one of the best places to tour.

The drive starts on Ramsey promenade, but before setting off be sure to take in the lovely sight of the bay and the slopes of Lhergy Frissel (Frissel's slope) – the hill with the tower set on the summit.

Driving along Mooragh Promenade you may get a glimpse of St Bees Head in Cumbria, the nearest mainland point to the Isle of Man. At the end of the promenade bear left up the hill and join the A10 by turning right. Follow this road to the lovely village of Bride. The church acts as a good landmark for miles around.

At Bride take the A16 marked for the Point of Ayre. Again it is an easy place to find because the lighthouse stands as a sentinel. This landmark was built in the early years of the 19th century by the great-grandfather of Robert Louis Stevenson. Definitely not the place to go swimming: the waters surrounding the Point are extremely treacherous.

On now to the Lhen, so reverse the route back as far as Bride and turn right and west at the church. Lovely country here with good farming land rolling down to the coast. Watch out for the sign to the Ayres Visitor Centre, well worth a visit but only open mid-May to mid-September, 2pm–5pm., Wednesdays to Sundays. Stay on the A10 and the Lhen is reached after a pleasant drive of a few miles. Watch out for the sharp turn at the Lhen Bridge. The little park close to the shore is ideal for a picnic.

Just a couple of miles further on is Jurby. Long ago this village was important to the Vikings and although it has lost something of its old eminence it is nonetheless a pleasant part of the Island, and well worth exploring for its beaches, church and crosses.

Carrying on still further on the A10, look out for The Cronk (The Hill), such as it is. Go straight on here at the crossroads, following the B9, and turn left at the second road down from The Cronk crossroads – but not counting any farm tracks or lanes. If you have it right, it's the road coloured yellow on the map taking you towards Dollagh Mooar, Black Lake and the Curraghs (mire or marsh).

Caution here because the roads are extremely narrow and there are lots of ditches awaiting careless drivers. Cross the A14, approximately half way between Sandygate to the north and Sulby to the south – and you are still following the

By car

yellow road to Kella and West Sulby.
 Turn left at the junction and for a brief distance you are on the TT course, on the famous Sulby Straight (A3). Just past Sulby Bridge is the Ginger Hall public house and you should turn right here on to the B8, which will bring you on to the Sulby Claddaghs, the river meadowland.
 Drive through the Claddaghs to the A14 or the Sulby Glen Road and begin the ascent of the glen towards Tholt-e-Will. This extremely scenic route brings you up

130

past the Sulby reservoir, built in the early 1980s to secure water supplies well into the 21st century. The upper reaches of the road roll across the shoulder of Snaefell and the scenery is typical of high moorland interspersed with plantation.

The end of the A14 joins the A18 TT course at the Bungalow. There is a Manx Electric Railway station here and during summer the Snaefell Mountain Railway operates regular services between Snaefell summit and Laxey, far below at the bottom of the valley.

Turn left and travel the 'wrong way' around the TT course – it is still a fast stretch of road. In clear weather, summer or winter, there are fine views of the Ayres, Scotland, England and Ireland. Take care on the final descent into Ramsey – there are some sharp corners. Once into Royal Ramsey it is easy to find your way around and the A18 takes you right into Parliament Square. Turn right just through the Square and you are into Derby Road and West Quay. Cross the swing-bridge and on to Mooragh Promenade.

Tour 4: 40 miles
Peel – St John's – Cronk-y-Voddy – West Baldwin – Ballasalla – Castletown – Foxdale

Peel is a must and if you are not actually staying in the town a visit should be a priority. This tour takes you from Peel through the Island's lovely hinterland and moorland, valleys and glens.

The starting point is the north end of Peel promenade in the vicinity of the Empire Garage. From here proceed up Stanley Road, turning right then almost immediately left into Church Street.

At the halt sign (the police station is across the road) take a left and head into Derby Road and the A20, signposted for St John's.

You'll know you're on the right road when you pass the Poortown quarry, and after about a mile and a half turn right down the small road marked Tynwald Mills Centre, which is well worth a visit.

Leave the Tynwald Mills Centre complex by the opposite end and bear left on to the TT course (A3). The exit on to the main road is narrow, and sometimes approaching cars from your right-hand side may be travelling at speed, so take care.

Now you are heading up the beautiful wooded Glen Helen road and if you feel like stretching your legs, stop and stroll up the glen.

From opposite the glen car park the road climbs steeply for a short distance, passing the famous TT landmark Sarah's Cottage and on up Creg Willeys Hill, Willy Syl's (or Sylvester's Crag) and on to Cronk-y-Voddy, which translated from the Manx means the Hill of the Dog. Here at the crossroads turn right for the undulating drive to Little London.

Long ago Little London was famous for fishing but nowadays its peace and tranquillity are disturbed only by the occasional passing car or walker. Before the Second World War the Old Smithy was the home of the renowned flyer Captain Pixton, who was the first British winner of the prestigious Schneider Trophy and the holder of many flying records. The road out of Little London skirts the south-west slopes of Sartfell, which is old Norse for Black Mountain or Dark Slope. In Manx it is known as Slieau Dhoo and joins the B10 about half a mile above Bayr Garrow (Rough Road).

Just before the minor road joins the main road is Sartfield Farmhouse Restaurant. The views from here are superb and at night you can see various

By car

Castletown harbour

Irish and Scottish lighthouses.

Turn up the hill and on the way look back at the view; on clear days there are fine panoramas of the Mountains of Mourne and the Mull of Galloway. You are now heading along the Brandywell Road with Colden Mountain ahead and to the right. There are a lot of cattle grids in the mountains, so be sure to take care crossing them and if you have to use the gates, please don't forget to close them after use.

Keep a look out for the B22 turning; it should be easy to spot because it is just before Brandywell Cottage – the only building on your left since you started on the B10. Turn off to the right and head along the Injebreck Road, and if you want a good idea of what the centre of the Island looks like, pull in just before the crest of the hill and you will see a countryside little changed in thousands of years.

Head down into the West Baldwin valley – an area not unlike the Scottish Highlands. At the upper end of this green and tree-lined cleft is Carraghan, which translates in English to rough, craggy or rocky place. It was chosen as an ideal spot for the Injebreck Reservoir, which has served Douglas and much of the Island for many decades.

On down the valley, keep to the B22 all the way until the Mount Rule halt sign, where a right turn puts you on to the A23 bound for the central village of Crosby. The road follows what was the edge of the south coast of the larger of the two northern islands that made up the Isle of Man at the time of the last ice age.

Go straight across the Crosby crossroads and up the B35 towards St Mark's. It is likely that at one time a cross stood somewhere near the site of the present-day village, because its name is derived from the Scandinavian word for Cross Village or Farm. The tour now follows one of the driveable parts of the Millennium Way.

St Mark's is a quiet little backwater and

Itineraries

lies peacefully on a rise and is visible for a good distance around the parish of Malew. Once a year it comes to life with the holding of the ancient St Mark's Fair.

A couple of miles or so further on you come to the busy village of Ballasalla. In more recent times there has been an upsurge in commercial activities here. There is plenty to do in Ballasalla, including a visit to Silverdale Glen, which is well signposted.

Go straight on at each roundabout, looking for the airport and Castletown signs (A5). Pass the airport on your left and drive into Castletown. The old capital is described in detail elsewhere in this guide, and when visiting remember that the town is a disc parking area.

The journey back to Peel is fairly straightforward. Retrace the route back along the harbour in Castletown to Victoria Road and the first roundabout, where you should turn left into Alexander Road and cross over the Alexander Bridge. Carry on for a quarter of a mile and turn right into Malew Road and the A3.

Stay on the A3, climbing up the Ballamodha Straight before dropping down through the old mining villages of Upper and Lower Foxdale. Approaching St John's, the road divides at a small hamlet called The Hope (not shown on many maps). Take the left branch and follow the A30 past the Forestry Department's nurseries, bearing right until you reach the halt sign in the middle of the village. A good guide as to whether you are on the correct route is that Tynwald Hill is across the road. Turn left at St John's for Peel and follow the A1 and the signs all the way to Peel promenade and the end of Tour 4.

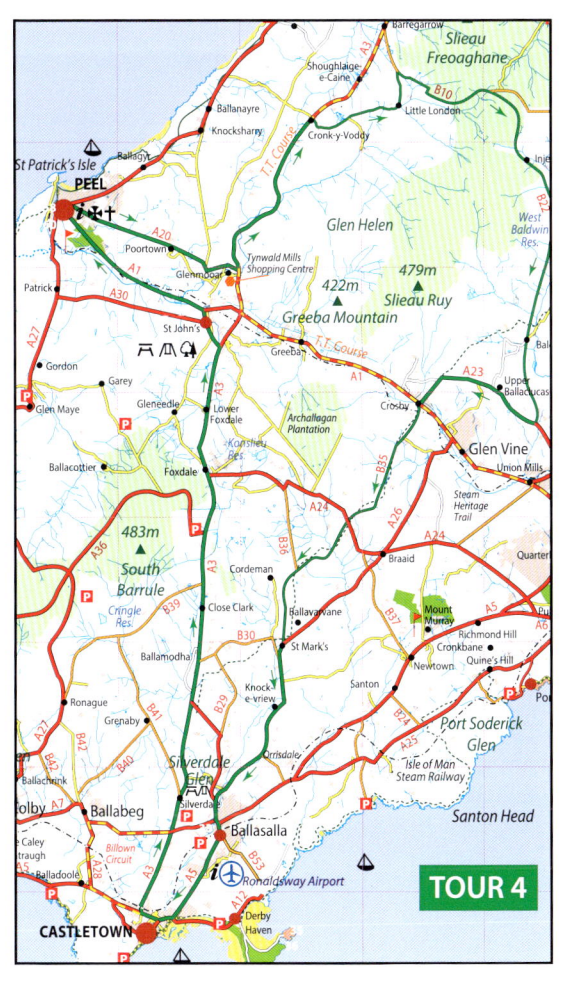

Tour 5: 42 miles
Port Erin – The Sloc – Niarbyl – Glen Maye – Foxdale – Braaid – Union Mills – Douglas – Ballasalla – Port St Mary – Cregneash

Pretty Port Erin is a good place to base yourself for a motoring holiday. Parking is easy and although parts of the village are disc zones, they present no real problems.

This drive starts on the upper promenade and covers the southern part of the Island. It takes you from the steep cliffs and hills of the south-west, through the gentle rolling hills of Glenfaba, Rushen and Middle Sheadings to the capital, and on to the old Manx hill village of Cregneash.

Drive up the hill away from the hotels and look for the signposts to Bradda. The village nestles on the slopes of Bradda Head and is divided into west and east, although the exact boundary between them is now somewhat blurred. This is the A32 and it brings you along a gradually widening road to Ballafesson, which appears on the ancient manorial roll as MacPherson's Farm.

At the junction you pick up the A7 for a short while and at the next crossroads – marked as a roundabout – turn left on the A36, up through Ballakillowey (McGillowey's Farm). It should be noted that the Manx usually exchanged the prefix Mac for the prefix Balla as far as place names were concerned.

Just before the junction with the B44 there is a nice open picnic area, with fine views over Castletown Bay and the sweep of the coast right round to the villages of the Howe and Cregneash high up on the Mull peninsula.

Driving on upwards on the Sloc Road, there are continually changing views of the landscape around almost every corner. There are many fine walks and picnic sites.

The Sloc Road takes you to the Round Table crossroads. Turn sharp left here on to the A27 and down to Niarbyl. Descending the hill into Dalby village, it is easy to see where the name Niarbyl is derived. Jutting out into the clear waters of the Irish Sea is a tail of rocks, which is how Niarbyl translates into English. Take the minor road down to the shore and spend some time on the rocky beach at the foot of the cliffs.

From Dalby the A27 continues on to Glen Maye, loosely translated meaning Yellow Glen on account of the muddy, almost clay-coloured waters of the streams running down the glen. There are a number of easy walks here.

From here carry on to the village post office. To the side of the building there is a narrow country lane which takes you up towards Garey, translated as rough or rugged river-shrubbery. If there ever was a river up here on the high ground it has long since disappeared; perhaps the road was the river, because in wet winter weather the road does seem to double as a stream. The road is also known as the Back of the Moon Road.

Rushen Mines soon loom up and even the isolation of the mines has a particular beauty of its own. Back on to the A36 and a left turn down the mountain to South Barrule Plantation and the junction with the A3.

Head left towards Foxdale, where you take the first right and join the A24. Skirt the edge of the Eairy Dam – watch out for the ducks crossing the road – and on to the Braaid, which literally translated means throat or windpipe, as applied in the sense of a glen or sheltered vale. Carry straight on at the roundabout, head up the hill for about half a mile, and look down and across into the central valley to the view known as the Plains of Heaven.

Carry on along this road until you arrive at a major road junction where the A24 bisects the A5. Cross over and drive to Kewaigue, which translates into Little Hollow. If you would like to revisit Douglas, continue on into town; if not then just past the headquarters of Isle of Man Breweries turn through an acute right-hander and head for Santon on the A25.

Santon – in older times it was spelt Santan – derives its name from Saint Sanctan. This road is known as the Old Castletown Road and there are a number of roads leading off it down to rocky bays and isolated coves. Try them when you have time, most are off the beaten track and are not accessible by public transport.

The road takes you in the direction of Ballasalla and rejoins the A5 at a spot where the railway line passes under the main road. Stay on the A5 by turning left at the Ballasalla roundabout – the Whitestone Inn faces you directly ahead as you approach it.

Drive past the airport and skirt the edge of Castletown. Leave the town behind by using the bypass (still the A5) and drive all the way along the edge of Bay ny Carrickey (The Bay of the Rock). Turn right up past the tall stone building along Beach Road, heading for the crossroads, where you go straight on using the A31. Ignore any other roads and make for Cregneash. From here carry on down to the Sound to enjoy the totally unspoilt scenery of the Isle of Man's equivalent of Land's End.

For the final stages of the drive you return back up the hill from the Sound towards Cregneash again. Just before entering the village from the south, turn sharp left on to the minor road leading past Mull Hill and its stone circles. Dating from Neolithic times, this unspoilt area remains much as the earliest inhabitants would have known it. This is a single-track

135

By car

road with passing places. Port Erin nestles quietly below as you drive down Dandy Hill and back on to the lower promenade.

Tour 6: 49 miles
Onchan – Baldrine – Laxey – Glen Roy – The Bungalow – Sulby – St Jude's – Andreas – Bride – Ramsey – The Gooseneck – The Hibernian – Dhoon – Laxey

Onchan started life as a small village to the north of Douglas and in recent times its growth has outstripped that of the capital. You could be forgiven for thinking that it is a suburb of Douglas, but the village has its own local government and is very much a separate community.

The drive starts at Onchan Head, just above Port Jack. Follow the A11 as it runs parallel to the track of the Manx Electric Railway and passes Groudle Glen. There is a minor road off to the right, approximately half a mile past Groudle station, and a detour up this road will bring you to Old Kirk Lonan Church, well worth seeing. Completing the detour brings you out on to the A2 just to the south of Baldrine village. Carry on towards Laxey via Fairy Cottage and Old Laxey Hill – bear to the right at the filling station – to the attractive harbour.

Laxey owes its origins to the Norsemen, who named it Salmon River. Give yourself time here as there's plenty to see. From the harbour travel up the glen beside the river and when you reach the woollen mills go up the hill, under the railway bridge and straight on at the stop sign looking for the Creg-ny-Baa signpost.

You are now on the Glen Roy Road (coloured yellow on the OS map) and about to experience one of the best glen drives on the Island. The glen was formed by the waters cascading down from Mullagh Ouyr, Slieau Meayll, Dun Summit, Bare or Bald Mountain and Windy Corner respectively. Care on this road is required as there are a number of blind corners, and the road is extremely narrow in places.

Eventually you rejoin a wider road, the B12, just above Social Cottage, and by turning in a south-west (right) direction, the road brings you to the well-known Keppel Hotel at Creg-ny-Baa. Turn right and head the 'wrong way' round the TT course (the A18), aiming for the Bungalow. Just past Brandywell is the highest point on the course at almost 1,400 feet.

The Bungalow actually bears no resemblance to a modern building of that name and the current site was home, until fairly recently, to a magnificent hotel made of wood and galvanised sheeting – very popular with TT fans. Watch out for the directions to Sulby and turn left on the A14.

If your passengers fancy a walk, pull up at the top entrance to Tholt-e-Will Glen. Allow them half an hour or so to walk down the glen and pick them up just outside the inn at the bottom of the hill. Alternatively, Sulby reservoir car park makes a good location for a picnic. The name of the glen translated from the Manx means Hill of the Cattlefold, and the inhabitants of the lower end of the bigger glen have traditionally been known as the Sulby Cossacks. At any time of year Sulby Glen has a beauty all of its own. In spring the east side of the glen is coloured with a haze of bluebells. At other times the heather and gorse lend their own particular splash of colour and the light always creates a special atmosphere.

A quarter of the way down the glen from the inn lies Irishman's Cottage and, high above the nearby waterworks, is the small feeder reservoir of Block Eary. The

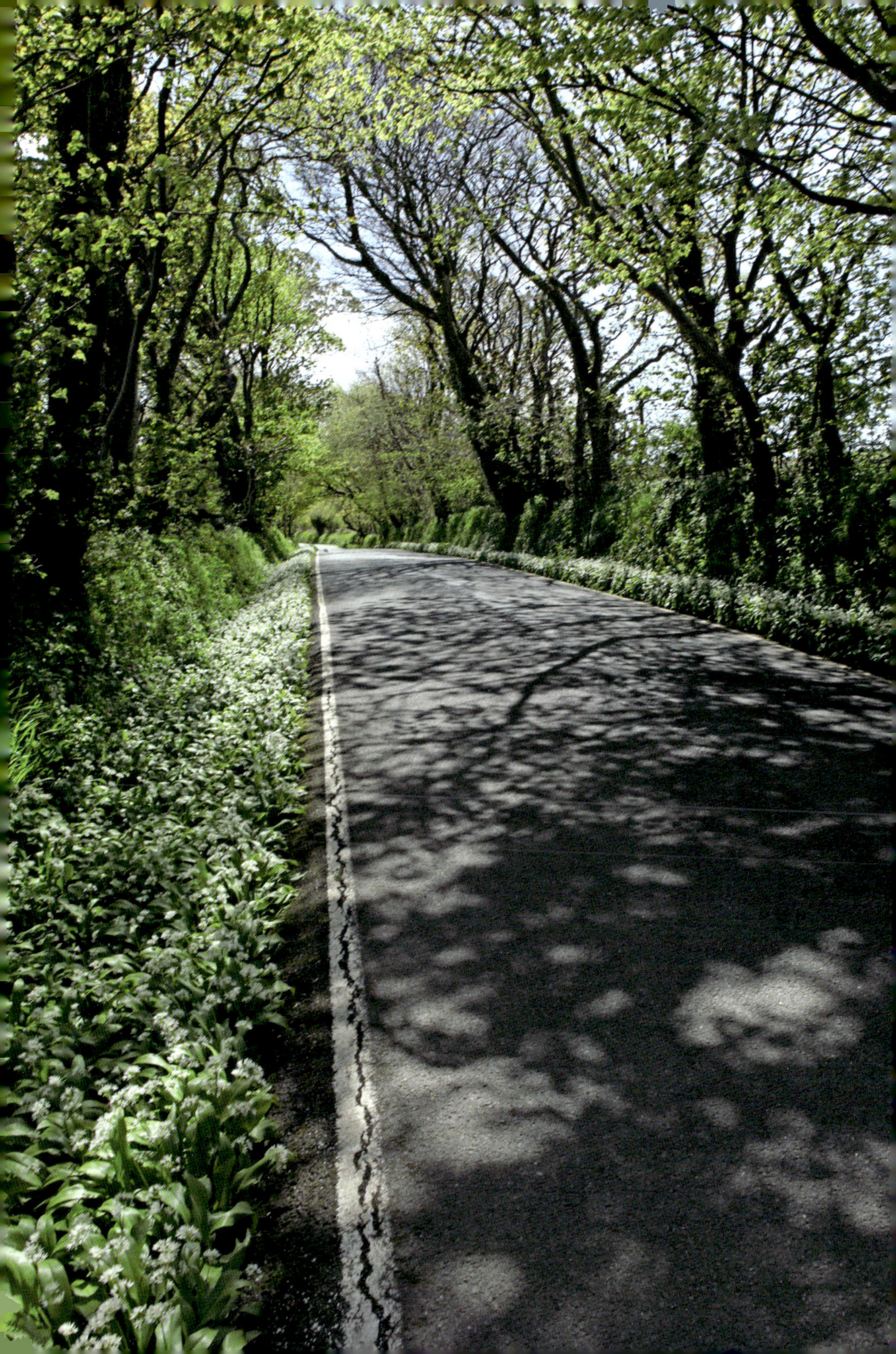

Ballaglass Glen in the spring

reservoir was built by German POWs and although it is a strenuous walk to reach it, it's well worthwhile. The name has changed somewhat from the original Scandinavian spelling Blakkarg but the meaning is still the same, Black Sheiling, from the peaty colour of the stream.

Carry on down the valley towards the Sulby Straight. Passing Sulby Mill go straight on to the main road and turn right on to the TT course at Sulby Methodist church. At the end of the straight, turn off the A3 on to the St Jude's Road (A17). From the West Craig crossroads stay on the A17 to Andreas. There is a subtle change in the scenery here as the landscape changes from moor and glen to low-lying well-drained marshland.

Andreas has a fine church dedicated to St Andrew, from whom the parish takes its name. The village is very much the centre of local agricultural activities. Leave Andreas by continuing on the same road, which takes you to the Island's northernmost centre of population, Bride.

The village lies in a little hollow of the Bride Hills and is one of the sunniest places on the Isle of Man.

Leaving Bride, travel along the A10 in the direction of Ramsey. The Bride road takes you right into Parliament Square and if you are not breaking your journey in Ramsey then carry on following the route marked for the TT course and Douglas. High above the town at the Gooseneck there is a minor road leading off behind the TT marshals' shelter. Careful negotiation of the turn is required to get on to what is known as the Hibernian Road. This is a delightful run across the lower slopes of North Barrule and whilst there seems to be no trace of the name's origination, it is most likely that it takes its form from the same meaning as South Barrule – Ward Mountain.

As you come off this road at the Hibernian, turn right on to the A2 – the coast road – and head for the Corrany. This name is a variation of Cornaa, which means Treen, the modern version of homestead. At the Dhoon is the glen, running down to the shoreline of Dhoon Bay, and the nearby earthworks of Kionehenin. It's an ideal place to stop – and if your passengers happen to be annoying you, send them back to Onchan on the Manx Electric Railway!

Leave the Dhoon car park area by the B11, the Ballaragh road. This is an interesting name and although its derivation is doubtful, there is reason to believe that perhaps its original meaning was Farm of the Spectre or Apparition. Just before the end of this road, King Orry's Grave is reached.

Turn right here and you are once again back on the A2. At Laxey, turn right and cross over the railway lines into Dumbell's Terrace, known to the locals as Ham and Egg Terrace, and park the car. Looking up the valley you will see the largest working waterwheel in the world – Lady Isabella, the Great Laxey Wheel (which incidentally has its own adjacent car park).

The final leg of your journey takes you from Laxey along the A2 to just south of Baldrine village, where you veer left after the railway level crossing lights and on to the A11 Groudle Road (watch out for trains!).

Passing through Groudle you may catch sight of the popular Groudle Glen narrow-gauge railway as it chugs around the headland. Soon the road grants you a fine view of Douglas Bay and then Port Jack is in sight – and so is your journey's end.

139

WILDLIFE & NATURE

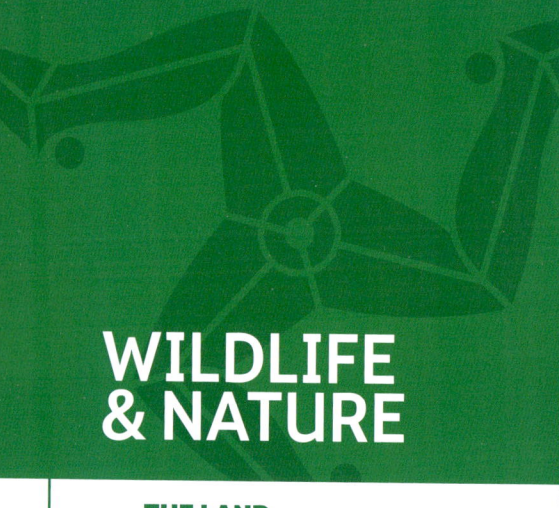

THE LAND
WILDLIFE ON YOUR DOORSTEP

From the scent and semi-alpine conditions of mountainous heather moorland to the music of the Irish Sea as it laps and pounds bays and beaches, the Isle of Man is a creation of breathtaking natural beauty. It's an environment which supports a rich diversity of wildlife – on the land, in the air and in the sea. And enhancing the appeal of this feast of flora and fauna is the fact that the Island's isolation from its mainland neighbours has had two positive effects: firstly producing a distinct Manx ecology, and secondly saving the resident populations of Atlantic and grey seals from the ravages of the two outbreaks of phocine distemper which killed so many of these endearing animals along the eastern shores of the UK.

Parks to visit
Parks and gardens

The Victorian tourist boom spawned a good number of parks. Many have lost their grandeur but are still very pleasant and relaxing, most with free access.

The **Tynwald National Park & Arboretum** at St John's is a fine spot for a picnic. The park's abundant trees and shrubs (along with many species of exotic trees), were gifted to the Manx nation by world governments in celebration of the Tynwald Millennium, the 1,000th year of the Manx Parliament, in 1979. Nearby are the **Manx Wild Flower Garden** and the nursery gardens of the Forestry Department.

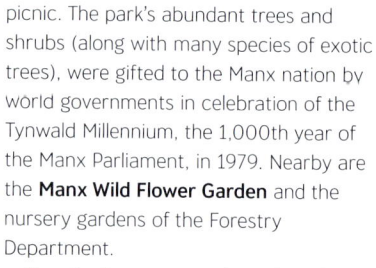

Douglas has many parks and gardens, tended with great pride. Best known are undoubtedly the **sunken gardens** which line the promenade. A riot of colour in spring and summer, the gardens often reflect the theme of notable anniversaries and other important occasions and are designed and planted accordingly. **Noble's Park**, with its sporting and leisure facilities, and the Villa Marina's attractive colonnaded gardens were donated to the town by Henry Bloom Noble.

From July to October, **Summerhill Glen** is a joy for children, the evenings brightened by fairy lights and illuminated animal displays. Douglas even has its own special rose – the Douglas Centenary –

which celebrated the capital's 100th year as a borough in 1996. To the north end of Douglas Bay, and within walking distance of most of the Douglas hotels, is **Onchan Park**, which offers a great variety of family entertainment through to late summer.

Laxey has fine natural gardens. The sheltered site of the old mine washing floors has been turned into a garden to blend in with the surrounding landscape.

The biggest park in Ramsey is **Mooragh** with 40 acres of parkland. It boasts a 12-acre boating lake with rowing boats, canoes, pedaloes and sailing dinghies for hire and you can learn to sail, canoe or windsurf. There are also a bowling green, crazy golf and putting green, and along the banks of the Sulby River you can enjoy the nature trails of the Poyll Dooey (Pool of the Black Ford) wetlands.

The attractions at **Silverdale Glen** near Ballasalla include the very popular Craftworks, where youngsters can create their own prized piece of art or craftwork based on local Manx designs.

Wildlife Park

The Isle of Man has yet more wildlife to show you. And although **Curraghs Wildlife Park** puts the emphasis on wetland birds and mammals from around the world, rather than on native Manx species, there is a strong natural connection – because the park edges and partly embraces the **Ballaugh Curraghs**, an important wetland habitat and wildlife environment which has international recognition. This Ballaugh Curraghs (pronounced khur-ucks) is an area of marshy woodland and grassland in the north – a surviving remnant of a habitat formed at the end of the last ice age as glacial meltwater was trapped against the hills. Over time the majority of the Island's other marshes have been

Wildlife Park

drained for farming, but these five hundred acres or so have defied all similar attempts. Ballaugh Curraghs is designated as both an Area of Special Scientific Interest and a site of international importance for birds and other wildlife. Most of the habitat types present in the Curraghs can be seen along the park's nature trail, along with an explanation and history of the area's origin, ecology and land use.

Curraghs Wildlife Park opened in 1965, purely as a tourist attraction. Today it is also a valued part of the international conservation scene, playing a role in explaining the need for wildlife conservation. The birds and animals are presented in suitably themed areas in a way designed to both entertain and educate. Kids particularly love the Humboldt penguins, the fervour at feeding time never failing to amuse an appreciative audience. The penguins' home is a landscaped enclosure, the rock work resembling the limestone slabs found around Castletown and Port St Mary. Their near neighbours are rheas, Patagonian hares, guanacos, geese, swans and flamingos, all happy to permit visitors to wander amongst them. The park has had great success in breeding flamingos from its modest population, defying the expert belief that this is only possible by keeping these long-legged birds in large numbers – a luxury the park doesn't run to. Similar success has been enjoyed with breeding demoiselle cranes, bar-headed geese and swan geese. They breed nearly every year and in summer months the downy young can be seen in the park's crèche. All the adults are exhibited in the Asian Swamp area, along with crab-eating macaques, short-clawed otters and fishing cats. In the wild, the macaques really do eat crabs and the cats really do go fishing, both species living in river valleys and swampy habitats, and surviving by foraging along the water's edge. The Flooded Forest of the Amazon presents several species of island-dwelling monkeys, including the breeding troop of rare black-capped squirrel monkeys. Other species here are capybara, king vulture, spectacled owl, red-handed tamarin, black spider monkey, agouti and the spectacular scarlet ibis.

Follow the North American Trail to see raccoons and otters, and step into the Australian Outback to encounter wallabies, emus, galahs and various Australian waterfowl. There are two species of wallaby here: the smaller Parma wallaby, believed to be extinct for a hundred years before an introduced colony was identified on a small island in New Zealand, and the rare brushtail rock wallaby. In the wild, these animals have been repatriated to Australia in an attempt to restore the local vegetation on Kawau Island. One of the park's most informative and eye-opening themed areas is Life on Islands – a unique living exhibit which highlights the very real threat of extinction now facing many island species under pressure from increasing human populations. Here you can see lemurs, fruit bats, waterfowl and other species which, rare in the wild, are part of international breeding programmes and in the front line of wildlife conservation. It's a sobering fact that more than two-thirds of known animal extinctions in the last 400 years have been of island species.

Education is a key part of the park's work, and habitat loss, rarity and conservation are explained in The Ark. There's also a schoolroom where children can learn about the incredible diversity of wildlife and why we should look after it for the benefit of future generations. All of which very much reflects Curraghs Wildlife Park's role as a member of both the British and European Zoo Associations – as does the fact that more than a third of the park's mammal species are in European breeding programmes. But while the future for much of the world's most precious wildlife is uncertain, Curraghs Wildlife Park remains a relaxing, enlightening and enjoyable place to visit.

NATURAL AREAS
Dark skies

It s official, the Isle of Man has some of the clearest skies in not just the British Isles, but in Europe. In January 2014, the Isle of Man was granted Dark Sky Discovery status by the UK Science and Technology Facilities Council, for a further 19 sites. This was in addition to the seven sites that were similarly granted this prestigious status by the Dark Sky Discovery network (DSD), based in Edinburgh, in October 2012.

In 2012, recognising the Island's unique aspect, the Island was visited by Alan Brown, the north-west coordinator of the Dark Sky Discovery network, and following a tour of the Island, seven sites were identified as suitable for consideration as Milky Way sites, the highest level of sites that are awarded by the DSD.

Dark Sky Discovery status is granted for sites that are fully accessible by the public, have good site lines, and are suitable for disabled persons. From an astronomical perspective, sites have to be able to see the Milky Way clearly on dark nights.

The seven sites identified in 2012 were at Axnfell Plantation, Smeale, Nairbyl, the Sound, Fort Island, Port Soderick Brooghs, and the Sulby reservoir car park.

The site landowners readily gave full support for the applications, and NASA Astronaut Nicole Stott also gave fantastic support with the following quote:

'I tried on many occasions to identify the Isle of Man from orbit, but I had great difficulty because it is so dark! I eventually captured an image and it shows how wonderful the night skies in the Island are. The Manx skies are fantastic for astronomy – great from above, on board the ISS and from below, on the Island.'

In October 2012, it was announced in London by the Science and Technology Facilities Council (STFC), that all seven sites had been successful in obtaining this highest level of Dark Sky status.

Following the success of the original seven sites, it was suggested that other sites be considered for DSD status and in September 2013 a further 19 sites were submitted, and all were subsequently granted DSD status in January 2014, making the Isle of Man an area with the highest concentration of Dark Sky sites in the British Isles. The full list of Dark Sky sites can be found on the DSD website www.darkskydiscovery.org.uk.

The night sky of the Isle of Man is, on cloudless nights, simply spectacular, and many astronomical sights can be seen through the naked eye and even more can be discovered through a telescope or binoculars. If you want to see the spectacular fainter objects, plan your trip around the new moon, so the bright moonlight will not affect your 'seeing'.

The Island is also ideally placed to see the magnificent sight of the Northern Lights on many occasions. The Northern Lights are normally only seen from northerly locations such as Alaska, Norway and Iceland, however the crystal clear northern horizon from the Island's north-eastern coast means this fascinating phenomenon can often be seen from the Island. The best chance to see the Aurora Borealis is normally around

Dark skies

Dark skies

February to March, or September to October, but it can often be seen outside these dates.

Visitors to the Island's Dark Sky sites can see some stunning sights in the night sky. With the naked eye you can clearly see the Orion Nebula – some 1,500 light years away, our Milky Way Galaxy, or 'Raad Mooar re Gorry', (the Manx name for the Great Way of King Orry) and the Milky Way's companion galaxy the Great Andromeda Galaxy whose light has been on its way to us for about 2.5 million years. With the aid of binoculars or a telescope the heavens will open for visitors the wonders of our cosmos.

Don't worry too much about not having a telescope with you, although do bring one if you have it. The best equipment for stargazing is the naked eye, just look up and marvel at the sights.

The Isle of Man Dark Sky locations mean you can expect some spectacular sights during an evening's stargazing. From our Island shores you can easily see, and thus become one of the few people in the British Isles to clearly see, the Milky Way which shows up as a fuzzy patch made up of around 500 to 700 billion stars!

As you look at the stars in the night sky you will notice that some of them make distinctive patterns and shapes or 'constellations'. Many different civilisations and cultures have seen these shapes around the world, have 'joined the dots' in the night sky and created many myths and legends about them.

Star charts (for example those found on the DSD website, www.darkskydiscovery.org.uk) show some of the clearest constellations that are easily viewable. Some constellations are only visible at certain times of the year so make sure you check the star charts for seasonal variations.

The lie of the land

There's no better place to appreciate the topography of the Isle of Man than from the top of the Island's highest peak. At 2,036 feet Snaefell is certainly no giant, but on a clear day you can see much of the Island itself and, across the Irish Sea, the Cumbrian Mountains to the east, the purple hills of Galloway to the north, Snowdonia to the south and, to the west, Ireland's Mountains of Mourne in the north and Wicklow Mountains in the south. The view from the top of Snaefell also throws light on the fact that more than forty per cent of the Island's land area is uninhabited.

Snaefell stands in the middle of the ridge of hills which runs through the Isle of Man on a north-east to south-west axis, from Ramsey to Cronk ny Arrey Laa (thought to mean 'hill of the day watch') south of Niarbyl, where the cliffs drop steeply into the sea.

Cutting across the ridge and dividing the uplands into north and south is a central valley extending from Peel to Douglas.

The large slate massif responsible for Snaefell also produced 25 peaks exceeding 1,000 feet in height. In the process it created a very pleasurable walk; you can spend a day striding across the uplands, through gorse and heather, taking in the wonderful panoramas of the Isle of Man's east and west coasts without any great rollercoaster variations in descent and ascent.

In fact, walking in the hills will take you to some of the wildest places on the Island. The scenery is spectacular, particularly with the purple heather of late summer, and the heath-land is a diverse wildlife habitat of international importance. Ling, western gorse, bell heather and bilberry are the dominant plants. Blanket bog is another globally-rare habitat found in the uplands.

Birdwatchers too will have a field day. Curlew, skylark, meadow pipit and wheatear are among the species which do well up here. The Island as a whole supports a great variety of birdlife and is recognised for its healthy populations of chough, peregrine falcon, raven and hen harrier, the latter representing somewhere in the order of ten per cent of the total hen harrier population in the British Isles. Since the 1960s the Calf of Man bird and nature reserve has been home to an officially-designated British Bird Observatory.

The hills have broad ridges with relatively smooth slopes merging into wide drainage basins. Streams cutting into the hillsides have produced the glens which collectively are one of the Isle of Man's great natural attractions.

Large areas of the uplands were once

The Sugerloaf

Calf of Man

covered in forest. Tree loss in Neolithic times probably resulted in water-logging and the formation of the peat on which the Manx people relied for fuel until relatively recently. In Viking times, many people lived on the uplands in summer, grazing livestock on the common pasture. The remains of their settlements, called 'sheilings', can still be seen.

Wildlife on the land

At the end of the last ice age, around 10,000 years ago, rising sea levels submerged the last land bridge between the Isle of Man and the rest of the British Isles. This separation is the reason why there are no native large mammals to be found on the Island. But although deer, badger, fox and otter are all absent, and there are no snakes, the upside is that many other species do very well here as a direct result.

For example, brown and mountain hares – both increasingly scarce in the rest of the British Isles – are relatively common. Polecats inhabit conifer plantations, and feral populations of goats, ferrets and even wallabies have established themselves, particularly in the north of the Island.

Along the 100-mile shoreline, several places lend themselves perfectly to spotting seals and animals of the deep, and birdwatchers flock to the Isle of Man to appreciate such ornithological delights as choughs, wild red grouse, peregrines, Manx shearwaters and a good number of other species.

A summer walk in an upland valley or glen is almost certain to show you at least one hen harrier, hunting along the lines of the old walls. In spring, a courting pair engaged in their aerial dance over the heather moor is a sight and sound to remember. But for a really unique view of these truly magnificent raptors, go to **Manx Wildlife Trust's Close Sartfield** nature in late autumn and winter.

Stand on the rooftop platform of the reserve's hide in early evening and you'll witness large groups of hen harriers flying in to congregate at one of the biggest winter roosts in Europe. During 2000, one hundred and ten of these rare birds were seen here in just one short evening!

Another rarity which visiting birdwatchers may have the good fortune to encounter is the corncrake. Now absent from almost all of mainland Britain, this species is pretty much restricted to the Scottish isles and Northern Ireland. But small numbers continue to breed on the Isle of Man and it always pays to keep an ear out for the strange 'crek-crek' call of the males in spring, especially when near hay meadows. To actually see a corncrake now is a truly unusual event.

Particularly good places for bird lovers and wildlife enthusiasts are Langness in

Niarbyl

the south, where many migrant visitors make their landfall, and the Ayres in the north.

The Ayres is of special note as it is one of those strange contrasts found on an island of this size. The northern plain is a post-glacial till and as a result has a low-lying rolling landscape not found anywhere else on the Island. The strong coastal currents and substrata of soft rocks and glacial sands have formed the huge shingle dune formation that is the Ayres. Along with slacks and lowland, the dunes back a wide, open beach, 4 miles long, which looks like a piece of the north Norfolk coastline tacked on to the rocky shores of the Isle of Man. And the lichen heath ecology is almost unique.

As well as the sight of hundreds of orchids and nesting little terns in spring, you can enjoy watching seals, basking sharks, porpoises and whales passing through the fast tidal channel that lies just a stone's throw from the beach.

Another rewarding location at which to see the rich coastal wildlife is **the Sound**, at the south-west tip of the Island. Here you can sit and look across another fast-flowing – and deep – tidal channel towards the Calf of Man and listen to the call of adult male seals as they bask on the rocks. Harbour porpoises, dolphins, minke whales and basking sharks are all regular visitors, and views of the Sugar Loaf Rock and its seabird colony are not far away.

Inland too there is an abundance of other wildlife to see. The Island is ringed with numerous rain-fed rivers tumbling down from the uplands, many of them cutting steep winding gorges as they pass. Apart from the Sulby they are modest in size compared with rivers of mainland Britain, but most support trout, salmon and a variety of aquatic life that is mostly free of pollution due to the lack of intensive industry. Many of these valleys were planted by the Victorians and are now classed as **National Glens**, freely accessible and open at all times. Awash

Oystercatchers at Ramsey

with bluebells, violets and primroses in spring, these wooded valleys hold a special place in Manx natural history.

For botanists too there are rare treasures to be discovered. Atop Snaefell you may be lucky in finding the small colony of alpine least willow, a last survivor of the ice ages, while lower down the mountainsides are cotton grass, bilberry, sundew and a variety of other upland species, sometimes in abundance. The dominant purple of the heathers in summer is characteristic of these habitats, but look closer below the heather's protecting arms and you'll find a miniature garden alive with mosses.

Also characteristic of the Island's lowlands are the areas known as **Curraghs** (pronounced khur-ucks). These low-lying wetlands are a combination of small scrub woodlands dominated by willows and alder, with wet grassland, sedges and rushes often mixed in. Important for a variety of wildlife, they are particularly critical for plants, including the royal fern, and for many species of orchid such as the heath-spotted, northern marsh, butterfly, twayblade and others.

The gem of these sites is the **Close Sartfield reserve** in the northern Ballaugh Curraghs area. Here in late May and June you can walk amongst a colony of over 100,000 orchids growing together. Curragh habitat also occurs at the bottom end of valleys throughout the Island, and little gems can be seen just a stone's throw from the centre of Douglas and Ramsey, as well as tucked away at the head of many river valleys and glens.

Out on the coastal cliffs and shores you can discover other wild flowers. The often steep rocky coastline is sometimes alive with the colours of a rock garden, decorated by a mosaic patchwork of thrift, spring squill, sea campion, harebells, maidenhair ferns and stonecrops formed around the exposed rocks and soil. Areas such as Scarlett outside Castletown, Marine Drive (Douglas Head) and the slopes around Niarbyl, to name just a few, can hold great swathes of these natural rock gardens in spring and summer.

Out on the open sand or shingle beaches, away from the steep rocky shores, look for the yellow-horned poppy as well as the scarce Isle of Man cabbage – a plant restricted to the Island and other shores fringing the Irish Sea.

And as you drive or walk or ride around the Island's roads, take a moment to look at the verges you pass. Traditional Manx sod hedges are solid, built of earth and stone, and home to a wide variety of plants and animals, typically orchids, foxgloves, lizards and butterflies.

Some hedges show handsome displays of bluebells, primroses and valerian, while others such as those around Archallagan Plantation east of Foxdale present an orchid show to shame many a nature reserve. You can also see good populations of elm – a tree that has all but disappeared from much of England due to the ravages of Dutch elm disease – and in spring the powerful scent of abundant wild garlic can seal the picture of these green roadsides in your memory for life.

Wildlife & nature reserves

Basking sharks, seals, hen harriers, choughs, gannets, mountain hares, wallabies – on the Isle of Man you can see them all, and in the wild at that. Then there are the more exotic bird and animal inhabitants of Curraghs Wildlife Park and the rare flora to be found in the Island's many and varied nature reserves.

Basking sharks are attracted to the waters of the south and west coasts from about mid-summer onwards and have been regular visitors for more than two decades. They feed just below the surface on microscopic plants and animals and are not difficult to spot – particularly if you take a boat trip to observe them at close quarters. There are several places where you're likely to spot seals, notably the Sound in the south and the Ayres in the north.

Manx Wildlife Trust has 24 nature reserves, including Close Sartfield in the north – the largest winter hen harrier roost in Western Europe. Details of the reserves are available online (www.manxwt.org.uk) and at the Trust shop, 7-8 Market Place, Peel, as are the seeds of native Manx wild flowers to grow in your own garden.

The **Calf of Man** is also a nature reserve and bird sanctuary, under the management of Manx National Heritage. A little over 600 acres in size, the island has been an official British Bird Observatory since 1962. A small flock of Manx Loaghtan sheep is kept here. This rare native breed is distinctive for its rams, which have four or even six horns. Grey seals can be seen all year round in the surrounding waters. Summer boat trips run to the Calf from Port St Mary and Port Erin, but visitor numbers have to be limited because of the island's sensitive environment.

Hen Harrier

Groudle Glen

The glens

From the Victorians to the many generations of holidaymakers since, these havens of peace and tranquillity have been high on the list of the Isle of Man's most visited attractions, several glens achieving fame for their spectacular waterfalls.

Seventeen designated national glens across the Island are owned and protected by the Manx government and preserved in their natural state. They vary in physical length, breadth and isolation but each is beautiful in its own way. In the east these glens are Summerhill, Groudle, Molly Quirk's, Laxey, Port Soderick and Ballaglass; in the south, Colby and Silverdale; in the north, Elfin, Ballaglass, Dhoon, Tholt-y-Will (Sulby), Bishopscourt and Glen Wyllin; and in the west, Glen Maye, Glen Helen and Glen Mooar.

The national glens are the largest areas of established broad-leafed woodland. Many are characterised by tumbling waterfalls, and the rushing waters of the steep glens were once put to good use for milling, mineral extraction and to drive turbines in the manufacture of paper. Relics of such enterprise can be found in the shape of disused mine shafts and buildings.

When Victorian holidaymakers started coming to the Island in large numbers, pleasure gardens, railways, follies and other attractions were created to further romanticise and popularise the glens.

A fine example of a mountain glen is Sulby (also known as Tholt-e-Will Glen). It starts from a spring in peat moss on the west slopes of Snaefell and runs down to Sulby. It is river-worn (the Sulby River is the Island's longest), deep and bold and represents an image of the grandest of Manx scenery in miniature. One of the glen's most charming attractions is the Tholton craft studio and shop. This produces only genuine Manx crafts, including the Isle of Man's only handmade teddy bears.

Glen Auldyn is perhaps the gentlest of Manx mountain glens and starts on the north of Snaefell as a trickling rill, then runs down through forest and a couple of hamlets to Milntown on the B17. The views at the top end are splendid.

One of the loveliest of the short coastal glens is Ballaglass, near Maughold Head in the north, and is easily accessible by the Manx Electric Railway. You can walk its total length or just a section of it nearer the sea. The lower wooded part is wonderful in spring, when coloured by bluebells, and the area is rich in folklore. Here you might just encounter the spectre of the giant Irish deer, the 'Londhoo'.

Dhoon Glen, a little further south and also on the route of the Manx Electric Railway, is typical of the quaint coastal glens. From the car park the walk down to the beach takes about half an hour.

THE COAST AND SEA
Coastal paths and the Isles of Man

The best way to appreciate the breathtaking beauty of the Isle of Man's 100-mile coastline is by following the Road of the Gull coastal footpath, as described in the walks section of this guide ... however, for the moment, you can think of the Island's coast in terms of two distinct sections.

Going clockwise from Maughold in the north-east to Peel in the west is maritime hardcliff. These rocky cliffs include some of the remotest places on the Island, least affected by human activity and idyllic breeding grounds for numerous bird species. The vegetation along the footpaths is also of interest. The tall cliffs at Douglas Head diminish incrementally all the way down to Derbyhaven. Between the two, on a low promontory above Port Grenaugh west of Santon Head, is a Celtic fort called Cronk ny Merriu (which means 'House of the Dead'). The Vikings subsequently used the fort and there are remains of a rectangular Viking house within the original fortifications. On Langness and around Derbyhaven, there are large populations of wading birds and Langness is a picture of wild flowers.

Further round the 'clock' are the dramatic sights of Spanish Head, the Chasms and the Sugar Loaf – the latter a solitary conical rock 100 feet tall favoured by breeding guillemots, razorbills and kittiwakes. Along the edge of Bay Fine look out for basking sharks feeding just below the surface – sunglasses are a useful aid for spotting them. Other points of note along this first of the two sections of coastline include Milner's Tower on top of Bradda Head at Port Erin; the Bradda Hills; the tall cliffs 1,400 feet high shot for the opening sequence of the feature film Waking Ned; Corrin's Folly on Corrin's Hill above Peel; and St Patrick's Well, where legend has it that the horse St Patrick was riding shed a silver shoe and spring water immediately gushed forth, forming the well.

The other section of coast, continuing clockwise from Glen Mooar to Ramsey, is not as dramatic as the rocky extremities in the south but is of vital importance for its ecology. Predominantly sand and shingle, and maritime soft cliff and dune, it embraces the Ayres, which has several special habitats unique on the Island and is both a National Nature Reserve and a designated Area of Special Scientific Interest (ASSI).

The Ayres derives its name from the old Norse word eyrr meaning 'gravelbank'. The soft cliff and dunes here are still changing as the hills to the south are being eroded and some of this material is being deposited. Marram grass (used locally as

Point of Ayre

All ROUND GUIDE ISLE of MAN

Basking shark

thatching and known as bent) stabilises the dunes. Just inland, heath has developed on the thin soil, and heathers, western gorse and other grasses grow here. The Ayres is notable for small breeding colonies of Arctic and little terns, and other bird species you are likely to see here include mallard, shelduck, lapwing, curlew, oystercatcher, gannet, shag and cormorant. The Ayres also has a visitor centre and nature trails.

Offshore, the **Calf of Man** in the south is the only true island, but there are a number of small islets and rocks which are of interest historically or ecologically.

The Calf of Man is a bird sanctuary and nature reserve managed by Manx National Heritage. There is a resident warden and a bird observatory, and the cliffs and springy turf are nesting grounds for an impressive variety of species including chough and Manx shearwater. At one time the latter was harvested for food and for oil used in the treatment of wool and for cleaning firearms. The ground-nesting shearwater population was decimated in the 18th century, most probably by rats escaping to the Calf from a ship.

It is possible to visit the Calf during summer months, weather and visitor numbers permitting. Regular sailings operate from Port Erin and Port St Mary. With a circumference of 5 miles and an area of 616 acres, the Calf can be explored easily in half a day – although such is the peace and tranquillity of the place that you may well find it difficult to leave!

Just off the Calf is Chicken Rock, unmissable for the lighthouse built in 1875 to steer shipping well clear of the treacherous reef on the edge of a steep descent deep into the Irish Sea.

Of much greater significance in Manx history is St Patrick's Isle, Peel – the site of the remains of Peel Castle and its medieval St German's Cathedral. 'No part of the Isle of Man has played so great and interesting a part in the history as has the islet known as Peel Island, or St Patrick's

Isle.' So spoke Canon Stenning. And in any historical account or modern photographic portrait of the Isle of Man, the isle is present, the first mention of it occurring in *Annals of Ulster* for the years 797–798. In addition to the castle, numerous periods of architecture are represented, from prehistoric earthworks to Napoleonic fortifications, and the islet has served as a garrison, an armoury and an ecclesiastical prison. Eight bishops are believed to have been buried here. The castle ruins are a big visitor attraction, and the grounds have staged summer concerts and theatre.

Offshore in Douglas Bay, and easily visible to all arriving at the Isle of Man by sea, is Conister Rock and Sir William Hillary's Tower of Refuge.

In the south of the Island, linked to the Langness peninsula by a short causeway, is St Michael's Isle. Here are the remains of a stone 17th-century round fort, built for the 7th Earl of Derby (Yn Stanlagh Mooar) and of much earlier earth embankments, thought to have been raised at the time of Magnus's landing here in 1250. There is also a ruined chapel, which stands on the probable site of an ancient keeill, and a close inspection of the building reveals alterations to its dimensions at different times. It is associated with the local legend of a priest who had a vision in which St Michael pointed to this location as the place for the building of a new church with a particularly fine altar. The church was duly built but to finance the altar the priest retrieved a hoard of gold buried in the churchyard by pirates – only to be later tricked and murdered by other pirates who knew of its existence. To this day it is believed that whoever strikes the walls of this ancient building will hear the moans of the priest and the jingle of coins.

Wildlife in the Sea

As dedicated and patient observers have discovered in very recent years, the variety and nature of marine wildlife which can be seen close to the Manx shoreline is greater and even more astonishing than anyone had previously suspected.

Seals have long been a familiar sight, particularly on the rocks and in the fast flowing waters of the Sound, and basking sharks – the world's second biggest fish, up to 11 metres/36 feet long and weighing 10 tonnes or more – are regular visitors to the Island's west coast waters from about the third week in May, saying their farewells in August, and best seen on an organised boat trip if you want to appreciate the sheer scale of these awesome creatures at close quarters as they feed on tiny plankton just below the surface of the water.

Much less familiar, except to the keenest observers, are rare dolphins and huge whales. They are drawn here by the abundance of their favourite foods – herring sprats, sandeels, mackerel, squid, cuttlefish and sardines – and they include fin whales, which are second in size only to blue whales as the largest animal ever to inhabit the planet.

In September, the perpetual quest to satisfy a healthy appetite also brings minke whales to the Isle of Man. Their prize is the herring which spawn on the sea bed from Langness to the Point of Ayre. Minkes are not shy of coming close to the shoreline, and an autumn afternoon spent at the bay at Laxey can prove a very rewarding experience for spectators.

Then there are other impressive whale species which are familiar to these waters, including the orca (killer whale) and the rare sei. Killer whales make no bones about feasting on grey seals and other cetaceans. Humpback and sei whales are seen only occasionally, as are white-beaked dolphins.

Of all marine wildlife, dolphins seem to share a very special affinity for mankind which goes way beyond their natural intelligence and playfulness. Bottlenose (most prevalent from October to April) and common (summer) are two species which frequent the Island's waters, but you could also catch sight of the wonderful and rare risso's dolphin.

The distinctive-looking risso's has a blunt snout, no beak and a torpedo-shaped body, and is very acrobatic. The Isle of Man is one of the world's few places where it can be seen close to shore. And it is here throughout spring, summer and autumn, feasting on a Manx diet of squid, cuttlefish and mackerel.

Not far behind dolphins in the must-see popularity stakes, certainly for children, are seals – and on the Isle of Man you're guaranteed to spot them at fairly close quarters by looking no further than the Sound. In fact, you can watch them in their natural habitat while you enjoy all the comforts of the Sound Visitor Centre and café, where the wide panoramic window gives you a fabulous view over the tidal channel to the Calf of Man nature reserve and bird observatory.

Within the tidal channel, close to shore, is the tiny Island of Kitterland, where seals bask openly on the rocks. This is an ideal and sheltered location for them, the water deep, fast-flowing and rich in fish.

Two seal species inhabit Isle of Man waters: Atlantic grey and common, the latter being slightly smaller and much scarcer. And it's not always easy to tell them apart, the main difference being that the common seal has a more distinctive dog-like rounded head compared with the Atlantic seal's longer, more Roman snout!

Both species breed here. Common seal pups are born in early autumn and able to swim within hours of birth. The pups of Atlantic grey seals are distinctive for their white furry coats, and during the three-week weaning period they gain up to 2kg a day in weight. After this the white coat is shed. Although it keeps the youngsters warm and protected in strong autumn gales, the fur is easily waterlogged and grey seal pups are poor swimmers to start with.

During weaning, pups are often temporarily abandoned, left ashore on small beaches and coves, while their mothers fish for food. Occasionally, a mother fails to return because of accident or falling victim to a predator such as a killer whale, and her pup is orphaned. But if you see a young seal pup alone on a beach or cove, do not disturb it or assume it has been abandoned – it is much more likely to be awaiting the return of its mother.

THE AIR
Wildlife in the Air

Boasting a unique avifauna, the Isle of Man is something of a paradise for birdwatchers. Here is an expert guide to some of the best locations.

1. THE AYRES

Beaches are pebbly and support good breeding populations of oystercatcher, ringed plover and little tern. In late summer, sands exposed at low tide attract flocks of sandwich tern and kittiwake, as well as sanderling, dunlin and the occasional knot. The terns are frequently harried by skuas, mainly Arctic. Sea-watching along the coast reveals good numbers of Manx shearwaters, common scoters and eiders, and gannets from Scottish breeding colonies nearby fish the shallow waters. Dunes separate the shore from the heath, with stonechats plentiful in both habitats. Flocks of golden plover frequent the heath and shoreline during winter months, when all three divers appear offshore.

2. GLASCOE DUB

Less than 4 miles south of the Point of Ayre, this little farm pond is the Island's best site for shoveler. Winter months attract pink-footed geese and several hundred wigeon.

3. RAMSEY

In winter the harbour can have up to 40 mute swans and over 50 Canada geese. Little grebes occur regularly, and kingfishers are often seen just above the stone bridge. You may even spot a black redstart around the harbour entrance. The attractions at Mooragh Lake include goldeneye, which can number more than 50.

4. BALLAUGH CURRAGHS

Not only the site of western Europe's largest communal hen harrier roost, but also the place to see (and hear!) water rails, greylags and long-eared owls. Summer attractions include wild orchid fields, grasshoppers, sedge warblers, blackcaps, redpolls – and maybe even a wild red-necked wallaby!

5. MAUGHOLD BROOGHS

From the car park, coastal paths lead east and west. Take care along the path towards Maughold Head to see colonies of kittiwakes and guillemots, scattered razorbills and fulmars, and peregrines, ravens and choughs. The path west gives views of black guillemots and maybe the odd puffin on the sea, but the main attraction is the Island's largest cormorant colony – now accommodating more than 150 pairs.

6. PEEL

An excellent year-round site. Summer views at Contrary Head include black guillemots, puffins, guillemots, kittiwakes, fulmars, stonechats, choughs and perhaps wheatears. Black guillemots nest in holes in the breakwater wall and there are usually eiders in the bay. Watching the sea from below the castle in late summer should yield plenty of gannets and Manx shearwaters, and possibly sooty shearwaters, storm petrels, Leach's petrels and skuas, with kittiwakes plentiful around the breakwater. For most of the year purple sandpipers and turnstones frequent the castle rocks, and during winter it's often possible to see all three divers in the bay.

7. THE FOXDALE DAMS

The two small dams – Eairy and Kionslieu – can attract an interesting variety of wildfowl: fair numbers of teals and tufted ducks in winter, along with the odd goldeneye and pochard and a

The Ayres

The air

Douglas Head lighthouse

resident ruddy duck. Whooper swans appear from time to time, and other recent visitors have included gadwall and goosander. Common sandpipers are regular transient spring visitors. Green sandpipers have also been seen. Two or three pairs of tufted ducks now breed here, and the songs of willow warblers, sedge warblers and whitethroats are constant in early summer.

8. MARINE DRIVE

Take the easy walk from Douglas Head to Port Soderick and you can't fail to see stonechats, choughs and ravens – with every chance of peregrines.

9. LANGNESS AND DERBYHAVEN

Arguably the best site throughout the year. In winter a flock of perhaps 60 choughs feed along the shore, and there are flocks of several hundred oystercatchers, golden plovers and curlews. Brent geese frequent Derbyhaven Bay in increasing numbers and it's also good for great northern divers and grebes, especially Slavonian and great crested. The principal wildfowl are wigeon, teal, mallard and shelduck, but any of the less common ducks may also turn up. At any time there's a fair chance of grey plovers, little egrets and black-tailed and bar-tailed godwits. Other waders appear on passage, especially little stints, curlews, sandpipers, whimbrels, ruffs, and perhaps spotted redshanks, greenshanks and wood sandpipers, while rarities have included avocets, little ringed plovers, Temminck's stints, both white-rumped and buff-breasted sandpipers, and long-billed dowitchers. Passerine migrants include flocks of skylarks and white wagtails, plenty of wheatears and, especially around the ruined farmhouse, a variety of warblers. Stonechats, linnets, reed buntings, ravens and both carrion and hooded crows (and their hybrids) are ever present.

10. POYLLVAAISH AND STRANDHALL

These two sites and the intervening coast are very similar to Langness and Derbyhaven and seem particularly attractive to shelduck, wigeon and eider.

11. CHASMS AND SUGAR LOAF

Spectacular for nesting colonies of kittiwake and guillemot, and excellent for chough and raven. On the Port St Mary side, black guillemots can always be seen and wheatears nest in the rocky field margins.

12. CALF OF MAN

For most of the year the Manx National Heritage bird observatory is manned by wardens, and basic accommodation is available. Summer boats from Port Erin and Port St Mary serve this islet nature reserve, where regular breeders are eider, fulmar, Manx shearwater, shag, peregrine, kttiwake, auks, stonechat, chough and raven. Occasional breeders have included hen harrier, water rail and short-eared owl. Thousands of passerine migrants are ringed and overnight visitors have a fair chance of seeing a trapped rarity.

13. THE HILLS

The variety of species is small, but driving through the hills is very likely to show you hen harrier, merlin, red grouse, wheatear and raven. In winter there's also the possibility of snow bunting. Particularly rewarding roads in the south are the A27 and A36, which meet at Round Table. In the north, you shouldn't ignore the narrow and mostly unfenced road which meanders from the head of the West Baldwin valley, through Druidale and down to Ballaugh. Recommended walking routes are the Millennium Way between Sky Hill and Crosby and – using the mountain railway – Snaefell summit to Glen Mona or Laxey.

Langness Point lighthouse

HISTORY

A proud history

The earliest inhabitants of the Island are believed to have been part of the original Celtic people of the British Isles. The Celts inhabited central and western Europe in pre-Roman times and in all likelihood derived, by assimilation, from the Neolithic people of Britain,

Not much survives from this period save for a few old names. In Manx Gaelic, the word for 'homestead' was 'balla' and there are still nearly 200 'balla' place names today. Of the original Manx place names, seventy per cent are Celtic. Many Manx surnames also date from the Celtic period, though they have been altered. Many begin with a hard C, K or Q – Corlett, Kelly and Quayle – which are all shortened versions of the Mac prefix. So Corlett is MacCorleod, son of the fierce one.

Excavations have revealed that the Celts were a prosperous and peaceful people, closely interwoven with the Irish. They lived in communities, with an idiosyncratic land tenure system which was largely unchanged by the feudal system, and they made the transition from pagan to Christian. They left behind monuments in the form of Ogham stones, and there are four fine examples on the Isle of Man dating from the 4th century.

The Romans certainly knew of the Isle of Man, but they never came as settlers and their influence, though profound on mainland Britain, was negligible here.

The Norsemen were a different proposition altogether. Essentially a maritime people, they found fame and plunder on the high seas. They harried Scotland and established colonies in the Orkneys, the Inner and Outer Hebrides and Northern Ireland. It was inevitable that they would eventually land on the Isle of Man and disrupt its peace.

What is thought to be the earliest recorded attack on the Island occurred in 798 when the Vikings landed on what is now St Patrick's Isle, off Peel. By the end of the 9th century there were Viking settlers and the Island became a pawn in the fight between Ireland and the Kings of Scandinavia.

Understandably, historical evidence is obscure, but a character from this period has formed a great part of early Manx history. Though his identity is disputed, 'King Orry' is attributed with establishing three important bulwarks of Manx society – the State, a legislative body and a standing army. The chronicles of the monks of Rushen Abbey favour the Viking King Godred Crovan, son of Harald the Black of Iceland, as the real 'King Orry'. He reached Mann in 1075 but was heavily defeated by the inhabitants. He returned with a strengthened army and landed in Ramsey Bay. Legend has it that on landing he looked up at the clear night sky and the Milky Way and declared, 'There is my path, running from my country to this place', or words to that effect.

Ever since, the Manx have called the Milky Way 'Yn Rad Mooar Ree Goree' (the great track of King Orry). King Orry was sufficiently fortified to defeat the Manx on this occasion, in battle on Skyhill. He spared his vanquished opponents and ruled for 16 years. The name of King Orry is still much loved and used on the Island.

Godred Crovan established the Kingdom of Mann and the Isles and with him begins the real recorded history of the Island. There are two important 'ship burial' excavations on the Island, at Knock-y-Dooney, near Kirk Andreas, and at Balladoole, in Kirk Arbory, which date from this time. Chiefs were buried in this way. Their ship was drawn ashore and equipped with everything they might need for the 'journey to Odin', including a sword, spear, fishing gear, a bowl and a sacrificial knife.

The second Scandinavian period, started by Godred Crovan, lasted from 1079 to 1266. It is a period of great importance for the development of the Manx system of government. Godred ruled the British islands, from Dublin and Leinster to the Isle of Lewis. His

Cashtal yn Ard

A proud history

St Michael's Island

descendants were to rule Mann for nearly two hundred years. At various times, the kings lived in Dublin, Northumbria and Mann. During the transition period from warriors of the seas to landowners and farmers, the Vikings left the Celts to run the farms and harvest the crops while they traded with the adjacent islands, Iceland and southern Europe.

The Cistercian Abbey of St Mary was built and constituted at Rushen Abbey during this period. It quickly became a source of great power on the Island and was a huge influence on the lives of the islanders. Another important development near the end of this period was the tying of the Island's fortunes to the English crown. Reginald, a tough Viking who reputedly spent three long years at sea, was desperate to hold on to Mann as part of his kingdom. In his anxiety, he swore to be a liegeman to Henry III of England, in return for two hogs' heads of wine and 120 crannocks of corn.

The Scandinavian influences have stood the test of time and still appear in a multitude of ways in everyday life on the Island. The most marked features are the land tenure system, the legislature and the Diocese of Sodor and Man, all of which differ greatly from their counterparts in Great Britain. There are many words of Scandinavian extraction including Snaefell, the Island's highest peak, which means 'snow mountain'. The Norse settlers used 'by' as the ending to many of their words and this remains a feature in many place names. Kirby meaning church farm, Colby meaning Kolli's farm, Jurby (Ivar's Farm) and Sulby are a few examples.

Although the Vikings eventually became Christians, it was not before they had extinguished the light of Christianity, which had burned brightly on Mann from the 4th century onwards. Around the beginning of the 11th century the Manx began, once again, to embrace Christianity. From the time of the founding of Rushen Abbey by the Cistercians of Furness Abbey in Barrow, it is possible to get a clearer picture of developments from the writings of the monks.

The Manx bishops are known as the Bishops of Sodor and Man, and the earliest reference to the Diocese of Sodor and Man seems to be in 1154. Consisting of the southern islands of Scotland, it extended from the Hebrides to Arran and the Isle of Man itself. Sodor owes its derivation from two Norse words meaning southern isles, so in fact Sodor and Man means 'the southern Isles and Man'.

Bishops have always played an important role in the history of the Island, sometimes leading the people by good example, at other times abusing their power and privileged position. In 1266 the connection between the Isles and Sodor came to an end, although the diocese continued to be under the rule of a distant Norwegian Archbishop until the 15th century. It was during this period that the Island was divided into parishes.

After Norse rule had come to an end, the Isle of Man was the subject of many struggles, which saw its ownership passing between the Scots and the English. It was not until 1346 that the Island came firmly and finally under English rule. During this period, immediately before the long reign of the Stanleys, the Island's people suffered grievously. Contemporary writings of the time report that the Island was 'desolate and full of wretchedness'. In another report the writer told of a great battle on the slopes of South Barrule, in which Irish freebooters who plundered everything of value heavily defeated the Manx. Only the purchase of corn from Ireland saved the people from starvation. So poor were the islanders that they could no longer afford to make the magnificent crosses for which they were renowned.

The Stanley dynasty ruled the Isle of Man from 1405 to 1736. The first King of Man, Sir John Stanley I, never came to the Island and was succeeded by his son Sir John Stanley II, a wise but somewhat

The Old Grammar School, Castletown

A proud history

despotic ruler, who at least conferred some benefits on the people. It is recorded that there were two revolts against his authority. To prevent a repetition, he increased the power of the governors and substituted trial by battle with trial by jury as a means of settling disputes. Many of his successors did not visit their kingdom, and those who did come often paid only a fleeting visit.

The next major turning point in the story of Man came with the arrival of James Stanley, the 7th Earl of Derby, referred to by the Manx as 'Yn Stanlagh Mooar' ('The Great Stanley'). In 1643 he was ordered to the Isle of Man by Charles I of England to put down a threatened revolt by the Manx. Hiding an iron hand in a velvet glove, he soon made himself popular. Although the people of this period enjoyed the peace, they had less liberty.

With Charles II on the English throne, Yn Stanlagh Mooar proved his loyalty once more to the Crown. Leading his troops, 300 of them Manxmen, he set off in support of the King but was defeated and executed.

At this time, the great Manx patriot William Christian ('Illiam Dhone' to the Manx) anticipated punitive action against the islanders and ordered the militia to take all military installations. Everything was captured, including Peel and Rushen castles – soon given up by Stanley's widow – and the Island eventually surrendered to the Parliamentarians.

William Christian paid a terrible price for his actions. After the Restoration, some ten years after leading the revolt against the Countess of Derby, he was executed by shooting on Hango Hill at Castletown.

The 18th century was a turbulent period for the Manx. The end of rule by the Stanleys, serious disputes with the English Parliament, and the destruction of the smuggling trade (the only way the Island had been kept afloat financially) all caused unrest. The period also saw the passing of the Act of Settlement in 1704, effectively the Island's *Magna Carta*, and in 1736 under the rule of the 2nd Duke of Atholl, the Manx Bill of Rights was introduced. This Act in effect did away with despotic government and replaced it with an oligarchic government – the Keys (or the Lower House) of Tynwald. Constitutional government was just around the corner.

Working hard for the people for more than half a century during this era was the much-loved Bishop Thomas Wilson, Bishop of Sodor and Man for 58 years. He fed the populace in times of crop failure, promoted education, established schools and libraries, and laboured long on behalf of the Manx State.

On 11th July 1765 the Island passed into the ownership of the British Crown. As the Manx standard was lowered at Castle Rushen and the Union Jack raised, George III was proclaimed King of Man. John the 3rd Duke of Atholl had sold the Island to the Imperial Parliament for £70,000. The prosperity of the Island, such as it was, disappeared overnight with the demise of the smuggling trade and London appeared well satisfied. This was not to be the end of the Atholl connections with the Isle of Man.

As the Island fell into decay and its people into despair, the government in London felt obliged to try and rectify this state of affairs and in 1793 appointed the 4th Duke of Atholl as Governor. This was not a success and in 1829 he severed his relationship with the Island for the sum of £417,000 and left.

George IV, King of Great Britain and Ireland, became Lord of Man. The period immediately after the Duke's departure saw little change. London continued to control the Island's revenue, and the House of Keys still largely ignored the peoples' wishes by electing one of their 'own' whenever a vacancy in the House occurred. Help was at hand though, in the name of Mr Henry Loch, later to be Lord Loch and after whom part of Douglas promenade is named.

Appointed as Governor in 1863, Henry Loch brought energy and a real sense of purpose to the position. Working closely with Tynwald Court, lengthy negotiations with Her Britannic Majesty's Government were eventually concluded in 1866 to ensure that after the running expenses of the Manx government were met, any surpluses could be retained on the Isle of Man for improvements to a fledgling infrastructure. Part of the agreement called for the House of Keys to be popularly elected and for the English Government to receive a sum of £10,000 annually from insular revenue as a contribution towards the defence of the realm, a payment that, although much increased, continues today.

Even before the arrival of Governor Loch, the Island had achieved popularity as a holiday destination. Certainly with more and more of the revenue being retained locally and spent on improving the infrastructure, it was not too long before the population increased and communications to and from the Island vastly improved. Towards the end of the 1800s, as the railways and their associated shipping companies opened up the adjacent islands to travel for all, a whole new industry mushroomed on the Isle of Man – tourism.

Much of the infrastructure that exists today owes its initial development to this period. Hotels, railways, piers, theatres, reservoirs, steamships and roads all played their part in thrusting the Island to the forefront of the domestic British leisure market, such as it was.

As the new post-Victorian era arrived, the Island rose to the challenge of mass tourism and for decades happily served the Lancashire cotton workers, Yorkshire miners, Scottish engineers, Geordie shipbuilders and many other working class families seeking annual escape from a life of hard work. During the 20th century the Isle of Man was not alone in experiencing huge changes to its economy with the decline of traditional industries and the lightning march of technology. It has been a period to challenge even the very cornerstone of Manx character and philosophy. As the inscription with the ancient Three Legs of Man symbol defiantly declares, 'Quocunque Jeceris Stabit' – Whichever Way You Throw Me I Stand.

Tynwald the oldest Parliament in the world

The Isle of Man is home to the oldest continuous parliament in the world. Tynwald, derived from the Norse word Thingvollr (which means assembly field), has ruled over the Island for over 1,000 years. According to the Chronicles of Mann Norse invaders first appeared as raiding parties on the Island around the years 800 880AD, however settlement seems to have occurred some time around 880 990, most likely during the turbulent times after the battle of Hafursfjord, when the Scandinavian Kings of Dublin extended their rule towards Man. From this time until 1079, and the rule of Godred Crovan, the Earls of Orkney largely took control of the Island. As the Vikings settled they brought with them their way of governing, under the principle that individuals would observe the laws

Tynwald Court

that were proclaimed, usually to an assembly that met in the open air at the midsummer solstice. Tynwald consists of the Legislative Council and the House of Keys, and is a unique parliament consisting of three chambers the House of Keys with 24 Members (presided over by the Speaker), the Legislative Council with 11 Members and the two chambers sitting together as the Tynwald Court (both presided over by the President of Tynwald, although the Speaker still sits as the Head of the Keys). When Tynwald is not in recess, Tynwald Court meets on the third Tuesday of each month; the Legislative Council and the House of Keys meet each Tuesday individually when the Tynwald is no gathered. Primary legislation is first carried through the House of Keys, with a first and second reading followed by Clauses then a final third reading. Once a Bill has passed its third reading it is given by the Speaker to the Secretary of the House who in turn passes this to the Legislative Council. Once taken before the Council legislation is passed in much the same way, although should any amendments be made these are passed back to the House of Keys for approval. Once passed by both branches the Bill must be signed by the majority of Members at a sitting of Tynwald before being submitted for Royal Assent.

Traditionally Midsummer's Day was the appointed day to meet, and on the Isle of Man July 5th is set aside each year as Tynwald Day, when the Island assembles for the Tynwald ceremony in the village of St John's, as it has done for countless centuries.

Although with the coming of the Vikings the Isle of Man fell under the auspices of the King of Norway, it was governed by a succession of chieftains. The most famous was Godred Croven who conquered the Island on his third attempt in 1079, and whose descendants ruled until the death of Magnus Olaffson, the last Norse King of Man, in 1265. During this time the Isle of Man was part of the Kingdom of Man and the Isles, along with Lewis, Skye, Mull and Islay, known as the Sudreys.

The House of Keys was created around the time of the Kingdom of Man and the Isles, with members acting as magistrates to enforce laws and settle legal disputes. Originally it is thought there were 32 members, one from each of the Island's 16 ancient parishes and four each from the four Hebridean Islands. At some point the Isle of Man was divided into six sheadings for administrative purposes ('sheading' derives from the Norse for 'sixth') and the other islands were lost from the administration, leaving four members from each of the Isle of Man's sheadings, bringing the members down to 24 in number. No one knows the true origin of the name House of Keys, however there are two possible origins: one is that the name derives from the Norse Kjosa, meaning 'chosen' while another explanation is that the name derives from Y Chiare-as-Feed, Gaelic for 'four and twenty'.

When Norse rule ended with the death of King Magnus, the Island was ruled by a succession of English and Scottish noblemen, until in 1405 Henry IV granted the Kingship of Man to the Stanley family. Sir John Stanley duly gave his son, also named John, the responsibility of the Island, and after a visit in 1414 he demanded that the Island's laws be written down. These earliest of records date from 1417. Although dropping the title 'King of Man' in favour of 'Lord of Man' in 1504, the Stanley family effectively ruled the Island until 1765 when the Duke of Atholl was forced to sell his title to the

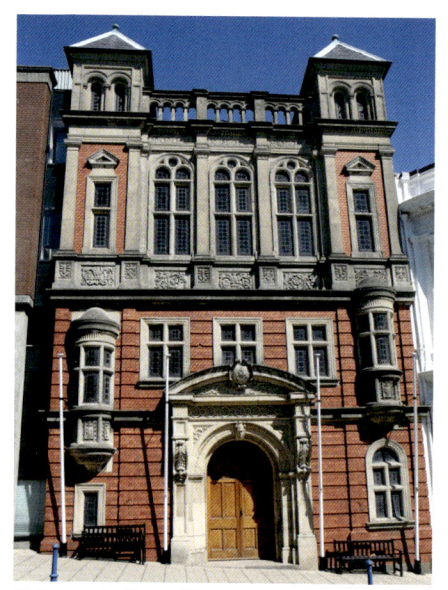

Entrance to Tynwald

British Crown. The Revestment Act ensured that Westminster took over the Island's finances and administration, effectively stripping Tynwald of its powers of public expenditure.

The Governors, who had been appointed as administrators of the Island by the Stanleys, continued in their role with the Island Council being responsible as advisers to the current Governor. Council members were appointed for life, but by the late 1800s Islanders were campaigning for reform, which took place in 1866 with the House of Keys Election Act, which ensured that House of Keys members were democratically elected. In 1881 voting was extended from property owners with a value of £8 to include property owning widows and unmarried women – the first country in the world to give women the vote in a national election.

A period of further reform took place after consultations began between 1904 and 1907 when the MacDonnell Report recommended a term of seven years for Governors, reform of the Legislative Council (where four Members should be elected by the House of Keys), and the formation of a Manx budget by the UK Government. In 1919 the Legislative Council was reconstituted to include the Bishop, two Deemsters, the Attorney General, four members nominated by the House of Keys and two members nominated by the Governor, and an act was passed to allow women to be elected to the House. Next, in 1921 the Governor's judicial responsibilities were removed. In 1922 Member's pay rates were set along with two committees, the Finance and Consultative Committees, being formed to look at more wide-ranging changes

During the years after WWII reform carried on, with more responsibility being handed over from the Governor to Tynwald, until by 1965 the majority of the Governor's powers were devolved. Alterations to the Legislative Council continued and by 1975 the Deemsters and Governors appointees, along with the Attorney General's right to vote, were removed. By 1980 the Governor was removed from the Legislative Council, and in the decade that followed restructuring occurred with a change towards a ministerial government. Finally 1990 saw the elected office of President of Tynwald being created

Tynwald Day

Every Tynwald Day thousands of Islanders and visitors congregate at Tynwald Hill to join in celebration of the Island's self-governance. It is thought that the Hill is a man-made structure created from sods of earth brought from all of the ancient parishes of the Island. Rushes are strewn along the processional way in symbolic tribute to the Island's mythical

House of Keys

protector, the sea god and shape-shifting magician Manannan, and the laws enacted in the past year are proclaimed by Deemsters (the Manx equivalent of British High Court Judges) in both Manx and English. The main feature of Tynwald Day is this promulgation of new Acts of Tynwald, which is the final stage in the Island's legislative process. Dignitaries in attendance include the Lieutenant Governor of the Island, who presides over the ceremony, and on occasion, as guest of honour and presiding officer, Her Majesty the Queen or a member of her family. But while the day is one of tradition and has a serious side, this is very much a day of celebration, with everyone enjoying themselves once the formalities are over.

The Millennium of Tynwald was celebrated in 1979 worldwide, and although no written evidence exists for the first parliament being staged in 979, it is highly likely that by the late C10th Scandinavian parliaments were meeting on the Island. When Queen Elizabeth II touched down on Manx soil at Ronaldsway Airport for the occasion she was given a piece of silver fern to ward off evil spirits. This, however, was not the first time a British monarch had presided over the ancient ceremony, that honour was given to King George VI and Queen Elizabeth (the later Queen Mother) when they visited the Island in July 1945.

The Tynwald ceremony, attended by Members of Tynwald, the judiciary, representatives of churches and other Tynwald Day dignitaries and guests, starts with a service in St John the Baptist Chapel taken by the Bishop of Sodor and Man and the Chaplain of the House of Keys. As winner of the highest music award at the Manx Music Festival, the holder of that year's Cleveland Medal is traditionally invited to sing at the ceremony. Once the formal service has ended those entitled to a seat on Tynwald Hill line the processional way allowing the

Governor, preceded by the Tynwald Sword Bearer carrying the Sword of State, to pass, before taking their seats. The Coroner of Glenfaba is then instructed by the Governor to fence the Court before the formalities of Tynwald can begin.

The Tynwald ceremony starts with the Coroners, or court officials, being invited by the First Deemster to come forward and take an oath to execute their offices. Then comes the Promulgation of Acts, where the laws that have been passed in the following year are read out, first in English by the First Deemster, then in Manx by the Second Deemster. Finally Petitions are presented to the Clerk of Tynwald, where those with grievances have the right of appeal to ask Tynwald to investigate. These matters are then conveyed to the Governor who refers them to the Standing Orders Committee of Tynwald.

Following the proceedings on Tynwald Hill the dignitaries return to the Chapel for a sitting of Tynwald to sign the Acts that have been presented. Finally the Tynwald Honour, the highest Honour that Tynwald can present, may be awarded to an individual who has made an outstanding contribution to one or more areas of Manx life.

Tours: Regular tours are held each week (excluding public holidays) on: Monday at 2.00pm and Friday at 10.00am

It is not usually necessary to book but if you wish to reserve a place you may do so by calling the Tynwald Library on (01624) 685520 or emailing library@tynwald.org.im. There is no charge for tours and they usually take approximately an hour and a half. It is also possible to pre-book tours at other times, including evenings and weekends. To request this please call or email the Tynwald Library giving an indication of the requested date, time and number in your party and we will contact you to confirm.

Please be aware that due to the age of

Tynwald Day

Hango Hill

the building, some parts of the tour are accessible only via stairs. Mobility impaired visitors can be accommodated via a different route but prior notice would be appreciated.
Tynwald parliamentary website: www.tynwald.org.im

Custodians of Manx Heritage

Manx National Heritage is one organisation responsible for six distinctly different and wide-ranging functions. It is at once the Isle of Man's Museum Service, Art Gallery, National Library & Archives, Ancient Monuments Service, National Trust and National History Recording Service. The purpose of these varied roles is to care for and to tell the history of the Island and to provide research facilities for students – and if you think you have Manx connections and are researching your family tree, you can access historical archives at www.manxnationalheritage.im.

Manx National Heritage is the Island's National Trust, and access to all National Trust land is free and usually without restriction (except for dogs and shooting). Some ancient monument sites are available for public viewing but many are on private property and therefore prior permission is required.

There are many sites to explore, not forgetting the Celtic and Scandinavian carved cross slabs, which are in the guardianship of Manx National Heritage but in general are found at parish churches around the Island.

Ancient sites & monuments

Many of the Island's ancient monuments stand on privately-owned ground and can only be viewed with prior permission, but among the freely-accessible sites are Balladoole (remains dating from prehistoric to Viking times) near Castletown, Cronk ny Merriu (Iron Age promontory fort) at Port Grenaugh between Douglas and Derbyhaven, The

St Michael's Island

Braaid (Iron Age and Norse settlement) west of Douglas, St Michael's Isle (12th-century chapel and 16th-century fort) at Langness, Mull Hill (a circle of Neolithic burial chambers) near Cregneash, King Orry's Grave at Laxey, 14th-century Monks Bridge at Ballasalla and the well-preserved Neolithic chambered tomb of Cashtal yn Ard near Glen Mona, overlooking the parish of Maughold.

Throughout the Island there are more than 200 decorated stone crosses of the type which have served as grave markers and memorial stones on the Isle of Man since the 5th century. Most of them remain in the churches and the churchyard cross shelters of their parish of origin, but cast copies of all the stones are housed in the Manx Museum in Douglas as a permanent record.

The Isle of Man has two historic castles – one, Peel Castle, a ruin and the other, Castle Rushen in Castletown, in remarkably good state of preservation. See under Peel and Castletown for more information.

Churches & religious heritage

From the cathedral in Peel to the Royal Chapel in St John's, the Isle of Man is richly endowed with many ancient and modern sites to visit, as detailed in the book *Sacred Architecture* available from Lily Publications.

The two most developed and active visitor attractions dedicated to telling the story of the Island's religious heritage are Rushen Abbey in Ballasalla and St Patrick's Isle, which is the site of Peel Castle and the ruins of the original medieval German Cathedral. The history and religious significance of St Patrick's Isle can be accessed via Peel's nearby House of Manannan heritage centre and the Manx Museum in Douglas.

Mining heritage

In the 19th century, the lead mines at

Laxey and Foxdale were highly productive and though the industry ceased in the early 20th century when it was no longer profitable, the Island's rich mining heritage is still very evident. Visitor attractions which reveal much about the Isle of Man's industrial archaeology include the Great Laxey Wheel, the Mines Heritage Trail, the restored surface section of the Laxey Mines Railway and the Snaefell Mine waterwheel. See also under Laxey on page 26.

Fairies, tradition and myth

If the British Isles is considered to be one of the most haunted and supernatural places in the world, then the Isle of Man can probably be thought of as the centre of this supernatural activity. Virtually every square mile of the Island lays claim to its own tales of fairies and other unearthly creatures.

The Isle of Man has a wide and varied folklore tradition but the most famous and well-known aspect of Manx folklore is its fairy belief. Manx fairies, or 'Themselves' as they are called by the Manx, are not the small pretty creatures with gossamer wings illustrated in children's fairy tale books. Instead, Themselves are described as small human-like creatures, often three or four feet in height and dressed in blue or green with red peaked caps, who most definitely do not have wings.

Traditionally they are neither good nor bad and can be quite helpful or spiteful depending on how the mood takes them. They also take offence easily, which is why you should never talk about them directly or call them by name but only use terms such as Themselves or Mooiney Veggey (Manx Gaelic for the Little Folk). Therefore, when crossing the Fairy Bridge on the main Douglas to Castletown road en route to and from the airport, it is always important to be extra polite and say hello to Themselves. It is uncertain how old this tradition actually is, but for several years

St Thomas's, Douglas

Santon church

locals and visitors alike have been very careful to observe it, and many have cautionary tales of what happens when you forget to say hello!

Tradition also has it that Themselves were particularly fond of hunting, feasting and fighting, with pitch battles between different bands of fairies. There are several sites on the Island specifically identified with such fairy activity.

The Fairy Mound in Rushen, next to Rowany golf course, was considered to be the home of one of these fairy bands. A young man walking home late one night was 'took' by Themselves into the Fairy Mound where he witnessed a great fairy banquet. He managed to escape to tell his tale, taking with him a fairy cup as evidence of his adventures. Most are not so lucky and are doomed to stay permanently in the Fairy Kingdom or to escape decades later, Rip Van Winkle style.

Another story of such a rare trophy relates to the Ballafletcher fairy cup given to the Fletcher family by the Lhiannan Shee (the 'peaceful spirit') of Ballafletcher. The Lhiannan Shee promised to protect the family and ensure no harm came to them as long as the cup remained unbroken and stayed within the family. The Fletcher family no longer lives at Ballafletcher, now known as Kirby, but the cup traditionally known as the Ballafletcher Fairy Cup still exists and can be seen on display at the Manx Museum in Douglas.

Fairy Hunts were considered to be a popular pursuit by Themselves, with various popular fairy hunting grounds being found around Douglas. A more physical relic of these nocturnal hunting parties is the 'Saddlestone' on the Saddlestone Road just outside Douglas. Here an apparently nondescript large stone protruding from a field wall is identified as being a saddle magically turned to stone.

The story is that the vicar of the parish

found his horse tired and sweating every morning although it appeared that no one had ridden it. Very early one morning, as he returned home from a late-night visit to a sick parishioner, he saw the reason why his horse was always exhausted. A group of fairies had ridden it all night and were taking the saddle off. When the fairies saw the vicar, they vanished in panic and horror and the saddle, which they had put on the wall, turned to stone! Maybe a more plausible explanation is that the stone was built into the wall to help people to mount their horses at the roadside – but the Fairy Saddlestone is the more popular and favoured version.

Another great fear and concern for the Island's people was that Themselves took human babies and exchanged them for fairy changelings. As a result there were several ways to protect babies from being 'took'. The most powerful form of protection was to have a child baptised as soon as possible. Another was to sew vervain, the potent and powerful Manx herb, into the baby's clothes. If all else failed, it was critical to always put the iron tongs across the cradle if the child had to be left alone for even a moment – iron was considered a great defence against Themselves.

Fairies were believed to be particularly powerful and active at certain times of the year, one of the most dangerous being the end of winter and beginning of summer, May Eve. This was the time when the cattle, who had been kept inside all winter, were put back out on to summer pastures. It was also when cows began to produce milk again. Milk was an important part of the Manx rural economy because of its versatility – used as a drink and for making butter and bonnag (Manx soda bread). So for a subsistence crofting community, the difference between a cow

Christmas on the Millennium Way

producing milk and not producing milk could be the difference between respectable poverty and borderline starvation – and there was understandable anxiety that Themselves could stop the cows from milking or stop the butter from being made by tainting the milk.

Therefore every possible precaution was taken on May Eve when Themselves were abroad. There were two main lines of defence. One was to spread primroses or other yellow flowers such as kingcups (the more powerful and effective Manx blutyn) on doorsteps and thresholds to stop evil spirits from crossing over; and the other was to make and put up over the doorway a crosh cuirn or rowan/mountain ash cross. The small crosh cuirn was made from two rowan twigs formed into a cross shape and tied together with a length of handtwisted sheep's wool.

175

Viking Festival at Peel

To make sure the cross was effective as a protective charm, no iron could be used in making it. So the twigs had to be broken by hand and not cut with a knife. To be extra sure of protection, the crosh cuirns were put up over the entrance to the cowshed and even tied to the cows' tails. People may not be so concerned now about protecting their cows from Themselves but many people on the Island still put up crosh cuirns on May Eve. When visiting Cregneash Village Folk Museum, have a look inside the doorway of Harry Kelly's cottage and see a crosh cuirn already positioned to do its work!

The Isle of Man has more than one type of fairy. A solitary and hardworking but potentially bad-tempered Manx fairy is the Phynodderree – a large hairy shaggy house elf. The Phynodderree is renowned for being a good worker and helper to any Manx farmer lucky enough to have one. The only problem is that if the Phynodderree is offered a new set of clothes by a farmer as thanks and payment for all his hard work, he will be mortally offended by the gift and instantly disappear.

Another potential problem is that sometimes he takes his work far too seriously. Visitors to the Island can see the mountain railway climbing to the top of Snaefell, but folklore tells of something far more alarming rushing around the mountain top. The Phynodderree was rounding up a flock of Manx Loaghtan sheep and, having easily caught 99 of them, proceeded to spend the rest of the long night on the slopes looking for the missing one. It took several hours but he finally made it, placing the last small Loaghtan back in the pen with the rest of the flock. Proud that he now had them all, the poor Phynodderree was dismayed to discover from the farmer that he only had 99 sheep and he had spent several hours trying to catch a mountain hare!

Not all Manx fairies are so hardworking or even mischievous, and one stands out as the most dangerous and terrifying of all – the buggane. This is the evil hobgoblin of the Manx fairy kingdom. Although there are various tales of bugganes around the Island, the most famous is that associated with the roofless church of St Trinian's on the main road between Douglas and Peel.

The tale is told that several attempts were made to complete the church but that each time it neared the final stage, the buggane would appear and tear off the roof. As the fearsome reputation of the buggane grew and a new roof was put on the church, a bet was made by the local tailor, Timothy, that he would stay in the church and make a pair of trousers regardless of what the buggane may or may not do.

As the tailor sewed, the buggane slowly emerged up through the church floor, uttering fearsome oaths. Undaunted, Timothy ignored the buggane's threats and only when the last stitch was sewn did he flee from the church. The buggane tore the roof off, leaving the ruin you can see today, and chased the tailor all the way to St Ruinius (Old Marown) Church, where Timothy dived over the churchyard wall for safety. In his fury at being outsmarted, the buggane tore off his own head and threw it in vain at the tailor. Although the tailor was safe and the tale has a happy ending, St Trinian's Church is still roofless.

In addition to fairies and hobgoblins, the Island has its own Black Dog – the Moddey Dhoo of Peel Castle. This is one of the oldest folk tales on the Isle of Man and was first published in 1732. The tale though is said to be older still and relates to a period in the 1600s when Peel Castle was a fortress with its own garrison of soldiers.

By all accounts, the soldiers on night guard duty had become accustomed to the fact that they were not alone and that they shared their guardroom with a spectral hound. One of them, under the influence of too much drink, announced that he was not afraid of the black dog. So when the castle keys needed to be returned to the Captain of the Guard, he was happy to do it on his own although his friends warned him strongly against it. Off he went, alone, followed by the Moddey Dhoo, which had left its usual resting place by the fireside.

Shortly afterwards, the guard's screams were heard echoing through the castle. Although he lived for three more days, the guard could not utter a single word or in any way describe what had frightened him, and the Moddey Dhoo was never seen again in Peel Castle.

Castle Rushen too has its supernatural side. There are stories of miles of underground passages, chambers and even magnificent mansions. The entrance to this mysterious underworld was apparently sealed up because all those who ventured down into the tunnels never returned, except for one brave soul who took the precaution of leaving behind him a trail of thread to lead him back out. This intrepid explorer, although courageous enough to travel through the underground passages, couldn't quite conjure up the nerve to enter the last mansion, where a great giant was asleep on a massive table.

After making his retreat he was informed that his act of discretion rather than bravery had saved him – and so he lived to tell his tale.

Manx folklore can be witnessed as a living tradition, both on Tynwald Day (Old Midsummer's Day, July 5th) at St John's and when White Boys perform the traditional Christmas mummers' play around the streets of Peel.

Tynwald Day is the Island's national day, when the Manx parliament holds an annual open-air sitting on Tynwald Hill for the reading aloud of all new laws. Part of this tradition is that rushes are strewn along the processional way as a symbolic tribute to Manannan, the mythical sea god and shape-shifting magician, who thanks to 21st-century technology is brought vividly to life in the House of Manannan heritage centre in Peel.

Christmas of course has its own special magic, and a variety of Manx festive customs are still practised. Traditionally, Christmas on the Isle of Man was never a single day's celebrations but rather 12 whole days (and nights) of festivities and merrymaking and was appropriately called 'Foolish Fortnight' (or Y Kegeesh Ommydagh in Manx).

The Christmas period would begin on Christmas Eve with the Oie'l Voirrey service, held in local parish churches decorated with seasonal hibbin as hullin (festoons of ivy and large branches of holly). After a short service, the clergymen would leave and the Oie'l Voirrey would begin in earnest with the singing of carvals (Manx carols) late into the night or early hours of the morning. Surprisingly, although written and sung at Christmas most of the carvals are not about Christmas or the Nativity but about less seasonal themes such as sin and repentance, a particularly notorious one being the Carval ny Drogh Vraane or 'Carval about evil women'!

The Manx carvals were especially long, 20 to 40 verses at least, and frequently the singing was not considered to be entertaining enough. As a result the parish clerk would act as Master of Ceremonies and try to ensure that the proceedings were not too unruly or riotous and that a certain degree of decorum was maintained. The young girls would go specially prepared with dried peas to fire at the bachelors. Pig tails would be routinely pulled and barracking of the singer would be considered standard practice. The parish clerk was also responsible for choosing who would sing and as a result would be strenuously lobbied by those wanting to sing their own carval. The clerk also had to ensure that no one sang for too long. So each singer was given a rush light (rush dipped in tallow), seemingly to provide light to sing by but also acting as a time limit. The service would carry on late into the night and it was not unknown for revellers to end up singing in the streets or along country lanes to greet the new dawn. Some would stop off at the public house for a traditional drink of hot ale flavoured with spices, ginger and pepper to prepare themselves for a long walk home.

Another essential part of a Manx Christmas was, and still is, the White Boys, who perform a mummers' play about St George and his battle with a series of saints – a greatly modified version of St George and the dragon. The characters wear white 'dresses' bedecked with all manner of ribbons, coloured papers, tinsel and matching tall cardboard hats, whilst the 'doctor' – who miraculously cures the dragon killed by St George – is dressed all in black. The 'doctor' collects contributions from the audience and also

Fairy Bridge

berates (and beats) them with an inflated pig's bladder on a stick if they approach too closely to the 'stage'.

The highlight of St Stephen's Day (otherwise known as Boxing Day) has for generations been Hunt the Wren, a very old custom once widespread throughout the British Isles, though its origins are unknown. The Manx ritual is one of many variations on the theme found throughout Europe and past antiquarians have attempted to trace its roots and symbolic meanings back to prehistoric times.

It was once a bloodthirsty ritual, gangs of youths scouring the countryside in search of a defenceless wren to trap and kill. Today an artificial bird is used. The wren became the centrepiece for a 'bush' – two wooden hoops set at right angles and placed on top of a pole and covered with ribbons and evergreens – carried from house to house in the hope that the singing of the Hunt the Wren song would be rewarded with money or treats. The song charts the demise of the poor wren as it is hunted, caught, cooked and eaten.

There are many suggestions as to why the wren should be singled out for such treatment. Some say it commemorates the martyrdom of St Stephen, others that the bird is the reincarnation of an enchantress who lured men to their death by drowning. The feathers of the wren are distributed amongst the 'wren' boys as a good luck charm, being particularly potent against witchcraft and to prevent a shipwreck (an important concern for Manx fishermen). The 'wren' is still 'hunted' every year by groups with a wren bush performing the traditional song and dance on St Stephen's morning.

The highlight of New Year's Eve on the Isle of Man is the Quaaltagh, a new year greeting similar to the Scottish First Footing, when groups of young men wander from house to house to bring good luck to each fortunate (or possibly unfortunate) household. To ensure good

Isle of Man Motor Museum

luck the first person to cross the threshold after midnight should preferably be a dark-haired man bearing a small gift or token, and woe betide anyone whose first visitor is a red-headed splay-footed woman!

Several of the traditional New Year's Eve rituals related to much more sober concerns, such as trying to discover who in the family might die during the coming year. For each member of the household a thimble of salt was laid out on a plate, or an ivy leaf put into water; if overnight a pile of salt had collapsed or a leaf withered, it was bad news for that unlucky individual.

Similarly, ashes from the fire would be raked over the floor last thing at night and in the morning checked carefully for any trace of fairy footprints. The direction of the footprints was critical; toes to the door would indicate someone would die, but heel to the door and the family could expect a new addition during the year. Extra care then needed to be exercised in sweeping the floor so that everything went into the chiollagh (hearth) and the good luck wasn't accidentally brushed out of the house for the year.

Then there was the notion that on New Year's Day nothing could be lent, otherwise the lender would be doomed to lend all year. So, fearful of this, even if the fire itself went out in the hearth no one would lend either a flint or a burning turf (peat) to make a new fire.

The Isle of Man's rich and colourful folklore heritage is not just part of the Manx people's past but also their present and future. Maybe you don't normally believe in fairies – but on the Isle of Man it is better to be safe than sorry and to say hello to Themselves as you cross that bridge, just in case!

Museums & art galleries

A.R.E. Motorcycle Collection. The Old Vicarage, Main Road, Kirk Michael, IM6 2HD. A collection of over 100 vintage motorcycles, held in a private collection. Open on Sunday afternoons 2pm – 5pm from Easter to September, and during the TT on non-race days from 10am–5pm.

Also open for parties throughout the year. Email tonyeastare@gmailcom or phone 07624474074 for more details.

Erin Arts Centre, Port Erin. Regular exhibitions are held at this important venue for the visual and performing arts. Each June the Mananan Festival is held in the last week of the month.

Grove Museum of Victorian Life, Ramsey. A Victorian time capsule of fine period furnishings in an elegant country house set in lovely gardens. A Manx National Heritage attraction.

House of Manannan, Peel. See Manannan and hear his own gripping story of how the early Manx Celts and Viking settlers shaped the Island's history. This interactive heritage centre uses audio, video and state-of-the-art display techniques to inform and entertain. A Manx National Heritage attraction.

i-Museum. Located in Douglas the i-museum is the repository for the Isle of Man's National Heritage collections. To complement the i-museum building, the digital collections website allows access to the Island's national archives, library and museum services. An important resource for historians, family historians, residents and visitors alike, the website brings the Island's history into your own home. www.imuseum.im.

Jurby Transport Museum. Created by the Manx Transport Trust on the redeveloping Jurby airfield, the museum opened at Easter 2010 and is dedicated to the Island's road transport heritage, particularly buses. The Trust's aim is to salvage, preserve and display as many vehicles as possible, and visitors will be able to see old buses and the like being restored on site.

Isle of Man Motor Museum. The Isle of Man Motor Museum is the home of the Cunningham Classic Car Collection. Concentrating on rare and unique models from all over the world, and from all eras, the collection boasts cars as well as commercial vehicles, one-offs and prototypes. The museum aims to keep things fresh by rotating exhibits on loan to complement the permanent collection.

Set in an exhibition space of over 70,000 sq. ft the ground floor displays a large number of vehicles, with motorcycles being housed on a mezzanine floor. Facilities include a gift shop, refreshment area, toilets, and a car club display area. There is full disabled access throughout.
www.isleofmanmotormuseum.com

Manx heritage

Moore's Traditional Curers, Peel

Kipper Factory & Museum, Peel. See a working demonstration of how herring are prepared and oak-smoked to produce delicious Manx kippers – a tradition dating back to 1770.

Leece Museum, Peel. The story of Peel as revealed in a unique collection of old photographs.

Manx Aviation Museum. Located next to Ronaldsway Airport, the museum records Manx wartime and civil aviation history.

Manx Museum & Art Gallery, Douglas. The excellent award-winning museum presents 10,000 years of the Island's history through a vast collection of artefacts. The art gallery is dedicated to works either featuring the Isle of Man or created by Manx artists. The museum shop displays many books and souvenirs, including jewellery fashioned in the style of Manxman Archibald Knox.

Manx Transport Museum, Peel. Located in the office of the former brickworks on a site now used by Peel power station, this is the Isle of Man's smallest museum – about 60 square metres in all. It houses artefacts representing all forms of Manx transport, including a P50 – the world's smallest road-legal car, made in Peel in 1964 – and features historical movie clips, photos and collectibles.

Museum of the Manx Regiment. Delve into the Isle of Man's military history at this museum in Tromode, near Douglas.

National Folk Museum, Cregneash. This authentic village of thatched whitewashed cottages, a popular film location, still uses traditional farming methods and shows how 19th-century Manx crofters lived and worked. It is also the home of the fascinating Harry Kelly's Cottage. Britain's first ever open-air museum.

Nautical Museum, Castletown. This small museum is dedicated to the amazing story of Peggy – an historic 18th-century vessel involved in local smuggling but walled up in her boathouse and undiscovered for a hundred years. The National Maritime Museum in Greenwich has listed this vessel as a ship of historic significance, meriting preservation.

The Old Grammar School, Castletown. Built as a chapel in about 1200, this small whitewashed building changed its role many times over the centuries. It was used as a school from 1570 and is best known for the Academic School – the forerunner of King William's College – and the Grammar School, which closed in 1930. Now restored, it is a Manx National Heritage attraction.

The Old House of Keys, Castletown. This restored 1820 building was once the assembly and debating chamber for part of the Manx Parliament. It gives an insight into the Island's unique political heritage and is a Manx National Heritage attraction.

Railway Museum, Port Erin. This small museum of railway memorabilia is located in the station building. Port Erin is the southern terminus of the Isle of Man Steam Railway.

Sayle Gallery & Arcade, Douglas. Named in memory of popular Manx artist Norman Sayle (1926–2007), the gallery is located within the Villa Marina & Gaiety Theatre Complex.

Douglas Railway Station

ACTIVITIES

All aboard!

One of the great joys of exploring the Isle of Man – particularly for children and families – is to experience the extraordinary network of Victorian railways and trams which is still so vital to the Island's public transport system.

You can travel all the way from Port Erin in the south-west to Ramsey in the north-east – a journey of about 33 miles – by a combination of steam and electric railways which meet roughly halfway at Douglas. You also have the option to stop off en route at Laxey and take the 5-mile electric mountain railway to the top of Snaefell. Not forgetting a 2-mile canter along Douglas promenade by horse-drawn tram!

It was the tourist boom of the latter half of the 19th century which inspired the creation of this surviving rail network, which is now well into its second century of operation and, amazingly, still using much of the original equipment, rolling stock and motive power.

At one time both Douglas and Ramsey were connected by rail to Peel on the west coast, as described in the walks section of this guide. For more information about railways and trams, see their individual headings (electric railway, horse-drawn trams, mountain railway and steam railway) and the separate chapter on heritage railways.

The Isle of Man's public transport system is not served exclusively by rail, of course. In fact, there are many more parts of the Island accessible by bus than there are by train or tram.

Electric railway

The Manx Electric Railway runs for almost 18 miles between Douglas and Ramsey, much of the route enjoying magnificent views along the east coast. At Laxey, roughly midway, you can transfer to the Snaefell Mountain Railway.

In operation since 1893, the Manx Electric Railway has the two oldest working tramcars in the world. With a 3-feet gauge double track, it is also the longest vintage narrow-gauge line in the British Isles.

A journey from Douglas to Ramsey and the sights and places of interest en route are described in the chapter Heritage Railways.

Horse trams

Horsepower has been keeping trams on the move along Douglas promenade since 1876. The horses were specially bred for the task and their working conditions are enviable: a two-hour shift per day in the summer season (with the rest of the year off to enjoy the grazing) and a Douglas Corporation pension scheme which on retirement guaranteed permanent residence and good care at the Home of Rest for Old Horses. The home, located at Richmond Hill on the Douglas–Castletown bus route, also welcomes families and children and has facilities for the disabled and ample car parking.

Offering a late March to early November service, the route runs for nearly 1.6 miles between the Derby Castle depot at one end of the promenade to the Villa Marina.

Miniature railways

Unlike the Island's other railways, the Groudle Glen and the Orchid Line were created purely as leisure attractions and are not part of the public transport system.

Lovingly restored to its former glory by the volunteers and supporters who run it, the Groudle Glen Railway is a marvellous little reminder of the feats achieved by Britain's great railway builders. The 2-feet gauge line just to the north of Douglas climbs up out of the glen's lower reaches and winds along the very edge of the hillside through trees, gorse, bracken and heather to the cliff-top terminus – a distance of about three-quarters of a mile. The views are fabulous. The railway celebrated its centenary in 1996, and the meticulously-restored carriages are still pulled by Sea Lion – the original 1896 steam engine. Opening hours are limited to certain times in summer and at Christmas

Manx Electric Railway

Horse tram at Douglas

only – you'll need to check with the Welcome Centre in Douglas.

On a smaller scale still – and great fun for children of all ages – is the Orchid Line in Curraghs Wildlife Park. The track gauge is just three and a half inches, making this one of the tiniest passenger-carrying railways anywhere in the world.

Mountain railway

Completed in 1895, the Snaefell Mountain Railway is the only electric mountain railway in the British Isles. The distance from base camp (Laxey station) to the summit (or more precisely, to within 46 feet of the summit) is almost 5 miles, up gradients as steep as 1 in 12, and the gauge of the track is three feet six inches.

The leisurely ascent up the side of Laxey Glen is slow and gradual, with changing views of Robert Casement's huge water-pump wheel Lady Isabella. The double line crosses the TT course at the Bungalow station and embarks on the long, final climb to more than 2,000 feet above sea level.

Journey's end is marked by the licensed Summit Café – as revitalising as the mountain air and amazing views. On a clear day you can see the Island spreading below you in all directions and, beyond, England, Scotland, Ireland and Wales.

The construction of the Snaefell Mountain Railway took just seven months. The task was aided by the steam locomotive Caledonia, which was despatched by sea from Ramsey to Laxey harbour and then moved on baulks and rollers through the village to Laxey station. The track width of three and a half feet for the new mountain railway had been chosen to accommodate a central Fell rail – a braking device for the electric tramcars when descending steep gradients. However, the much heavier

Caledonia was not equipped with the caliper brakes needed to grip the rail and so had to steam up and down the mountain in its somewhat hazardous daily work, dependent entirely on the hand and steam brakes.

The effort and vision required to build the Snaefell Mountain Railway has been rewarded many times over – as anyone who has ever travelled on it will tell you.

Steam railway

The sense of wonder evoked by the sight of a living, hissing, fire-eating steam locomotive is timeless and hypnotic – as you can discover simply by standing on the station platform in Douglas or Port Erin and enjoying the magic of the Isle of Man Steam Railway.

The unique cocktail of sights, sounds and smells is as exciting to today's kids as it has been to generations before them. Thomas and the Magic Railroad was filmed on the Island – and you could say that the title and the location were made for each other.

Opened in 1874, this is the oldest of the Isle of Man's surviving railways and the longest narrow-gauge (3-feet) steam line in the British Isles. The restored Beyer-Peacock 2-4-0 locomotives date back to this time. But far from nearing the end of the line, the railway has been granted a new lease of life since the turn of the millennium and is enjoying all the benefits of the largest reinvestment in renewal, improvement and maintenance since the railway was built.

In July and August, the peak months of the holiday season, there are seven return trains a day, each leisurely one-way journey snaking through some of the Island's prettiest countryside in about an hour. The station at Port Erin has a café and a museum of railway memorabilia. The Douglas terminus also has a café.

Get active
Adventure parks

Ape Mann is an adventure park suitable for both children and adults (from the age of 5 years), located in the South Barrule Plantation. Walk through the trees on rope courses, compete with pedal go-karts or climb a tree up to 12 metres high – just some of the activities on offer to make the most of the great outdoors.
www.apemann.info

Bowls

Bowling of all kinds is very well catered for, including annual festivals. There are venues in Douglas (crown green), Onchan Park (crown and flat green), the National Sports Centre (indoor flat green and short mat), and crown greens in Port Erin, Port St Mary, Castletown, Peel and Ramsey.

Bowling

Head down to Ramsey seafront and you'll find Pepsi Max Bowl. With 10 lanes, pool tables, table tennis, air hockey and a soft play area for the little ones it's a great way to spend some quality indoor time. See the section on Ramsey for more information.

Cycling & mountain biking

From family groups to committed cyclists and mountain bikers, the Isle of Man's beautiful coast, countryside and varied terrain are a sheer delight for everyone on two wheels.

Mountain biking is the perfect way to see the Island, and whether you want to stick to the natural trails or mix it up with a bit of road cycling you are certain to see sights that others rarely do. Mountain Biking on the Isle of Man details twenty routes that will guide you around, published by Lily Publications.

Diving

Based at Port St Mary, Isle of Man Diving Holidays promise you some of the best diving in the British Isles – a combination of great natural beauty, diverse marine life and a fascinating variety of wrecks. The weekly and long-weekend packages include 4-star accommodation, and a wide choice of courses is available.

Experienced divers making their own arrangements to visit the Isle of Man should note that many of the wrecks are protected by the wreck laws and some are owned by local people or sub-aqua clubs and should not be dived without permission.

Festivals of sport

The Isle of Man's action-packed calendar of annual events is never short of exciting sporting festivals and tournaments (as well as less serious competitive events such as tin bath and Viking longship racing) and typically includes yacht racing, soccer, rugby, table tennis, walking, marathon and fell running, darts, motorsport, motorcycle racing, angling, hockey, crown green and flat green bowling, drag racing and street kart racing.

Fishing

No wonder anglers are hooked on the Isle of Man: two annual festivals, more than 20 great locations for sea angling (conger eel, wrasse, ray, tope, cod and mackerel), a dozen rivers and streams (rainbow and brown trout and migratory sea trout and salmon), and five reservoirs (rainbow and brown trout). Rivers and reservoirs, good until the end of September and October respectively, require licences but these are widely available on the Island. Late summer and autumn are the ideal time to land salmon and sea trout.

A challenge for experienced sea anglers is the Point of Ayre, where fast-flowing tides and the Gulf Stream call for every ounce of strength and concentration, though the rewards can be fabulous. For details of boat hire and offshore fishing grounds, contact the Welcome Centre in Douglas.

Geocaching

A treasure hunt by any other name, geocaching is still a popular outdoor pursuit, and what better way to get to know the countryside? Armed with a GPS device or a GPS-enabled mobile phone, visit the official geocaching site to get started on your hunt, locating hidden items around the Island, and enjoy a great day out. www.geocaching.com

Golf

The Isle of Man is something of a golfers' paradise. In a week you can play all nine courses, particularly as each is open to visiting players, and the game is very much part of the Manx way of life. Queues are rarely a problem here and the mild climate makes it a year-round sport. The links course at Castletown was used for the 1979 PGA cup matches against the USA. It was laid out by golfing legend Mackenzie Ross in the late 1920s and early 1930s and provides some of the best links golf anywhere in the British Isles. The infamous 17th calls for a 185-yard drive across a gaping sea gully. King Edward

Steam Railway

Bay at Onchan has magnificent views across Douglas Bay, although the 6th tee at Port St Mary (the Island's only 9-hole course, designed by 1920 British Open Champion George Duncan) boasts one of the finest views of all.

Health, Beauty & Fitness

If you want to address mind, body and spirit, and engage in personal luxuries which hectic lifestyles too often forbid, the Isle of Man is the perfect place to indulge yourself. Opportunities include beauty salons, stylists, well-equipped venues such as the National Sports Centre and Mount Murray's total Fitness Club. A new experience for many people awaits you at Brightlife – a leading centre for holistic learning, stress therapy, yoga, reflexology and other aspects of personal care and development.

Kayaking

A sea kayak is unbeatable for exploring the Island's coastline and taking you into otherwise inaccessible coves and bays and close to grey seals, dolphins, basking sharks and other marine wildlife. Tuition is available from Adventurous Experiences and the Venture Centre.

National Sports Centre

This is the flagship of the Island's sports and leisure facilities, incorporating a first-class water sports complex. You can make quite a splash here: as well as the 25-metre competition pool, there are leisure pools and fun features such as bubble tub, flow pool, jets and geysers, water cannon, mushroom sprays and a toddlers' slide.

There's also a fitness zone and health suite, a 5-rink indoor flat green bowling hall, a secondary sports hall, 6 competition-standard squash courts, an athletics stadium and Astroturf pitch, and a licensed café.

Other sports and leisure facilities can be found at two large municipal parks and at Onchan Park & Stadium.

Noble's Park in Douglas has tennis courts, bowling greens, BMX track and skate park and a children's play area, while Mooragh Park in Ramsey is best known for its 12-acre boating lake – ideal for beginners to learn the ropes in canoeing and sailing – and also has a bowling green, minigolf, tennis courts, BMX track and children's playground. Onchan Park, just north of Douglas, has tennis courts, a bowling green, pitch'n'putt and a children's playground.

Outdoor pursuits and Extreme sports

There's probably no better way to appreciate the Isle of Man's natural attributes than through its great outdoors. Maughold's multi-activity Venture Centre on the north-east coast offers an impressive range of activities and professional tuition starting, alphabetically speaking, with abseiling, archery and the assault course and going right through to raft building, rock climbing and supervised activity days for children – with lots more in between. The Island's other dedicated centre for outdoor pursuits and extreme sports is Adventurous Experiences, specialising in sea kayaking and offering British Canoe Union courses for absolute beginners and upwards. Other activities include coasteering.

If climbing's your thing, HotRocks in Douglas houses an indoor climbing wall!

Pony trekking & riding

Whether you're new to the saddle or an experienced rider, seeing the world from horseback gives you a unique perspective. Isle of Man establishments such as GGH

Peel Castle

Equestrian Centre and Ballahimmin Riding and Pony Trekking Centre cater for all abilities and take you from the quiet lanes of Manx coast and countryside to the Island's more challenging and expansive open moorlands and high hills. Horse riding establishments can be found on the government's website (www.gov.im) under leisure and entertainment.

Quad biking and Trikes

Quad Bike Trail Rides at Ballacraine Farm (01624 801219) are a fabulous and fun way to enjoy the great outdoors. Full instruction and protective clothing are all part of the deal.

IOM Trike tours can also take you around the island on three wheels, including a tour of the TT circuit. www.iomtriketours.com

Sailing & water sports

One of the big attractions for sailing enthusiasts is the Isle of Man's varied conditions – the relative calm of Ramsey and Douglas bays for novices, and the more rugged north and south coasts for those sailors who relish a challenge and the chance to put their experience to the test.

Cruising, racing and dinghy sailing are all very popular and the Island has six sailing clubs. Port St Mary is home to the Isle of Man Yacht Club and is the main sailing centre. The star event of the sailing calendar is the Round the Island Yacht Race, supported by numerous competitions throughout the year.

The abundance of safe harbours also makes the Isle of Man a regular stopping-off point for vessels crossing the Irish Sea. Harbours information and telephone numbers are included at the back of this guide.

As for water sports, surfing in Gansey Bay is really taking off in a big way and Derbyhaven on the Langness peninsula is an ideal spot for windsurfing.

Taste of the Sea – Round the Island Yacht Race

Held every year in early May by the Manx Sailing and Cruising Club (www.msandcc.org), this annual race sees competitors racing anti-clockwise around the Isle of Man. Currently sponsored by OMA Fund & Investment Management Ltd, the race sets off from Ramsey, with a number of trophies to be won in numerous classes. The most prestigious trophy being the Coronation Cup, first awarded in 1953.

With a full social calendar to complement the race, this festival to shows that not all excitement is attached to two wheels!

Walking

If you really want to discover the Isle of Man, on foot is the perfect way to do it. If you want to go it alone Lily Publications has a number of books available to help you find you way, ranging from a walker's guide to the Isle of Man to short walks, Other books include favourite walks, hill walks, glen walks and holiday walks. For more information on out titles: www.lilypublications.co.uk

Go-Mann Adventures

Based in Port Erin, Go-Mann Adventures arranges guided walks and tours throughout the Island. With half-day and short-day walks or full-day hikes for varying levels of fitness there will be an adventure to suit everyone. You can also brush up on your outdoor skills, map reading and navigation. Booking is essential, and a full calendar of events is available on their website go-mannadventures.com tel: 07624 480129

The Isle of Man Walking Festival

The Isle of Man Walking Festival was introduced in 2004 and was so successful that it celebrated its 10th anniversary in 2014. Each year the Isle of Man Walking Festival is due to place in the early summer. The festival brings together walkers to indulge in the great outdoors and take advantage of the Island's breathtaking scenery. Covering a wide range of abilities, experienced guides will lead you along the routes while providing interesting information about the areas visited, which are some of the Island's best kept secrets.

The festival programme is available on request from the Isle of Man Tourist Board (www.visitisleofman.com) or online at issuu.com/visitisleofman.

Phone 01624 664460 for more information

The Parish Walk

If endurance walking is more your thing, whether participating or cheering along those taking part, then the Manx Telecom Parish Walk is for you. Competing along the 85-mile Parish Walk course in the space of 24 hours each June, race walkers from all around the world must reach check points at each of the Island's parish churches to complete the course. Over the years, and the race recently celebrated its centenary, times have been steadily eroded to find the latest race winners stepping over the line in magnificent times of less than 15 hours.

With a number of classes available, entrants must be 21 years of age and over on the day of the walk, with a junior race being available for 18–21 year olds, at a distance of 32.5 miles. Further information is available from www.parishwalk.com.

Motorsports
TT racing: how four wheels became two

The world's only surviving motorsport event to be run on a long circuit of public roads, Isle of Man TT racing celebrated a remarkable centenary in June 2007 as fans, spectators and competitors from the world over converged on the famous Mountain Course to savour the high excitement and party atmosphere of TT Festival Fortnight.

At 37.73 miles per lap, this legendary circuit is still acknowledged as the ultimate test of rider skill and machine durability. For many competitors it is the fulfilment of a lifetime's ambition to race on it, while for others it is simply being here that matters. Whatever their motivation, to compete on the gruelling course requires absolute concentration, an almost photographic memory of the circuit, and the ability for riders to become one with their machines.

Men such as Stanley Woods, Geoff Duke, Mike Hailwood, John Surtees, Steve Hislop and Joey Dunlop are among the legends who have tasted TT success, and anyone who competes in either the TT itself or the amateur Grand Prix races has to be just that little bit special and, as some would say, just that little bit crazy.

To watch the racing costs nothing, as there's no ticket to buy or admission to pay. Regular spectators tend to have their own favourite vantage points, the best being those that enable you to move around during the races, and all the festival action is supplemented by entertainment such as vintage and custom bike shows, sprint racing, extreme stunt riding and displays by the Red Arrows aerobatic team.

To trace the beginnings of Manx TT racing, you have to go back to the last

TT Races at the Ginger Hall

years of the 19th century and a wealthy American living in Paris. James Gordon Bennett, son of the owner of the New York Herald, had gone to the French capital to establish a continental edition of the newspaper. He quickly embraced the European way of life and particularly the passion for automobiles.

The French were already elevating the status of the horseless carriage to something far more exciting than a rich man's toy. In the summer of 1895 they staged a road race from Paris to Bordeaux and back to Paris – a distance of 727 miles. It was the first of several such contests in that decade, and Bennett wanted a piece of the action, not least to promote this thrilling new sport to his fellow countrymen back home.

In 1900 he instituted his first competitive event – the Gordon Bennett Cup Race, open to countries which had national automobile clubs. His sponsorship over the next 5-year period was to play a significant role in the development of international motor racing.

In Britain, a speed limit of 14 mph meant that such foolhardiness on public highways was a non-starter, and the Automobile Club of Great Britain and Ireland cast envious eyes across the Channel to the achievements of their continental cousins and the emerging superiority of their cars and drivers.

Undaunted, the great English racing driver and motoring entrepreneur S.F. Edge, representing Ireland, drove his much-improved Napier to victory in the 1902 race – the only starter to complete the 351-mile Paris–Innsbruck course. As it was down to the winning nation to host the following year's event, the Emerald Isle seized the opportunity and passed new legislation to permit racing on public roads.

The 1903 race duly took place in County Kildare, over a distance of 327 miles, and was won by the German driver Jenatzy. Despite the failure of the British team, and the prohibitive speed limit (by now increased to 20 mph), interest in the sport in Britain was very much on the up. For the sake of national pride and the

Gaiety Theatre

future development of the British automobile industry, one man believed he could redress the balance. Julian Orde, cousin of Lord Raglan and later to be knighted, had an ace up his sleeve. That ace was Raglan himself – Governor of the Isle of Man.

Orde reasoned correctly that this small island nation, with its own parliament and a fledgling tourist industry, was ideally placed to host the eliminating trials to decide the British entries for the 1904 and 1905 Cup races. To permit such road racing on the Isle of Man, Tynwald passed the Road Closure Act, which remains in force to this day.

On 10th May 1904, the Gordon Bennett Cup Eliminating Trials began on the Island and paved the way for a long tradition of Manx motor car and motorcycle racing. The teams competed in three separate events – a hill climb, speed trials on Douglas promenade, and a high-speed reliability trial over five laps of a 51-mile course.

This automobile spectacular was a great success and repeated a year later for the 1905 eliminating trials. But this was to be the last of the Gordon Bennett Cup Races, and the Automobile Club of Great Britain and Ireland (forerunner of the RAC) decided to fill the void by introducing its own Tourist Trophy races to aid development of touring cars for the benefit of ordinary motorists.

It was also in 1905 that the Auto Cycle Club (later to become the Auto Cycle Union) held eliminating trials on the Isle of Man for the International Cup event in France. This race event too was short lived and so the Club followed the lead of the cars and in 1907 launched its own Tourist Trophy motorcycle races. The winner's trophy – a silver statuette of Mercury poised on a winged wheel – is the same in every detail as the trophy awarded today to the winning rider in the Senior TT Race. In 2013 this was John McGuinness – his 20th TT victory overall and his 6th Senior. McGuinness also holds the lap record for the fastest person around the TT course for the longest period of time.

Who in 1907 could have believed that this pioneering event would not only go on to achieve global cult status, but also endure for more than a century?

Manx road racing and motorsport

◆ The winners of the first TT motorcycle races (1907) averaged under 40 mph. The current lap record is more than 131 mph, with the biggest bikes hitting 200 mph on the straights.

◆ The TT circuit is known as the Mountain Course and on each lap (37.73 miles) riders have to negotiate towns, villages, railway tracks, river bridges, hairpin bends and more than 220 corners.

◆ The Prep-TT Classic and TT Festival Fortnight kick-start a whole series of summer motorsport events on the Isle of Man.

◆ The Isle of Man Festival of Motorcycling: a motorcycle event for amateur riders keen to experience and master the difficult Mountain Course. The festival features the Manx Grand Prix Races, Classic TT, Two-Day off-road trials, Festival of Jurby and the Vintage Motor Cycle Club Rally. It is held in late summer.

◆ Manx National Two-Day Trial: the biggest event of its kind in Britain, staged in some of the Island's remotest places. Around 300 competitors test their ability to control a motorcycle on the most extreme terrain, including rocks, gullies and slithery mud.

◆ Southern 100 series: motorcycle racing on the 4.25-mile Billown road

TT Races 2022

circuit near Castletown. Usually held in July, and sponsored by the Isle of Man Steam Packet Company.

◆ Manx motorsport also includes motorcycle meetings at Jurby airfield and Jurby South road circuit, motocross, beach cross, long-distance Enduros off-road motorcycle competitions, car rallies (Rally Isle of Man, RBS International Manx Rally and the Manx Classic), karting at Jurby airfield and the Peel Kart Racing Grand Prix, and summer stock car racing on the 400-yard oval stadium track at Onchan Raceway – the Island's smallest motor racing circuit.

Entertainment

One of the Isle of Man's proudest boasts is the magnificently-restored **Gaiety Theatre** – a wonderful example from the age when family entertainment was one of the highlights of a great British seaside holiday. Painstakingly restored over a 10-year period, and a listed building since 2002, the Gaiety Theatre on Douglas seafront is a magnificent example of the work of Frank Matcham (1854–1920) – one of Britain's most revered Victorian theatre architects. The Gaiety is also very popular for its fascinating tours, taking you behind the scenes to the Edwardian era.

Nearby is the seafront **Villa Marina** – a thoroughly modern venue for live music, comedy and dance, and home to the Sayle Gallery.

Villa Marina & Gaiety Theatre Complex. Tickets 01624 600555. For information and what's on: www.villagaiety.com

Erin Arts Centre in Port Erin is another important and long-established Manx venue for the performing arts, regularly hosting major international festivals of music and song. And don't miss Peel's lively Centenary Centre.

FOOD & DRINK

Island hospitality

Over the centuries, the Manx population has depended heavily on the land and sea to put food on the table. Farming and fishing were the traditional staple industries. But in a changing world which even touches these independent shores, finance and insurance now top the economic menu as the Island's main breadwinners.

This shift in fortunes means that today eating out on the Isle of Man promises more choice than ever before – a veritable feast of taste sensations. Now you can enjoy the best of fresh local produce, dishes and seafood alongside a banquet of popular international cuisine.

Although agriculture has slipped overall in the Island's income rankings, farming is still very healthy. There are around 450 commercial farms. Their meats, dairy products and cereals are much in demand, both on and off island, and flower exports are blooming.

The quality of Manx beef and pork is exceptional and consistent. But the biggest success story is the native breed of Loaghtan lamb. Awarded the prestigious and coveted EU Protected Designation of Origin status, the dark meat has a distinctive flavour and significantly less fat and cholesterol than conventional lamb.

The long tradition of cheese-making on the Island dates back to the Viking era. The variety of mature full-flavoured cheddars includes oak-smoked and black peppercorn and you can now buy them off island at many UK supermarkets, particularly in the festive season.

The Manx sea fisheries fleet is now less than a hundred strong, about half of which are smaller part-time vessels. Quota restrictions mean that the catch is focused mainly on shellfish, and the Island's twelve-mile territorial waters are patrolled by a fisheries boat.

Most of the shellfish is processed on the Island prior to export, but fresh crab, lobster, scallops and fish are served up daily in many Isle of Man restaurants. There are two varieties of scallop – small but delicious queenies in summer and larger king scallops in winter. Other food producers on the Isle of Man make heather honey, Manx preserves, chocolate, ice cream, pâté (kipper and

COFFEE CLUB
TUE - SUN 9:30AM - 12PM
ENJOY NOA'S COFFEE & A GREAT RANGE OF HOT DRINKS. HOT & COLD MORNING BITES INCLUDING HOMEMADE CAKES, BISCUITS, PAULA'S KITCHEN GLUTEN FREE TREATS, TEACAKES, TOAST, SCONES, & SAUSAGE ROLLS
SILVER SURFERS
IF YOU HAVE A 'GO SILVER' BUS PASS THEN WE HAVE A SPECIAL OFFER COMING SOON! ENJOY DISCOUNTED MENU FAVOURITES AT LUNCH
LIGHTER BITES, LIGHTER PRICES
YOU'VE EARNED IT!
20 19
BOATYARD
PEEL
WATCH FACEBOOK UPDATES
FIZZY FRIDAYS
ENJOY 20% OFF PROSECCO BY THE GLASS EVERY FRIDAY
SUNDAY LUNCH
OPEN EVERY SUNDAY 12 - 4pm
SERVING OUR NORMAL A LA CARTE LUNCH MENU INCLUDING A DELICIOUS ROAST OPTION
MID WEEK 'DATE NIGHTS'
BOOK FOR A 'DATE NIGHT MEAL' & ENJOY A SUPPER TO SHARE, & GET TALKING WITH FUN COUPLES TABLE TRIVIA. COMING SOON

Island hospitality

14North

crab are specialities) and mineral water. There are also breweries and distilleries. Homemade Manx offerings you may come across on your travels round the Island are bonnag (made with soured milk and sultanas or other dried fruit) and blaeberry pie.

Davison's Ice Cream

Adding to the holiday feel, the Island is home to the award-winning Davison's Ice Cream. Winning numerous awards and over 90 industry diplomas, the company makes good use of the Island's famed dairy produce, using the finest locally sourced Manx double cream, milk and butter, to create tasty ice cream in over 100 flavours. And if you fancy creating a new flavour let them know, they may just make it! Pop along to their website www.davisons.co.im to see a list of flavours they have made so far, you may be surprised. With the addition of a large selection of their handmade chocolates, a visit to one of their parlours in Douglas and Peel is sure to brighten any day.

Kippers – a Manx delicacy

Globally, the most famous Manx offering of all is the humble but delicious kipper, still in year-round demand despite the decline in the Island's fishing industry. At its height in the 1870s and 1880s the fleet provided the daily bread for one in every five of the population.

Isle of Man kippers are still prepared in the traditional time-honoured way – an art which is becoming increasingly rare. The herring are gutted, soaked in brine and smoked over oak chippings for exactly the length of time required to create that very distinctive flavour. Eating kippers with butter or marmalade, as they often are, is a sheer delight to the taste buds.

◆ Kippers, eaten the world over, are smoked herring: split, gutted, cleaned, soaked in a brine mixture, hung on racks in kilns and smoked according to their size and oil content.

◆ In the 19th century the staple Manx diet was spuds and herring – mashed potato on a wooden platter with herring and butter, eaten with fingers and no cutlery! In the 1840s almost 12 million herring a year were on local tables.

◆ Kippers are rich in nutrition. Oil-rich fish (which also includes mackerel and sardines) are unique in supplying the special Omega-3 polyunsaturated fats proven to help reduce cholesterol levels. They are also an important source of vitamins A & D, calcium, iodine, flourine and protein.

◆ Vacuum-sealed kippers can be kept in a fridge for up to 10 days. Loose kippers will keep in a fridge for 4-5 days. Both vacuum-sealed and loose kippers will keep in a deep freeze for up to 18 months.

♦ The home of Manx kippers is Peel. Devereau's was established in 1884 and in 1972 Peter Canipa, having worked for the company since the age of 13, bought the small kipper curing factory and shop. Today it is a Canipa family business with two shops and a factory four times the size of the original.

Isle of Man Food & Drink Festival

When the Isle of Man Food and Drink Festival returns every year, September sees the Villa Marina, Douglas transformed into a gastronomic delight, highlighting the best local produce, food and drink on offer. Aimed at families and serious foodies, visitors can sample a vast array of edibles on offer, watch cookery demonstrations, visit the Farmers' Market and take part in a large number of family friendly activities. When it's time to for a meal or snack there is also an abundance of eateries situated around the festival.

Regularly attracting celebrity chefs, the festival highlights the amazing range of quality food and drink that the Island produces. Visit www.visitisleofman.com to find out more.

Eating out on the Isle of Man

Visitors to the Isle of Man are spoilt for choice when it comes to fine dining. The finest and freshest local produce is lovingly and expertly prepared in restaurants and cafes all over the Island; from simple to extravagant there is something to suit every taste. Making the most of local availability you will find many of the establishments change their menus to suit seasonal fare, supporting local growers, farmers and fishermen. A

Milntown, Ramsey

selection of establishments can be found under each area at the beginning of this book.

Island Breweries
The Ale of Man – A Real Ale Utopia!

The Isle of Man is regarded by many as a beer drinker's paradise, which spoils the visitor with an array of traditional pubs, showcasing the products of no fewer than four breweries. The Island's brewing traditions go back centuries, with clear, pure water and rich soils enabling top quality barley to be grown for use in beer making. These factors are enhanced and underpinned by the Island's own unique Beer Purity Act, which (globally along with Germany and Switzerland alone) prohibits by law the use of any inferior ingredients. Passed by Tynwald in 1874 it states: 'NO BREWER SHALL USE IN THE BREWING, MAKING, MIXING WITH, RECOVERING OR COLOURING, ANY BEER OR LIQUID MADE TO RESEMBLE BEER, OR HAVE IN HIS POSSESSION ANY

COPPERAS, COCULUS INDICUS, NUX VOMICA, GRAINS OF PARADISE, GUINEA PEPPER OR OPIUM, OR ANY ARTICLE, INGREDIENT OR PREPARATION WHATEVER FOR, OR AS A SUBSTITUTE FOR MALT, SUGAR OR HOPS'.

It really makes an observer wonder what was going on in the brewing world of that time, that such exotic ingredients were having to be prohibited by law – and we think alcopops are bad nowadays!

The local breweries are extremely varied in size and style with a host of awards being won regularly. Most will show visitors around with a little notice. Listed here in order of age are the details of each:

O'Kells (1850)

The longest established brewers with the lion's share of tied pubs, producing a solid, steady range of beers. www.okells.co.uk.

Bushy's – The Ale of Man (1985)

Brewing the Island's largest range of beer styles, including the only local craft lager (Nörseman), with many seasonal and event related beers, they are also the only brewery to use Manx-grown barley. The favourite tipple with TT and MGP fans – look out for the famous bottle cars. www.bushys.com

The Island boasts more pubs in CAMRA's bible The Good Beer Guide than a city like Leeds with a population of over 2 million – 25 times that of Mann. The following pubs are dotted evenly around the isle and between them have pretty well won all the local CAMRA awards over the last 20 years or so. They all host beer festivals at differing times of the year and are all easily reached using public transport:

The Albert Hotel, Athol Street, Port St Mary.
Overlooking the bustling harbourside this friendly family-run hostelry has been wowing beer lovers for generations and especially appeals to fishermen and yachties in the three distinctly different bars.

The Bay Hotel, Shore Rd, Port Erin
Overlooking the Island's most picturesque and popular beach, The Bay is a great spot to enjoy a well-kept local ale (try a sampler tray) from the outside deck while keeping an eye open for passing basking shark. Great food too.

The Rovers Return, Church St, Douglas
A traditional unspoilt backstreet alehouse with lots of small rooms tucked away waiting to be discovered. Crammed with interesting memorabilia and well-kept beers it's well worth seeking out.

The Sidings, Station Rd, Castletown
Located next to the steam railway station this friendly local ticks many boxes for beer and train enthusiasts alike. The house brew is Castletown Bitter – a faithful throwback in memory of the town's much missed historic brewery (RIP 1986).

The Sulby Glen Hotel, Main Rd, Sulby
Situated on the fastest straight on the TT course this place is a Mecca for race fans and anyone else that enjoys good hospitality. Well appointed en suite rooms make it a great place to stay with beautiful views up the valley.

The Trafalgar Hotel, West Quay, Ramsey
A very friendly locals' pub on the quayside, serving well-kept real ales. Being so cosy it's a great spot to spend quality time while the other half shops.

The White House, Tynwald Rd, Peel
Winner of CAMRA pub of the year for an unprecedented 3 years running this wonderful multi-room hostelry captures

Dining Car experience at Douglas Railway Station

1886 Douglas

all that is good about the Manx pub with a good mix of local and guest ales on offer.

The Island has rather unkindly been referred to as '80,000 alcoholics clinging to a rock' and 'Alcytraz' and while these are obviously humorous jibes, they seems even more undeserved when the fact is known that the Island's beer drinkers tend to favour lower strength 'session' ales with Mild and lighter Bitters stealing the limelight. This is mainly down to the fact that, having no munitions factories, the IOM's pubs never suffered the ridiculous afternoon closing that the rest of the British Isles endured for so many years (Sunday hours excepted) following the original WWI enforcement. Local drinkers used to watch with amusement the antics of unknowing UK visitors 'cramming' their quota of drinks into a lunch hour and then paying the price soon after the 3 o'clock bell never rang, while the locals sipped away steadily.

The Isle of Man now leads the way in alcohol related matters following the formation of its unique Manx Licensing Forum – a body consisting of Home Affairs, Police, Law Society, Brewers, Pub operators, LVA, Nightclubs, Off-Licences, Pubwatch and other interested parties, which meets regularly to discuss all matters relating to this subject and debate any proposed changes in the trade. This is one of the benefits of living in a small close-knit community.

The Forum demonstrated the benefits of this multi-agency approach when about ten years ago it took the bold steps of abolishing licensing hours completely (for alcohol, not music) and thereby creating one of the most liberal drinking environments in the world. Far from becoming the 'free for all' predicted by some, if anything pubs are now open fewer hours than previously as the freedom to close when quiet often makes more economic sense. In addition statistics have proven that many other problem areas improved following the changes and authorities from throughout the UK and beyond come over to study how it has been achieved, with a view to following suit.

Please go out and support the pubs and enjoy Manx beer and hospitality responsibly – cheers!

Dr Okell and the science of beer making

Beers bearing the Okell's label rank amongst the best in Britain and they've been produced on the Isle of Man since 1850.

Owned by Heron & Brearley, the business was started by a man whose profession was more akin to scars than bars. Dr William Okell, a surgeon from

Cheshire, opened his first brewery at Castle Hill in Douglas.

Within twenty years or so, after buying up many of the island's pubs – a considerable number of which had brewed their own beer until then – he was unable to meet the demand of his outlets and he set about the task of building not just a new brewery, but a model brewery based on his own ideas using advanced scientific principles. His handwritten book, which is now one of Heron & Brearley's most treasured possessions, described in great detail the brewing process, the ideal equipment to use and the specifications for his new brewery.

When it was built in 1874 at Glen Falcon – in those days a greenfield site on the edge of Douglas – he called it the Falcon Steam Brewery. He opted to use steam to boil the brewery coppers rather than the more usual and accepted direct coal fire because he calculated it would cause less charring and caramelisation of the sugars during the boiling process. He figured correctly that this in turn would eliminate any unwanted burnt flavouring and give the final beer a much cleaner and superior taste.

It speaks volumes for Dr Okell's forward thinking that the brewery far outlived him and stayed in production until 18th August 1994, when the last brew was mashed – and for the best possible reason. Fifty barrels of Okells Bitter was also produced on this date. The time had come to move the business on to yet another advanced new production plant, at Kewaigue on the outskirts of Douglas.

This separately produces both ale and lager. The ale facility was built first and went into full production in August 1994, lager brewing commencing in September 1995.

Production is highly automated, most of the brewing process controlled by programmable logic controllers and computers. If you have a passion for, and understanding of, the technicalities of brewing you may be interested to know that the majority of the ale production is cask conditioned, the brewhouse consisting of a mash conversion vessel, lauter tun, copper and whirlpool. The brew length is 60 barrels.

The copper is of unusual design, having a vapour condenser to prevent steam and any aromas escaping into the outside air. It is also heated by an external heater – not uncommon in itself, but in this case utilising a very rare wide gap plate and frame heat exchanger. The fermentation facility for ales consists of four 60-barrel fermenters and one 30-barrel.

A well-equipped laboratory backs up the quality control and production functions.

No doubt Dr Okell himself would approve of such advanced technology – particularly as Okell's Bitter has since become the winner of at least one prestigious International Brewing Award. Okell's beers were awarded seven medals in 2014.in The World Beer Awards, SIBA NW and the British Bottlers Competition, and continue to produce award-winning beers, being finalists in the 'Champion Beer of Britain' awards in 2017.

205

Island Distilleries
Seven Kingdom Distillery

This award winning gin came on the market in 2017. It's major ingredient in 2019 was Manx gorse, handpicked locally, Manx heather honey, citrus and pure Manx water. Delivering a tropical top note with a peppery base, the result is a well-balanced but complex gin.

Available all over the Island in its distinctive bottle it is now making headway into England. However, when you are on the Island, the best way to savour the gin is in the bar on North Quay, the home of Seven Kingdom.

The distillery has created a number of

Seven Kingdom Distillery

new gins recently, including apple and citrus zest gins. Gin tours and tastings in the distillery can be arranged by appointment. Tel: 07624 302236.

Fynoderee Distillery

The multi-award-winning "Fynoderee Distillery" is the Island's largest craft distillery and can be found in Ramsey in the North of the Island. Founded in 2017 by local couple Paul and Tiffany Kerruish, the production of their signature range of seasonal "Fynoderee Manx Dry Gins" featuring hand-foraged local botanicals took the Island by storm.

Since then, the distillery has evolved and expanded to now include "Manx Bumbee Vodka", the "Glashtyn Manx Rum" range along with their recent historic commencement of "Isle of Man Single Malt Whiskey" production.

The Distillery is located in a converted Victorian warehouse opposite the 'end of line' tram stop on the Manx Electric Railway. Catching a vintage tram from Douglas or Laxey is a wonderful way to arrive at the distillery as you can enjoy the spectacular scenery on the way. However, if you are visiting by car, there is a carpark right next door and also the town's main bus station just a very short walk away.

The craft spirits produced at Fynoderee can be enjoyed island-wide in many pubs, bars and restaurants, however the most engaging and informative place to enjoy a "perfect serve" Fyn & Tonic or Fynoderee cocktail is undoubtedly at the distillery's own bar, "The Fyn Bar" - a charming and cosy cocktail bar adjoined to the main distillery. Here, you can also browse the shop shelves and chat to the knowledgeable team and enjoy some free sampling.

The Fyn Bar is opening a new outside seating area in 2023 known as "The Ginny Patch" so there will be even more reason to call in at Ramsey for 'al fresco' summer tipples. The distillery hosts regular pop-up events with visiting food vendors and live traditional music evenings so be sure to visit the website to see what's on the agenda! The Fyn Bar is also the 'meeting point' for all Distillery Tours as well as the location for its "Cocktail Masterclasses".

The Distillery operates bookable Tours at various times throughout the year with extra tours available at peak seasonal times. Tours must be booked online via the distillery

DISCOVER THE
SPIRITS OF MANN

The multi-award-winning Fynoderee Distillery based in Ramsey produces a range of craft spirits, including gin, rum and vodka.
We are also the home of Isle of Man Single Malt Whiskey.

Book a Distillery Tour or call in for a cocktail at the legendary Fyn Bar & Shop.

OPENING SUMMER 2023
THE GINNY PATCH
OUTSIDE TERRACE

Find us at the end of MER Railway Line on Parsonage Road, Ramsey

Ramsey Heritage Centre
Waterloo Road (A2)
Manx Electric Railway Station
Manx Electric Railway Line
Albert Terrace (A18) TT COURSE
Cruickshanks Corner

Fyn Bar, Shop & Distillery Entrance
PARSONAGE ROAD
RAMSEY,
ISLE OF MAN
IM8 2EE

For opening times and to book tours please visit www.Fynoderee.com

Contact us: 01624 812756

THE FYNODEREE DISTILLERY

Laxey Wheel

website www.fynoderee.com, however visitors are welcome to call in anytime when the "Fyn Bar & Shop" is open for a drink, a cocktail, coffee and to peep through the glass window in to the main distillery floor.

Distillery tours are a fun and engaging way of learning all about the methodology the distillery uses to create it's range of spirits. The Fynoderee team operate three very different Still systems including traditional Copper Pot stills used for Gin and Vodka production, a Dual Kettle Column Still used exclusively for its Isle of Man Single Malt Whiskey and an IStill 2000 which is a high tech still system used primarily for its Rum production. The Distillery is one of only a few in the British Isles who ferment and distil their own Rum from scratch using Fair-Trade, organic Panela Cane Sugar.

During the tour you will also delve into the unique fairy folklore that inspires the distillery's name and branding and exquisite artwork used within its labels. The Fynoderee Distillery is dedicated to promoting Manx culture, folklore, language and music and you will hear a re-telling of the story "Kitty Kerruish & The Fynoderee"

which is set in a location just outside of Ramsey which has special significance to the team. A Fynoderee is a character from Manx folklore – a big, strong satyr-like creature with large horns who is reputed to dwell within the Manx landscape. BUT, he didn't start out his life this way....All will be revealed during your tour!

Distillery Tours will cover the full range of spirits produced at Fynoderee and include a tutored tasting.

However, if you are particularly interested in learning about the distillery's Whiskey production, then do look out for their dedicated Whiskey Tours. The Fynoderee Distillery is proud to be a partner business to the Isle of Man UNESCO Biosphere.

Island Wines

Foraging Vintners is a small craft-winery overlooking Port Erin Bay. It specialises in making non-grape based sparkling wines, ciders, ginger beer and sparkling wine cocktails. The winery has a small cosy bar and an outdoor terrace which overlooks one of the British Isles most stunning bays. For more information email them at celebrate@foragingvintners.com

Looking from the Calf of Mann across to The Sound

ALL ROUND GUIDE ISLE of MAN

ESSENTIALS

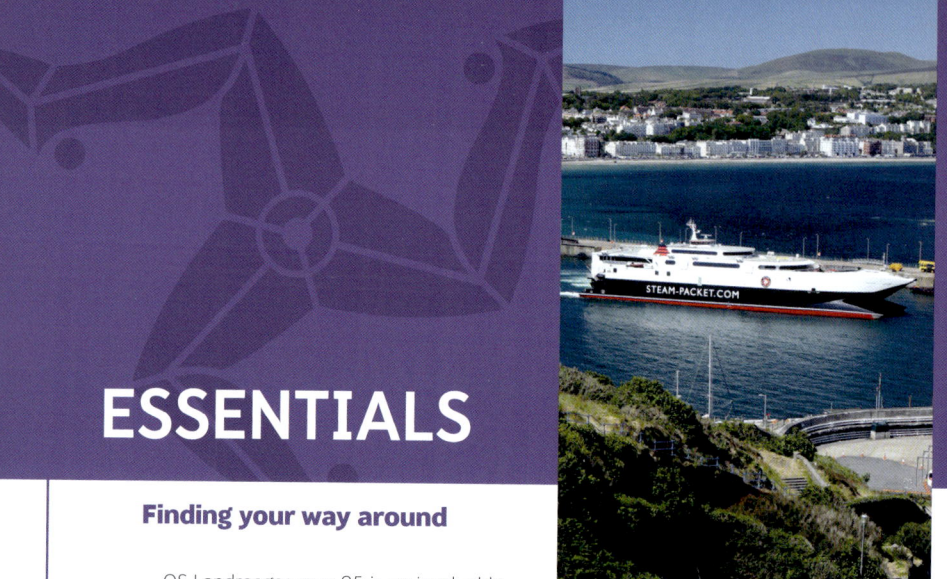

Finding your way around

OS Landranger map 95 is an invaluable source of reference and information for discovering and exploring the Isle of Man.

Getting around the island
Motoring

Discover more than 500 miles of roads. Driving is on the left and road signs are in English. Car hire is widely available. Parking discs (free of charge and easily obtained) are required in towns. Touring caravans are prohibited because of the Island's narrow roads and winding country lanes.

Public transport

The Isle of Man is famous for its remarkable vintage railways and trams: the Isle of Man Steam Railway (Douglas–Port Erin), Manx Electric Railway (Douglas–Ramsey, via Laxey), Snaefell Mountain Railway (Laxey to the summit) and Douglas horse trams (promenade, end of March to the beginning of November).

Frequent bus services operate all over the Island. Money-saving Explorer tickets cover all bus and public transport train travel as listed here.

Bus & train services

For up-to-date timetable and fare information call Isle of Man Transport on 01624 662525 or the Welcome Centre on 01624 686766, or look online at www.iombusandrail.info.

Single and return tickets (valid on day of issue only) are available from your bus driver. One Day Saver and Go Explore (unlimited bus and rail travel for 1, 3, 5 and 7 days) or Go Explore Heritage (5-day unlimited travel plus admission to all Manx National Heritage attractions) tickets are the best way to get around the Island and are available online, at the Welcome Centre, airport and at main bus and rail stations. See www.bus.im for more details.

Getting to and from the Island

The Isle of Man is in the Irish Sea, off the coastlines of Lancashire, Galloway, Northern Ireland and North Wales, and is well-served by airports from across the British Isles (flights are as short as 20 minutes) and by sea from England and Ireland (average time 3 hours 45 minutes

The new Steam Packet ferry the Manxman is due enter service during 2023

by conventional ferry, 2 hours 45 minutes by fastcraft). Flying gives you obvious time advantages, whereas a ferry can accommodate your car too. If you're travelling in the high season, or busy school holiday periods, it's sensible to book your flight or sailing well in advance.

The information given in these pages was correct at the time of going to press (February 2023) and is intended as a general guide, but contacting individual operators will give you a completely up-to-date picture.

Travelling by sea

Ferry services (for vehicles and foot passengers) are operated by the Isle of Man Steam Packet Company, based at the Sea Terminal on Douglas harbour – your arrival point on the Isle of Man whether you're travelling from England, Northern Ireland or Ireland by sea.

Services from England give you a choice of two departure ports – Heysham or Liverpool. The average crossing time from Heysham is 3 hours 30 minutes by the conventional ferry *Manxman/Ben-my-Chree*. The average crossing time from Liverpool, by the fast craft *Manannan* which operates between March and November, is 2 hours 45 minutes.

Services from Belfast and Dublin usually operate from March/April to September and are mainly by fast craft (2 hours 45 minutes and 2 hours 55 minutes respectively). Occasional services by conventional ferry take 4 hours 45 minutes from or to either port.

Contact details:

Isle of Man Steam Packet Company
Tel: 661661 (IOM), 08722 992 992 (UK) or 0044 8722 992 992 (ROI & Outside UK) Calls from numbers outside the Isle of Man are charged a 11p per minute plus telephone access charges. Book online at www.steam-packet.com

easyJet fly to Isle of Man from London, Bristol, Belfast, Liverpool and Manchester

Travelling by air

The Island of Man is accessible directly via a number of UK airports, with flights taking as little as 20 minutes. As at March 2023, airports and airlines regularly serving the Isle of Man were as follows:
- Belfast International (easyJet)
- Birmingham (Loganair)
- Bristol (easyJet)
- Dublin (Aer Lingus Regional)
- Edinburgh (Loganair)
- Liverpool (easyJet and Loganair)
- London City (Loganair)
- London Gatwick (easyJet)
- London Heathrow (Loganair)
- Manchester (easyJet and Loganair)

Contact details:
- Isle of Man airport:
  tel: 01624 821600 www.gov.im
- Aer Lingus: www.aerlingus.com
www.easternairways.com
- easyJet: www.easyJet.com
- Loganair: https://www.loganair.co.uk/

A-Z of the rest
Disability services

For information about disabled facilities on the Island
Disabled Go http://www.disabledgo.com
CIRCA (Centre for Information Resource Care and Assistance)
www.circa.org.im. Tel: 01624 679153

Harbours

- Douglas. Good shelter except in NE winds, very heavy seas in NE gales. Harbour Master 01624 686923.
- Laxey. Sheltered except in strong NE/SE winds. Harbour dries out. Port Manager 01624 861663.
- Peel. Good shelter except in strong NW to NE winds, when entry should not be attempted. Harbour Office 01624 842338.
- Port St Mary. Very good shelter except in E or SE winds. Inner harbour dries out.

Port Manager (also for Port Erin and

Castletown) 01624 833206.

◆ Ramsey. Very good shelter except in strong NE/SE winds. Harbour dries out. Port Manager 01624 812245.

Landscape

With much of it given over to farming, and more than 40% of it uninhabited, the landscape is largely unspoilt – a haven for wildlife, supporting a great variety of habitats. Tranquil countryside, wooded glens, high hills, uncrowded beaches and dramatic coastlines are the main features. The highest point is Snaefell (2,036 feet – 635 metres), accessible on foot or by mountain railway. Much of the 100-mile coastline can be walked on Raad ny Foillan (Road of the Gull) – the signposted coastal footpath (95 miles/153km).

Law

The Isle of Man has a strong anti-drugs policy and illegal possession of banned substances can lead to imprisonment.

Licensing laws

The Isle of Man permits 24-hour opening for pubs, bars and off-licences. This means that all licensed premises, including nightclubs, restaurants and the Douglas casino, now have the option to serve alcohol 24 hours a day but only within their stated pre-arranged opening times.

Manx National Heritage

For opening times, admission prices (where applicable) and other information about Manx National Heritage sites and attractions, call 01624 648000 or visit manxnationalheritage.im.

Manx Wildlife Trust

The Trust's shop at Peel has a great variety of books, maps and other information about Isle of Man wildlife and habitats. Call 01624 844432 or visit www.manxwt.org.uk.

Medical

A reciprocal healthcare agreement is in place between the Isle of Man and the UK, which allows for free emergency treatment should you fall ill. However, it is advised that you have adequate healthcare insurance arranged before you visit, to cover repatriation to the UK if this becomes required. More details: www.gov.im/categories/health-and-wellbeing.

Motoring Laws and Information

◆ Drive with care. Isle of Man roads and lanes are narrow and should be negotiated with care and consideration.

◆ Mobile phones. It is an offence to use a hand-held mobile phone while driving.

◆ Parking discs. These are required in some of the larger towns and villages and are available free from Isle of Man Steam Packet vessels, the Sea Terminal, airport, car hire companies and local commissioner's offices.

◆ Seatbelts. Similar seatbelt laws to those in the UK and elsewhere apply.

◆ Touring caravans are not permitted on the Isle of Man without a permit, but tenting campers and motorhomes are welcome.

Postal Services

The Isle of Man Post Office, like the UK Post Office, sells Manx stamps (much prized by collectors worldwide) and coins, arranges foreign currency, bill payments and vehicle licensing. www.iompost.com

Telephone

The area code for the Isle of Man is 01624, with the Island using the same telephone numbering system as the UK, however, some telecommunications companies may charge higher rates to phone the Island from outside. While visiting it is recommended that you check whether your mobile phone company charges extra for calls within the Island, which may not be covered by your provider's free texts and minutes.

Tourist Information: The Welcome Centre

Located at the Sea Terminal, Douglas, and formerly known as the Tourist Information Centre, the centre is open 7 days a week: Monday to Saturday 8am–6pm and Sunday (May to September) 10am–3pm.

For information call 01624 686766, fax 01624 627443, or email tourism@gov.im

From the Republic of Ireland call +44 (1) 8744455.

TOURIST INFORMATION POINTS
Open all year:
- Airport 01624 821600
- Castletown 01624 825005
- Onchan 01624 621228
- Peel 01624 842341 or 845366
- Port Erin 01624 832298
- Port St Mary 01624 832101
- Ramsey 01624 812228

Seasonal only:
- Ballasalla (March–October)
- Laxey Heritage Trust 01624 862007

Visitor Websites

The main website for visitor information – including details of accommodation, events, attractions, activities, TT and motorsport, travel information, special offers and much more – is www.visitisleofman.com.

The Isle of Man Government website is also a mine of information and has a comprehensive index: www.gov.im.

Calendar of Events

The Isle of Man hosts numerous annual events throughout the year, to cater for all tastes, from flowers to fast cars. Below you will find a small selection, correct as of February 2018, please check websites to confirm dates.

January
Peel New Year's Dip: www.peeldip.com

March
Internationals Darts Festival:
www.bdodarts.com
www.visitisleofman.com

April
Manx Classic Car Sprint and Hillclimb:
www.manxmotorracing.com
Cyclefest: www.iomcyclefest.com
Isle of Man Beer & Cider festival:
www.iombeerfestival.com

May
Isle of Man Walking Festival:
www.visitisleofman.com
Manx National Rally:
www.manxautosport.org

May/June
TT Races : www.iomtt.com

June
Crown Green Bowling Festival:
www.visitisleofman.com
Longest Day, Longest Ride: www.ldlr.im
Parish Walk: www.parishwalk.co.uk
Mananan International Festival of Music and The Arts: www.erinartscentre.com

July
Tynwald Day: www.tynwald.org.im
Yn Chruinnaght: Manx National Festival) www.ynchruinnaght.com

Looking towards South Barrule from Cronk ny Arrey Laa

Southern 100 Races:
www.southern100.com
Isle of Man Flower Festival:
www.flowerfest.im

August
Royal Manx Agricultural Show:
www.royalmanx.com
Festival of Motorcycling:
www.iomfom.com

September
World Tin Bath Championships
www.castletown.org.im
Manx Litfest: www.manxlitfest.com
Isle of Man Food and Drink Festival:
www.gov.im
Rally Isle of Man: www.rallyisleofman.im
Crown Green Bowling Festival:
www.visitisleofman.com

October
Hop Tu Naa Festival:
www.manxnationalheritage.im

November
PokerStars Rally:
http://www.manxautosport.org/

Manx place names A-Z

Manx place names are often of Celtic or Norse origin, linking back to the Island's earliest inhabitants. Here you will find a small number of translations to help you understand more easily the names associated with the places in this book.

Aldrick	old people's creek
Awin Ruy	red river
The Ayres	derived from the old Norse word 'eyrr' meaning gravelbank
Baie ny Breechyn	bay of the breeches – so named because it resembles a pair of blue trousers laid out on the sea

Manx names

Baldrinea	derived from Manx Gaelic meaning the place of the blackthorns	Carraghyn	meaning scabby, with reference to its stoney top
Balla	homestead	Cashtal Kione ny Goagyn	meaning the castle of chasms' head
Ballabeg	Begson's Farm	Cass Struan	stream end
Ballagarey	farm of the river thicket	Chibbyr Vashtey	the Well of Baptism
Ballagrawe	Balla ny Groa – farm of the cotes or coops	Chibbyrt Catreeney	Catherine's Well
Ballajora	farm of the strangers	Cleigh yn Arragh	stone rampart
Ballaleece	Leece's farm	Cletts	rocks
Ballalough	farm of the lakes	Closemooar	great enclosure
Ballamodha	farm of the dog	Colby	Kolli's Farm
Ballamore	More's farm	Congary	rabbit warren
Ballanass	Balla n eas is Manx Gaelic meaning farm of The waterfall	Cooilingill Farm	low nook
		Cornaa	an ancient treen name meaning land division
Ballaragh	of doubtful origin but best seen as derived from Balley arraght meaning farm of the apparition	Creg y Whallian	rock of the whelp
		Creggans	literally rocky place but describing a small rocky outcrop
		Cregneish	
Ballasalla	the place of the willows	Cregneash	meaning Rock of Ages
Ballatersen	farm of the crozier	Crogga Hill	from the Norse Króká meaning winding river
Ballaugh	a corruption of Balley ny Loughey – lake farm	Cronk Brec	hill of many colours – literally piebald
Ballawyllin	Byllinge's farm		
Ballure	Balley euar meaning yew tree estate or farm	Cronk Keeill Abban	the hill of St Abban's church
Bay ny Carrickey	bay of the rock	Cronk Mooar	big hill
Bay Stakka	a corruption of Baie yn Stackey, referring to the stack of Sugar Loaf Rock	Cronk ny Arrey Laa	thought to mean 'hill of the day watch'
		Cronk ny Irree Laa	hill of the dawn
		Cronk ny Moghlane (or Mucaillyn)	hill of the sows and the River Glass (green river)
Beg	meaning little		
Beinn y Phott	very loosely interpreted as turf peak		
Block Eary	from blakkärg meaning black shieling	Cronk ny Merrui	literally the hill of the dead people or house of the dead
Bollyn Road	Boayl ein – spot of the birds	Cronk y Feeagh	meaning hill of the raven
Burroo Ned	nest hill	Curragh	bog

BAYR DREEYN SKERRY
ROAD OF THE SCARFFE'S RIDGE

Dalby	glen farm	Glenchass	an English corruption of Glion Shast meaning sedge glen
Darragh Road	place where oak trees grow		
Dhoon Rhennie Mine	Dhoon is probably derived from an Irish word meaning fort and rhenny is a ferny place	Glenfaba Mill	a mixture of English and Manx; it should be Myllin Glenfaba meaning Mill in the glen of the Neb
Dollagh	a corruption of Doufloch, meaning black lake	Glion Booigh	the dirty glen
		Glion Cam	the winding glen
Douglas	convergence of the River Dhoo (black river) and the River Glass (green river)	Gob Ago	literally edge headland
		Gob ny Rona	headland of the seals
		Gob ny Ushtey	headland of the waterfall, although the literal translation means beak of the water – the early Manx often described headlands as looking like the bill or beak of a bird and so the description came into common use
Eary Cushlin	Cosnahan's shieling		
Ellan Bane	white island		
Ellan Rhenny	ferny island		
Ellan Vannin	the Manx name for the Isle of Man		
Feustal	precipice		
Fleshwick	green creek		
Foxdale	an anglicised corruption of Forsdalr, a Scandinavian word meaning waterfall dale	Greeba	an obscure Scandinavian word meaning peak
		Groudle	narrow glen
Garwick	from the Norse Gjarvik, meaning cave or creek	Hango Hill	The Norse name for the hill was Hangaholl, or Hill of Hanging
Glen Lough	literally Lake Glen		
Glen Maye	Glion Muigh, yellow glen		
Glen Mooar	the great glen	Jurby	Ivar's Farm
Glen Wyllin	glen of the mill		

219

Keeill	church or chapel		below
Keeill Catreeney	Catherine's chapel	Laxey	Laxa, 'Salmon River' in
Keeill Vreeshey	the church of St Bridget		old Norse
Kenna	Aodha's hill – Aodha being a name of Irish descent	Lhen Mooar	meaning great ditch
		Lhiattee ny Bienee	literally meaning summit on the side
Killane	from the Scandinavian kjarrland, meaning brushwood land	Mona	name given to the Island by Caesar in his book Gallic Wars
Kion e Hennin	KioneKione ny eaynin – headland of the cliff; Kione literally means beak or bill of a bird but by common usage has come to mean headland	Mooar	meaning big
		Mooragh	meaning waste land by the sea
		Mull	Meayll in Manx, meaning Bald or Bare Hill
Kione ny Garee	literally meaning the end of the thicket	Niarbyl	Manx name Yn Arbyl literally meaning the tail – from the tail of rocks stretching out to sea
Kirby	Scandinavian in origin and means church farm		
Knockaloe	Caley or Allowe's hill	Northop	a Scandinavian word meaning north village
Lag Birragh	literally the sharp pointed hollow – referring to the rocks	Onchan	the patron saint of the parish was St

	Christopher, better known by his Gaelic name of Conchenn, meaning dog-head or wolf-head	Rjoofjall	Norse for Ruddy Mountain
		Scarlett	cormorant's cleft
		Shellag	the original Norse name means seal creek or bay
Orrisdale	from the Scandinavian Orrastör, meaning estate of the moorfowl pasture of the lapwing		
		Shenharra	meaning Old Ballaharra possibly referring to an ancient earthwork
Park ny Earkan			
Perwick	old Scandinavian for harbour creek	Shenvalley	old farm
Phurt	port	Skerisdale	or more correctly Skeresstaör from the Norse meaning rocky farm
Pooyldhooie	pool of the black ford		
Port e Vullen	harbour of the mill		
Port Erin	translated means either Lord's Port or Iron Port, In Manx Gaelic is written as Purt Chiarn		
		Skyhill	the Norse named it Skógarfjall the wooded hill
Port Mooar	the great harbour	Slieau Chiarn	the Lord's mountain
Port Soderick	sunny or south-facing creek	Slieau Managh	mountain of the monks
		Slieau Ruy	red mountain
Port Soldrick	sunny creek	Sloc	Slough, meaning pit or hollow
Poyll Dooey	pool of the Black Ford		
Poyll Vaaish	pool of death or bay of death; the name's origin is obscure but one likely explanation is that a slaughter house associated with the farm drained into one of the many sea pools	Snaefell	snow mountain
		Surby	a Norse word – 'Saurbyr' meaning moorland farm
		Tholt-y-Will	probably a derivative of the Celtic Tolta yn Woalilee meaning the hill of the cattle fold
Purt Veg	little port	Traaie Vane	white beach
		Traie Cabbag	cabbage shore – so named after the wild cabbage that grows there
Raad ny Foillan	Road of the Gull		
Raad ny Quakerin	the Quakers' road		
Ramsey	Ramsa, seemingly drawn from the old Scandinavian language and meaning wild garlic river	Traie Coon	narrow beach
		Traie Fogog mountain	or more correctly Traie Feoghaig – meaning periwinkle shore
Rhenny road	boayl y rhennee – place of the fern		
River Dhoo	black river		
River Glass	green river		

Further Reading

Other Isle of Man books published by Ramsey-based Lily Publications, the Island's leading publishing house, include:

All Round Guide to Wildlife of the Isle of Man
Knockaloe Internment Camp
Hidden Gems Isle of Man
Then and Now - Around the Isle of Man
Looking Back – Isle of Man Holidays
Profile of the Isle of Man
Made in Summerland
The Folklore of the Isle of Man
Tram, Train & Foot
Spectacular Isle of Man
Isle of Man -Britain's Treasured Island
Favourite Manx Walks
Glen Walks
Isle of Man Summits
Isle Of Man Countryside, Coast & Churches
Isle of Man Holiday Walks
Isle of Man Hill Walks
Isle of Man Short Walks – Northern Section
Mountain Biking on the Isle of Man
Mountain Biking on the Isle of Man – Book 2
150 years of Manx Railways
Lifeboats of the Isle of Man
The Silence of Summerland
Wild Flowers of Mann
Trains - Ailsa Years
Trains - Post-Nationalisation
Ferries of the Irish Sea
Ferries of the Isle of Man
Manxman

All titles listed are available direct from Lily Publications, Ballachrink Beg, Jurby East, Ramsey, Isle of Man IM7 3HD. Tel: 01624 898446.

Email: sales@lilypublicayions.co.uk
Website: www.lilypublications.co.uk

223

Index

Activities 184–197
Ancient sites & monuments 171–172
Birdwatching 156–159
Breweries 202–205
Bus & train services 212
Calendar of Events 216–217
Castles 38, 42, 44–46, 56, 61, 172, 177
Chapels and churches 6, 172
Curraghs Wildlife Park 17, 141–143
Currency 2
Cycling & trails 111–115
Dark Skies 143–145
Distilleries 206–209
Driving & tours 123–139
Eating out 17, 31–34, 47, 55, 61 see also Food & drink
Entertainment & the arts 23, 197
Essentials 212–222
Events 216–217
Fairies & folklore 173–180
Fishing 188
Food & drink 3, 198–209 see also Eating Out
Further reading 222
Glens 150–151
Golf 189–190
Government 2
Harbours 214–215
History 160–183
Horse trams 185
Itineraries 64–139
Landscape 215
Language 2
Laws 215
Manx National Heritage 171, 215
Manx Wildlife Trust 149, 215
Mining 28, 58, 76–77, 100, 122, 172–173
Motorsports 3, 193–197, 191
Museums & art galleries 180–183
Nature reserves 149–150
Parish Walk 193
Parks & gardens 140–142
Place names (Manx) 217–221
Places to go 12–17, 29–31, 44–47, 54–55

Quad biking 192
Railways 115–122, 184–187
Sailing & water sports 190, 192
Sport 187–197
Towns & villages
   Andreas 8-9
   Ballabeg 42–43
   Ballasalla 41–42
   Ballaugh 12
   Bride 8–12
   Castletown 38–47, 105–107
   Colby 42–43
   Cregneash 52–54
   Derbyhaven 44
   Douglas 20–35, 102–105
   Foxdale 58
   Glen Maye 57
   Jurby 8
   Kirk Michael 60-61
   Langness 44
   Laxey 26–28
   Maughold 12
   Niarbyl 57
   Onchan 28–29
   Peel 56-58, 107–109
   Port Erin & Port St Mary 50–57
   Port e Vullen 12
   Port Soderick 29
   Ramsey 6-8, 12–17
   St John's 58–59
Town walks 102–111
Trams 185
Travel information 212–215
TT & motorsport 193–197
Tynwald 165–171
Useful information 212–222
Walking & walks 64–111, 192
Watersports 190
Welcome Centre & Tourist Information Points 216
Wildlife & nature 140–159
Wildlife Trust 149, 215